Out of Mouths Of Serial Killers

"Why did you kill?"

MARY BRETT

WILDBLUE
PRESS

WildBluePress.com

OUT OF THE MOUTHS OF SERIAL KILLERS published by:
WILDBLUE PRESS
P.O. Box 102440
Denver, Colorado 80250

ISBN 978-1-952225-47-5 Trade Paperback
ISBN 978-1-952225-46-8 eBook

Interior Formatting/Book Cover Design by Elijah Toten
www.totencreative.com

Out of the Mouths Of Serial Killers

It is not normal behavior to kill and mutilate, in multiples, to satisfy an inner dark lust.

This book is based on one simple question posed to over 70 of America's most prolific Serial Killers: *Why did you kill?* Read the response from hand-written letters, court testimony, interviews, and interrogation statements that will give you, the Reader, an eye-opening insight into the mind of these monsters that walked among us.

In loving dedication to The Yo-Yos, lifelong serial friends: Ellen, Ginny, Joan, Jutta, Pennie, and Randi…plus honorary Yo-Yo, Wayne

A special thank you to Stevan Gould and Patty Gordon, plus WildBlue Press and their amazing staff: Steve Jackson, Michael Cordova, Ashley Kaesemeyer, and Rowe Carenen

Table of Contents

PROLOGUE

OUT OF THE MOUTHS OF SERIAL KILLERS: *An in-depth look into the reasons some of the most notorious serial killers killed through their own words.*

Insane or Pure Evil?

What makes one human being kill others, usually strangers, in such vile and methodical ways? While murders attributed to serial killers account for less than 1% of all slayings committed in the United States per FBI statistics, these killings are extremely disturbing. Serial murders are not done in the heat of passion, for revenge, and are rarely executed solely for financial gain. They are committed simply because the killer is compelled by something dark and broken inside himself. To the serial killer, other humans are nothing more than objects, the vessels required to fulfill their sick desires.

America is not the only country to produce serial killers. Quite the contrary. There is no country in the world that has not prosecuted and sentenced their own serial killers, but America leads the world in the number of serial killers captured. This is either a negative mark on our society or a positive statement suggesting our law enforcement agencies work harder and are more effective than other nations' patrolling forces.

Only during times of war will a civilized society murder with the complete lack of compassion and empathy for human life that defines the serial killer. During times of war, however, there is a patriotic or self-preservation rationale involved: for "*love of country*" or the "*kill them before they kill me"* reasoning. The serial killer kills for no other reason than he likes it.

Most legal systems allow certain cases that result in the death of another individual to be forgiven fully or punished less severely if warranted by acceptable circumstances. Examples would be self-defense, accidental death, manslaughter, or by reason of insanity. When we read or hear in the news of the horrific acts committed by an apprehended serial killer, it is not unusual for the average citizen to conclude that this perpetrator must be insane, insanity defined legally as not being able to discern right from wrong. However, the majority of our world's serial killers are not absolved by reason of insanity in a court of law. Being evil does not necessarily equate to being insane.

How Many Are Out There?

A serial killer is roughly defined as someone who has killed three or more people, usually in separate incidents. Most victims are complete strangers. Estimates vary, but on any given day it is believed that there are between 50 and 100 serial killers roaming America. That translates to one to two serial killers per state, although for some unexplained reason, California, Florida, and Texas seem to have had more than their fair share of known culprits. Surprising, considering Florida and Texas' known penchant for the death penalty. Serial killers are most often married with families or in a long-time relationship, but there are a relatively few described as loners, incapable of maintaining a successful permanent connection to anyone.

Some serial killers like Tommy Lynn Sells (known 22 kills, most likely many more) roam the country while others such as John Wayne Gacy, (known 33 kills, suspected of two more) and Dennis Radar (known 10 kills) stuck close to home, blending undetected into their communities. A few serial killers have become household names, but most remain relatively obscure, known only to the families and communities they so tragically affected.

Most victims of serial killers have left themselves open to the possibility of extreme harm by the lifestyles they have chosen: drug sales or drug addiction, alcoholism, prostitution, hitch hiking, or homelessness. This in no way makes it right, but it does explain how they could become an easy target and generate marginal alarm should they go missing. A minority of victims are innocents in the wrong place at the wrong time or simply too trusting of the stranger who approached them. Most victims of serial killers are adult women, but men and children have also fallen prey.

Most serial killers are males, but there are women and even children serial killers. Ages vary from the young to the elderly. We originally believed most serial killers were Caucasian but that trend started to change in 1990. By 2010, 59.1% of serial killers were black as opposed to 32.3% white and 8.6% Hispanic. If asked, the average person would categorize the typical serial killer as a white male in his mid to late 20's, but that description only represents 7.4% of all serial killers in the U.S. from 1990-2015. It is important that law enforcement personnel and the public rethink the profile of a serial killer.

Some cases involve two or more relatives killing together: cousins, brothers, uncles and nephews, a parent in concert with a child or children. Male and female killer teams are especially lethal and they tend to torture their victims who are most often young women, in the wrong place at the wrong time, or innocents related to the killers.

Trending Down

The recent trend in serial killing is down, but that is because we are becoming a savvy public. We are more skeptical about offering or accepting rides from strangers and most people have cell phones to call for help if a car is disabled or trouble perceived. We lock our doors and install security systems. We are a society that watches our children more closely, not allowing them to walk to and from places unattended nor play in parks without supervision. Our police are better trained with sophisticated methods of processing evidence. Jurisdictions can interact with one another through computer systems. DNA has made the hunt for offenders easier, quicker, and almost foolproof. Media and social networking bring crime stories to the public's eye immediately.

According to the Bureau of Justice statistics, approximately 75% of released prisoners will be arrested and behind bars again within five years. In most cases, the seriousness of the crime escalates each time they return to the prison system. We are justified in seeking stricter legal penalties for repeat offenders. We cannot arrest an individual until the crime has been committed, even if all the red flags are in place, but better access to mental health services is desperately needed in this country. There are and always will be monsters that walk among us. One thing is certain, however. Once a serial killer escalates to that first kill, he or she will not stop until apprehended or dead.

Nature vs. Nurture

Opinions vary, but most experts in the field claim that roughly 50% of serial killers showed serious warning signs as children, the majority resulting in juvenile convictions. Approximately 40% of serial killers were, at some point in time, convicted of a sex crime. There is a push in many localities to establish an animal abuse registry since researchers have found overwhelming evidence that animal abuse is a particularly good indicator and predictor of future violence towards humans. (Jeffrey Dahmer, 17 kills). Starting fires is another action signaling an extremely troubled individual. (David Berkowitz, 6 kills and Ottis Toole, 6+ kills). Bed wetting at an inappropriate age is considered an indicator of a difficult childhood by many psychologists and a child who has been abused or badly neglected is more likely to commit serious crimes as adults. (Gary Ridgway, 71+ kills, Derrick Todd Lee, 7+ kills). Still, not all children or young adults who abused the neighbor's pets, set fires, or had a difficult childhood become a serial killer, and convictions for sex crimes, ranging from public exposure to violent rape, don't guarantee this person will eventually kill multiples of people.

Most serial killers had rough childhoods and unloving homes, but not all. Some come from loving homes. (Charles Albright, 3 kills, Robert Reldan, 2 kills, David Berkowitz, 6 kills) Some have below normal IQs (Henry Lee Lucas, 11-50+ kills, Danny Rolling, 8 kills, Coral Watts, 80+ kills) but the vast majority have average intelligence. A few are considered highly intelligent, registering genius or near genius levels. (Patrick Wayne Kearney, 21-43 kills, Stephen Stanko, 2 kills and 1 left for dead, Lawrence Bittaker, 5 kills, Edmund Kemper, 10 kills).

At trial, a severe head injury affecting the frontal lobe of the brain is often cited as a possible cause for the antisocial or even violent behavior of many serial killers. (Wayne Ford, 4-6 kills, Richard Ramirez, 14 kills). Defense attorneys may point to a childhood accident that resulted in hospitalization, serious parental abuse, or a vehicle wreck that family and friends claim negatively affected the defendant's personality, however, the majority of people who have suffered a severe head injury never kill, much less kill in multiples.

All serial killers are psychopaths but not all psychopaths become serial killers or even a murderer. It is estimated that one in 100 people are psychopaths, usually described as a person with amoral and antisocial behavior, extreme egocentricity, and the inability to love or establish meaningful, prolonged personal relationships. During the past few decades, researchers have begun studying the brain scans of vicious murderers and psychopaths in the hopes of discovering tangible proof that can explain why a person could and would commit such vile deeds. To date, no study has been able to pin-point concrete findings that would allow us to recognize the next serial killer in time to stop the carnage.

Simply put: There is no set formula to predict who will become a serial killer or why they kill.

This book is going to look at some of the most notorious serial killers who ever walked among us and seek to explain why *that* individual killed. We will explore the crimes they committed, their backgrounds, and delve deep into their mind **through their own words**. As a society, we may never be able to accurately predict who will kill in the future, but we will discover why the serial killers included in this book say they killed and killed on a such a heinous level that they have earned a permanent place in dark history… and hell.

Parting Shots:

The sentence from a judge condemning a man to death for the premeditated murder of his girlfriend and their infant son: ***"I conclude that you, under the laws of the state of Florida, have forfeited your right to live"***

Presiding Judge John O'Malley said at Lorenzo Gilyard's sentencing, ***"He's forfeited any right to live here among the rest of us. That's the comfort we can derive."***

Florida's Assistant Attorney General Christina Pacheco replied during a last minute bid by defense lawyers to keep convicted serial killer Bobby Joe Long, who suffered from epilepsy, from being executed on grounds that Florida's lethal drugs could cause him a painful death from a possible seizure: ***"He's not entitled to a pain-free death. Michelle Simms certainly didn't have one in this case."***

"I hope they put you so deep in the penitentiary that they'll have to pipe sunlight to you." Texas judge sentencing Coral Watts to 60 years behind bars.

The judge sentencing Patrick Kearney to 21 counts of life: *"I can only hope the community release board will never release Mr. Kearney. He appears to be an insult to humanity."*

"The first request of civilization is justice." Sigmund Freud

At Randy Kraft's sentencing, Superior Court Judge, Donald A. McCartln proclaimed, *"I can't imagine doing those things in scientific experiments on a dead person much less someone alive."*

Los Angeles Superior Court Judge William Keene pronouncing sentence upon William Bonin: *"He had a total disregard for the sanctity of human life and a civilized society. Sadistic, unbelievably cruel, senseless, and deliberately premeditated. Guilty beyond any possible or imaginary doubt."*

Thomas Johnson, speaking at member of the Prisoner Review Board at William Heirens' 2007 hearing while denying him parole: *"God will forgive you, but the state won't."*

California's then-Governor Pete Wilson rejected a clemency plea from serial killer William Bonin's attorney prior to his execution and remarked that Bonin was the *"poster boy for capital punishment"*.

"The vast majority of prison inmates will claim they are innocent, that they have found God, and that they have changed for the better. If released from prison, few will remember or honor their claims," Mary Brett, Author of this book.

According to the conclusive belief of mental health professionals, psychopathic criminals such as Serial Killers cannot be cured.

AN EXAMPLE OF THE BASIC LETTER
MAILED TO EACH SERIAL KILLER.
Minor changes were made on a few letters.

ADDRESS:

DATE:

Dear ,

I am a published research writer working on my fourth book. My last book (Schiffer Publishing, Ltd. ISBN13:9780764348457) was released late last year.

My next book will be a study of why serial killers killed in their own words. I am simply posing the question to each person I write asking *"Why did YOU kill?"* I can assure you the book will not be written with the intention of forgiving nor exploiting the crimes. The mission of this book will be to try to understand the act through reading the participant's actual statement. Each letter and/or statement will be included in the book **unedited.**

I was hoping that you might be interested in being included in this book but I will completely understand if you choose not to participate. I thank you in advance for your time and consideration regarding my request. However, you may feel that you have something important to contribute to this project or a message you would like to leave, in print, for the victims' families, your family, or society in general. Often information is published that is not true. This book will provide you the vessel to clarify any and all statements you feel are not accurate. You will be remembered in history. I hope to give you an opportunity to make sure that history gets it right.

Kindest regards,

Mary R. Brett

The FBI estimates that on any given day in America, there are between 50-100 Serial Killers walking among us

CHARLES FREDERICK ALBRIGHT
"The Eyeball Killer" 1+ KILLS

DOB: 8/10/1933 TX

SENTENCE: LIFE WITHOUT PAROLE

Facility: John Montford Psychiatric Unit, Lubbock, TX
Inmate 00606168

THE CRIME and CAPTURE: The killings were characterized by the removal of the victims' eyeballs with expert precision using an X-ACTO knife. Between 12/13/1990 and 3/18/1991, three Dallas prostitutes from the seedy Oak Cliff district were found dead from gunshot wounds. Each had been shot with a .44 caliber gun and all were missing their eyes.

Charles Albright, a 57-year-old known petty criminal with an extensive rap sheet, was arrested on 3/22/1991 based on information provided by other prostitutes and circumstantial evidence found during a search of his Oak Cliff residence. He was tried by a jury and convicted on the third murder charge only. There was insufficient evidence to try Albright of the other two killings but, to date, he remains the only suspect in those murders. After his arrest, no other bodies were found with the eyes removed.

A ballistic comparison of the bullets found in the body of the first and third victims matched although the gun was never located. DNA evidence evaluation had not progressed to today's standards. A pubic hair found on the third victim was from a Caucasian male and an expert testified it matched Albright's hair but not uniquely. A hair from the tail of a squirrel was found on the third victim's borrowed raincoat that was left in the field where she was killed. A squirrel's tail hair was also found in the vacuum cleaner bag at Albright's home. Albright's live-in girlfriend gave Albright an alibi for the time of one murder. Evidence was lost and a star witness for the prosecution, a drug-addicted prostitute named Veronica Rodriguez, changed her testimony.

Ultimately, Albright was convicted of one murder based solely on hair and circumstantial evidence. The jury deliberated for only a brief time before rendering their verdict. However, there are a few skeptics who firmly believe that Albright was not the killer. Albright still claims to be innocent of all charges.

BACKGROUND: Charles Albright was adopted from an orphanage when he was three weeks old. His adoptive mother doted on her only child and his well-being was a top priority. However, she was "old-school" strict and at times punished Charles severely by physically tying him down or shutting him inside a dark room. Good manners were especially important in the household she dominated. Charles was taught piano and he was expected to practice daily. He became an accomplished painter under her direction.

The mother and son shared a fascination and love for the same hobby: taxidermy. His mother encouraged Charles in this pursuit, imagining her son as a future doctor or surgeon. They would search for dead birds and small mammals to mount, spending hours on each meticulously crafted project. After Charles received his first gun, he would shoot small animals to mount. However, to Charles' dismay and disappointment, his mother insisted that each piece of taxidermy be completed with black buttons instead of the expensive glass eyes used by professionals. Many authorities proffer this as the root of his arcane fascination with eyes.

Charles' mother relentlessly pushed him in his academic studies. As a result, he was able to skip two grades and graduated from high school at 15. Unfortunately, by 13, he was already on a pathway to crime. Relatives report that even as a young child, he was always "a handful." By age 17, his thievery had escalated to the point that his crimes earned him a two-year sentence in a detention center. He served six months.

Upon release, he appeared to have changed for the better. He enrolled in Arkansas Teachers College and his charismatic personality and good looks earned him the coveted role of "big man on campus." Albright exceled in academics, sports, social clubs, and was elected to the student council. However, he was also known for outrageous pranks that bordered on the bizarre. In one instance, a good friend ended a relationship with a classmate and threw all photographs of his lost love in the trash. Charles retrieved the photos and cut out the woman's eyes from the torn-up pictures. He pasted them on the ceiling of his friend's dorm room above his bed and around the bathroom. In 1954, 20-year-old Albright was expelled from college before graduating for stealing from the school.

Real life was quite different from his college days. He married his college sweetheart, a teacher, but again seemed to prefer cheating, stealing, and lying over upstanding and legal behaviors. He pursued many avenues to earn a living but failed or quickly tired of each endeavor. In 1968, he faked his credentialing and academic record to falsely obtain a position at a high school teaching biology and coaching. He was well-liked by students, parents, administrators, and co-workers, but his deceit was eventually discovered. He was fired, prosecuted, and received probation.

All through the 1970's, he continued his petty larceny, cons, and illegal habits but with little repercussion. Even when he was charged and convicted of molesting a nine-year-old girl in 1981, he only received probation. He continued to shun lucrative employment, usually lasting on a job for only a few months. He relied first on his wife, Bettye, and then on a girlfriend, Dixie, to support him even after inheriting $96,000 from his father along with rental properties. When he was arrested, he was a part-time carpenter and delivered newspapers during the early morning hours. Reportedly, he frequented the Oak Cliff "bedroom motels" many days, a secret he successfully hid from his partners.

OUT OF THE MOUTH OF THE SERIAL KILLER: An UNEDITED letter to the author dated 6/22/2016:

Dear Ms. Brett,

Congratulations for your past published feats. I would certainly like to read about the freaks of film: I'm an avid Film Fancier- (that's supposed to read fancier). At one time, I had over 10,000 old movie posters, with over 300 of them, autographed- some by 6 to 8 members of some casts.

I enjoyed your letter. You said all the right things, if you forgive my opinion; (with a dollar, might just get you a cup of coffee, somewhere). Unfortunately, I'm no "killer", and there was never any evidence to show otherwise. It may be hard to believe, but everything, that makes me seem to be a killer, is simply a lie. I had "air-tight" alibis for all the times of all the crimes, and these were suppressed. I could not have been the killer- I was 700 miles away, in one case, and this was never dropped from the charges against me, and it was used at trial, as an extraneous offense, and the Court-Appointed Lawyer, who had worked for the D.A.'s office, over 10 years, betrayed me, in many different ways. I was arrested, without any warrant. Grenades were fired into the house, twice, starting fires, and no warrant. Fake evidence was "planted" in my house, and taken, without search warrant. There's more, a lot more, that the world needs to know.

I'll tell you a little bit more, believe it or not! I was accused of one crime, that was a "(9) hour ordeal" for her, it was said. This crime supposedly began at 5:00 P.M., and lasted until 1:00 A.M., (or there about). I was at home, when my lady "roommate" (Dixie) got home from work, at 5:30 P.M., so there was no way I could have been the culprit in this crime-which never happened.

The corrupt D.A., didn't go to the trouble of inventing a live victim. She just talked about at trial, as if she did exist. "When it was over, she made her way to a phone, and called the police." (But there was no record of this.) "Then she called a taxi, to go to the hospital." (No record of this either.) "Then, she went to a Hospital." (Which one? No record anywhere.) I had been Xmas shopping that day, and I had wrapped presents, most of the afternoon, until Dixie got home at 5:30.

Now, picture a clock face, and mark the 9 hours, starting at 5 pm, and going to 1:00 am. If I had done this crime, I had an alibi for the next crime which supposedly happened between 8:30 P.M., and 10:30 P.M. (the same night). I kidnapped this girl, and held her at knife point, and at gun point. (How do you drive, with weapons in both hands?) Then I drove her out in "the country" somewhere, and she got away, not shot, but slashed on the throat. And of all the houses she could run to, for help, she luckily ?? ran to a rent house of mine (Axton Schindler was the renter).

Now put 2:30 a.m. to maybe 6:am, and I was supposed to have picked up a girl in her Motel, and killed, and dropped her somewhere, during these 4 (?) hours. (My, is anyone that dedicated to doing dirt?) This 1st victim was last seen-leaving her motel, with a large Mexican man, with a moustache, in a blue and white, Chevrolet Pick-up, at 2:30. (I had no blue & white pick-up, nor did I have a moustache. I'm not a Mexican, and I only weight around 180 lbs., at 5'10" high. Nothing fit me.) This victim's body was found only a few blocks from my rent house-mentioned above. (I lived a mile away, from this house).

At trial, the supposed victim a local Prostitute, came to the stand, and said, "I've never seen Albright, and this crime never happened. I was coerced by the Police, until I finally agreed to "help" them, by lying about the crime. They threatened me with 10-20 years in the Penitentiary, if I didn't 'help' them! (We had a tape of the Coercion session, and the Judge wouldn't let us play it, for the Jury/ Court.) This was never dropped, even after her testimony, and the Judge let a lying Cop come in, 7 months later and say, "Now this case didn't really happen on "that night", it really happened the next day, from 8:30 to 10:30. I remember it quite well, and she wasn't cut, she had what you might call an abrasion -I remember it quite well. (He was the lying Cop who filled out the lying Police Report, that they used for an excuse to arrest me, (with no warrant).)

This new time, 8:30 'til 10:30 a.m., put me right into another alibi. I was 20 miles away, in a Volleyball game, and my "Judas" lawyer didn't even make this alibi, known.

The Prostitute, who was supposedly kidnapped, and who told the truth, at trial, was named Veronica Rodriguez, was actually taken to my Renter's house (Axton Schindler) by her Pimp, on the night of the 1st murder. He was in a blue and white Pick-up, and he was a huge Mexican man. (I don't know about the moustache, but he left her there, and left later, to go Where?? The Police looked for a big, robust Mexican Man, for several weeks; I was told.

I was refused "Truth Tests" of their choice, (3) times, and I will close this letter now. I am definitely interested in a book, but I'm not a killer, and this must be shown. I'm sorry for the handwriting. I have a legal type summary, (typed), being copied at present. Let me know if you want one.

Sincerely,

Charles Albright

Additional Facts:

• Albright was charged with the three "Eyeball Killer" murders as well as an unsolved 1988 murder of another prostitute who was stabbed to death, even though her eyes had not been removed. He was cleared of the 1988 murder when he presented an airtight alibi.

• He frequented prostitutes regularly and was known to many of the local Oak Cliff working women. During an initial police interview, however, he stated he had never used the service of any prostitute.

• His first experience with a prostitute had been when he was 15-years-old. He caught "the crabs" from the liaison.

• His adoptive mother died in 1981. His adoptive father died in 1986.

• After World War II ended, there was a building boom in America. Albright's mother began to sell real estate and he helped her. The parents bought their son a rental property when he was only 14-years-old. In total, he was left four rental parcels in Oak Cliff after his father passed. When the parents purchased the properties, Oak Cliff was a safe district with well-maintained homes and low crime.

• His adoptive mother reportedly kept goats in the back yard of their home so Albright would have fresh milk each day. She was obsessively concerned about his health.

• He married his wife on 12/27/1954. She left him in 1975 but did not divorce him until 1987. They had one daughter. In 1986, he began living with a woman, Dixie, whom he was still living with when he was arrested in 1991.

• Members of his senior soft ball league described Albright as having a great sense of humor and one who avoided physical altercations. He was well-liked. Dr. Irving Stone, a forensic scientist who was investigating the murders, played on the same team.

• When authorities searched his home, they found a hidden cache of almost a dozen guns but none matched the gun used in the murders. They did however find, .44 caliber ammunition, several X-ACTO knives, and the brand of condoms found with both the second and third bodies. His girlfriend was past child-bearing years and knew nothing of the condoms.

• He has always suggested that a renter in one of his homes was the killer. The man's name was Axton Schindler. The police searched Albright's rental properties after his arrest and found no incriminating evidence in the rental home where Schindler lived nor in any of the other properties.

• All the bodies were dumped in open residential areas. The third body was dumped miles away from the first two bodies. Each was crudely staged, either nude or with the victim's breasts exposed. The third victim was left in clear view near a public school.

The MO from the first two kills changed with the last kill. The first two victims had been Caucasian. The last victim was black and she had also been savagely beaten about the face. An earring had been ripped out of her ear. The removal of her eyes was done in a much less precise, almost blundering manner and part of the blade of an X-ACTO knife was still lodged in an eye socket. The authorities suggested the killer had been forced to rush during his macabre ritual or had worked himself into a violent frenzy.

• Albright admitted that he had a fascination with eyes, but always claimed that did not make him the killer. *"I got 3 books that gave references about taking out eyes. One of them is Stephen King."* **("Thinner")**

DAVID BERKOWITZ *"Son of Sam"*
".44-Caliber Killer" 6 Kills

DOB: 6/1/1953 NEW YORK

SENTENCE: 6-25 LIFE SENTENCES

Facility: Shawangunk Correctional Facility, Wallkill, NY INMATE 78A1976

THE CRIME and CAPTURE: Berkowitz was arrested on 8/10/1977 after a year-long killing spree, randomly shooting into occupied parked cars, or approaching victims on the street. Left in his wake were six innocents murdered, seven wounded, two of those impaired for life, and New York, a city of sixteen million people, in the grip of fear. A simple parking ticket brought the killer to justice. A witness described the man and the car leaving the shooting scene area and remembered a parking ticket on the windshield. The police were able to trace the ticket to Berkowitz. *"What took you so long?" "Well, you've finally got me."* In custody, he claimed he had been given the order to kill by his neighbor's dog that was possessed by a demon.

Berkowitz later confessed to two attempted murders on 12/24/1975. He claimed he tried unsuccessfully to stab two females to death. One victim has never come forward but the second female, age 14, was hurt seriously enough to be hospitalized and named. Reportedly, his failure in these two crimes prompted Berkowitz to change his MO weapon from a knife to a gun. He has never been charged with either crime. When authorities searched Berkowitz's residence after he was arrested, they located notebooks that recorded numerous arsons in the city he claimed were his doing.

He was never charged with the arsons. The apartment was in total disarray and had alarming and macabre sayings written all over the walls in magic markers.

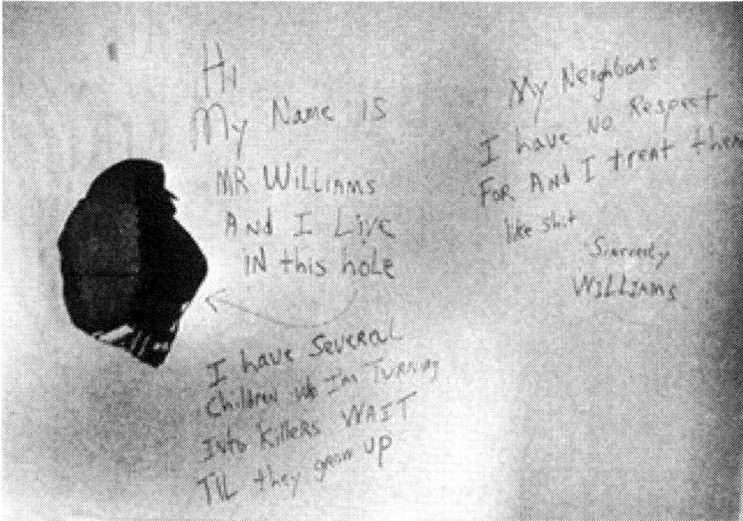

David Berkowitz's alarming and macabre sayings written all over the walls in magic markers.

(Photo source: www.people.com)

BACKGROUND: David Richard Berkowitz was born Richard David Falco to a divorced Jewish woman who was having an affair with a married man. The biological father wanted nothing to do with the child so his mother, a waitress, put the infant up for placement within days of his birth. He was adopted by a childless middle-aged Jewish couple of moderate means who spoiled their only child. He was especially close to his mother who doted on him. Berkowitz was bright but did not do well in school. He was described as difficult, disrespectful, at times violent, and prone to playing only with smaller, younger children he could bully and control. Early in life, he stole and set fires.

His adoptive mother died when Berkowitz was 14. He was devastated. His father remarried and Berkowitz immediately took a disliking to his stepmother.

In 1971, his father and stepmother moved to Florida and David, 18, joined the Army. He served in Korea and was honorably discharged in 1974. He returned home to New York and located his birth mother but was deeply disturbed to learn of his illegitimacy and of his biological father's absolute rejection. Deep depression and a feeling of worthlessness followed. He severed all ties with his biological mother and remained mostly estranged from his adoptive father and stepmother.

His only sexual intercourse experience was with a prostitute in Korea when he was 19 years old. He contracted a venereal disease from the encounter. He dated briefly, but was considered a friend by females, never a boyfriend.

OUT OF THE MOUTH OF THE SERIAL KILLER: Below is the UNEDITED wording of the hand-written letter from Berkowitz that was found dropped at a crime scene to taunt police on 4/17/77. He had just killed an 18-year old woman and 20-year-old male. (The errors in spelling and grammar are the killer's:)

"I am deeply hurt by your calling me a weman-hater. I am not. But I am a monster. I am the "son of Sam." I am a little brat. When father Sam gets drunk he gets mean. He beats our family. Sometimes he ties me up to the back of the house. Other times he locks me in the garage. Sam loves to drink blood. "Go out and kills" commands father Sam. Behind our house some rest. Mostly young - raped and slaughtered - their blood drained - just bones now. Pap Sam keeps me locked in the attic too. I can't get out but I look out the attic window and watch the world go by. I feel like an outsider. I am on a different wavelength then everybody else - programmed to kill. However, to stop me you must kill me. Attention all police: shoot me first - shoot to kill or else keep out of my way or you will die. Papa Sam is old now. He needs some blood to preserve his

youth. He has too many heart attacks. "Ugh, me hoot, it hurts, sonny boy." I miss my pretty princess most of all. She's resting in our ladies house. But i'll see her soon. I am the "monster" - "Beelzebub" - the chubby behemouth. I love to hunt. Prowling the streets looking for fair game - tasty meat. The wemon of Queens are prettiest of all. I must be the water they drink. I live for the hunt - my life. Blood for papa. Mr. Borelli, sir, I don't want to kill any more. No sur, no more but I must, "honour thy father". I want to make love to the world. I love people. I don't belong on earth. Return me to yahoos. To the people of Queens, I love you. And i want to wish all of you a happy Easter. May God bless you in this life and in the next. And for now I say goodbye and goodnight. Police: Let me haunt you with these words: I'll be back. I'll be back. To be interpreted as - bang, bang, bang, bang - ugh. Yours in murder, Mr. Monster."

A portion of a letter written 5/30/1977 to a journalist and published in the newspaper. Per police request, some parts of the letter were omitted from the public:

"Hello from the gutters of N.Y.C. which are filled with dog manure, vomit, stale wine, urine and blood. Hello from the sewers of N.Y.C. which swallow up these delicacies when they are washed away by the sweeper trucks. Hello from the cracks in the sidewalks of N.Y.C. and from the ants that dwell in these cracks and feed in the dried blood of the dead that has settled into the cracks..."

"Stacy was a whore" presumably referring to murdered Stacy Moskowitz, his 20-year-old innocent last victim. Berkowitz chanted this continuously under his breath in court 5/22/1978 at his sentence hearing. The judge postponed the hearing after the courtroom erupted in response. Berkowitz was required to have additional psychological testing.

An excerpt from a letter to the then-governor of New York in 2002 regarding a parole:

"In all honesty, I believe that I deserve to be in prison for the rest of my life. I have, with God's help, long ago come to terms with my situation and I have accepted my punishment." He has been up for parole every two years since 2002 and always denied he wanted to be released until 2016 when he declared in an effort to obtain parole that (His crimes were) *"...beyond my comprehension"* and cited his good work with fellow inmates.

"Jesus has already freed my heart, soul, and mind and has forgiven me.'" 2014.

"I just felt like I had no mind; I felt something else was controlling me." "I became an animal."

"I became virtually a killing machine. A machine of destruction."

"... prison is not easy, but over the years, God has given me a lot of strength and a lot of hope to make it and to endure and to survive. He has brought me -- he's done some miracles in my life, and he's brought me through a lot of things that maybe others would not have survived."

"...there were several times that at the beginning, when I first came to prison, I was very suicidal."

Additional Facts:

- Berkowitz has an older half-sister, the daughter of his mother and her divorced husband.

- He was over-weight as a child and teased. He remained "chubby" throughout adolescence and into adulthood.

- Reportedly, he killed his adoptive mother's beloved pet parakeet because he saw it as a rival for her attention and habitually burned bugs.

- Low self-esteem ruled his social world and employment choices. He felt totally frustrated around women, especially attractive women, and even though highly intelligent, he always gravitated toward jobs or job positions well beneath his abilities.

- As an adult, he claimed that knowing he was adopted made him feel inferior and different than other children.

- At 20, he briefly adopted the Baptist faith and was baptized. A few years later, he briefly became involved with a Satanic cult. In both experiences, he later claimed he was looking for acceptance and a faux family unit.

- He was cleared to work as a security guard and to drive a cab. He also worked as a duct installer for an air conditioning company. At the time of his arrest, he had recently quit his job as a postal worker.

- He attended Bronx Community College but did not graduate.

- He tended to choose young female victims with long, dark hair or couples together in a car.

- The task force assembled in 1977 to apprehend the serial killer consisted of over 300 law enforcers. It was dubbed operation Omega. At the time, it was the most intense man hunt ever launched in New York.

- Berkowitz now blames pornography for his killing spree.

- In 1979, he admitted to law enforcement and in a press conference that he never heard voices from any dog but had been seeking an insanity plea. The dog that Berkowitz claimed was possessed by a demon and ordered him to kill was a black lab named, Harvey. His owner was a former neighbor, Sam Carr, hence "Son of Sam". According to Carr, in 1977, he received two threatening letters about Harvey's barking and someone shot and wounded the dog. The handwriting later proved to be Berkowitz's.

• In 7/1979, a fellow Attica inmate slashed his neck with a razor so deeply that the wound required almost 60 stitches and left an 8-inch scar still visible today. Berkowitz refused to press charges and the inmate was relocated. *"...the punishment I deserve."*

• In 1987, Berkowitz became a born-again Christian, "Jews for Jesus," while incarcerated. He now prefers to be called "Son of Hope" in lieu of "Son of Sam".

• In 1993, Berkowitz broke almost 14 years of silence with a shocking new confession from jail. He now claimed he only killed three people and the rest were killed by members of a Satanic cult. He also claimed he confessed to all killings to get out of the cult with no repercussions for his family.

• Currently Berkowitz spends his time in prison administering to other prisoners and writing reflective memoirs based on his Christian convictions. His book, *"Son of Hope: The Prison Journals of David Berkowitz"* was published in 2006. He receives no royalties. In the 1980s, several states, including New York, put into place the "Son of Sam" law that allowed all profits to be diverted from the criminal and directed to the victims as compensation. The Supreme Court struck down the law in 1991 as unconstitutional.

• While most believe that Berkowitz was the sole perpetrator, there are still some respected professionals that doubt the single gun theory and believe that Berkowitz had one or more accomplices.

• In 1999, film director Spike Lee's movie, "Summer of Sam" portrayed Berkowitz's crimes and fearful grip on New York City. The movie was a critical and financial flop.

• www.AriseandShine.org is the official web site of Berkowitz. He personally has never seen the website since prisoners are not allowed internet access.

ANGELO BUONO & KENNETH BIANCHI
"The Hillside Stranglers" 10 Kills/12 Kills

BUONO DOB: 10/05/1934 NY DOD: 9/21/2002 CA (age 69)

DIED IN HIS CELL FROM A HEART ATTACK

BIANCHI DOB: 5/22/1951 NY

SENTENCE: LIFE WITH CHANCE OF PAROLE

Facility: Washington State Penitentiary, Walla Walla, WA INMATE 266962

THE CRIME: From 10/17/1977 until 2/16/1978, the two cousins, related by adoption, raped and strangled to death 10 females in the Los Angeles area, then dumped their nude bodies alongside deserted highway embankments or in isolated locations. Some of the victims showed signs of torture and some were sodomized. Buono and Bianchi pretended to be police officers to lure most of their unsuspecting and naïve victims. The murdered ranged in age from 12 to 28.

THE CAPTURE: Bianchi and Buono separated at Buono's request to avoid detection. He was worried that Bianchi was becoming too careless. Bianchi moved to Bellingham, WA and was hired as a security guard. However, he was quickly arrested for the rape and murder of two women there. Bianchi agreed to plead guilty and testify against Buono in exchange for leniency after his failed attempt to claim insanity.

BACKGROUND: Angelo Anthony Buono, Jr. exhibited an unusually high level of interest in anything of a sexual nature from an early age. He bragged to peers that he had raped several girls and idolized serial rapist, Caryl Chessman, "The Red Light Bandit", but faulted his hero for not killing his victims. At 17, he wed his pregnant girlfriend, but left her before their son was born and refused to financially support the child. He fathered five children by his second wife and two children by his third wife. Both women claimed he sexually molested one of their daughters. He married a fourth time in prison before his death but was not allowed conjugal visits.

Buono would have most likely remained a low-life, low-key offender if he had not met Kenneth Bianchi in 1975. Together the two became an evil force sustained and fueled by one another. On 10/17/1977, 43-year-old Buono and 26-year-old Bianchi killed their first victim. The sexually sadistic and psychopathic duo, working in concert, abducted, raped, and strangled to death their first victim, a 19-year-old waitress and prostitute they felt cheated them out of money.

Kenneth Alessio Bianchi was adopted after his birth mother, a teen-age alcoholic and prostitute, placed him for adoption shortly after birth. He never knew the identity of his biological father. Bianchi was raised in a middle class, two parent home as an only child. From the beginning, he showed signs of psychiatric problems. His adopted mother once complained that Bianchi started telling lies the same day he started to talk and remained a compulsive liar his entire life. At age 5, he was diagnosed with petit mal seizures, causing the young child to briefly lose consciousness. He was a bed wetter and was diagnosed with a passive-aggressive personality disorder by age 10. He often had violent and uncontrollable tantrums in school by age 11.

OUT OF THE MOUTH OF THE SERIAL KILLER:

"Was it wrong to get rid of some fuckin' cunts?" Kenneth Bianchi

(At Bianchi's sentencing in 10/1979:) *"To even begin to try to live with myself, I have to take responsibility for what I've done and I have to do everything I can to get into the modem and to devote my entire life, to do everything I possibly can to give my life so that nobody else will hopefully follow in, will hopefully won't follow in my footsteps."*

(Kenneth Bianchi interviewed *after* he was tried, sentenced, and serving time, claiming no memory of any crime:) *"I really have no memory of having murdered anybody. Even to satisfy other persons' allegations at one time. I attempted to think about what it might feel like and I have never been able to do that."*

When Kenneth Bianchi was asked if he could live his life over, what would he change: *"I really wouldn't change anything."*

Additional Facts:

- Bianchi pled NGRI (Not Guilty by Reason of Insanity), claiming he had another personality named Steven Walker who had committed the crimes. His claims were debunked and he eventually admitted to faking the disorder.

- Victoria Compton was 24-years-old when she fell in love with the incarcerated Kenneth Bianchi. She planned a copycat killing to get Bianchi out of jail but was caught and sentenced in 1981 for attempted murder. *"There I was with the Manson women and Carol Bundy. All I could think was, what the hell have I done? This isn't me."*

• Victoria Compton escaped from jail in 1988 but was caught 10 days later. She was released on parole in 1996, but that parole was quickly revoked after she failed to comply with its terms. She has since been released from jail.

• Bianchi's sperm that was to be used in the murder by Compton was concealed in a plastic glove and passed to her during a jailhouse visit, hidden in the binding of a book.

• On 8/27/1989, while incarcerated, 33-year-old Victoria Compton married 60-year-old James P. Wallace, a retired professor. Their daughter was born while Compton was in jail.

LAWRENCE BITTAKER & ROY NORRIS
"The Toolbox Killers" 5 Combined Kills

BITTAKER DOB: 9/27/1940 PA

DOD: 12/13/2019 in prison, natural causes (79)

SENTENCE: DEATH PLUS 199 YEARS, 4 MONTHS

Facility: San Quentin, San Quentin, CA

NORRIS DOB: 2/02/1948 CO

DOD: 2/24/2020 in prison, natural causes (72)

SENTENCE: 45 YEARS TO LIFE

Facility: R. J. Donovan Correctional Center, San Diego, CA

THE CRIME: In total, the sexual sadistic pair would abduct, rape, sodomize, torture, and kill five innocent teenage girls, relishing in affecting intense fear on their faces before they died. Three victims were tape-recorded during their horrific ordeal. One was photographed as she pleaded for her life.

The killing spree spanned from June 1979, through November. Their hunting ground was usually a 20 mile stretch in Southern California from Redondo Beach to Santa Monica. They had equipped their 1977 silver cargo van to accommodate their gruesome needs. The vehicle was windowless on both sides and had a large sliding side door on the passenger side. Inside was a platform bed with a storage area below where they kept tools, a change of clothes, plus a cooler filled with chilled beer and soft drinks.

Bittaker and Norris, who first met in prison, became known as the "Toolbox Killers" because most of the instruments the sick duo used to torture and murder their victims were items that normally would be found in any typical toolbox or kitchen.

BACKGROUND: Lawrence Sigmund Bittaker was born to parents who considered the child a mistake. They gave him up when he was an infant to a couple who were distant relatives and he was raised an only child. Bittaker would later claim his adoptive parents were cold and unloving.

He was an extremely bright child, did well academically in school, but did not make friends easily among peers and had several run-ins with juvenile authorities. At 17, he dropped out of high school before graduation. Shortly afterwards, he was arrested for auto theft, hit and run, and evading police. He was sent to the California Youth Authority and released in 1959 but was constantly in and out of prison.

In 1974, Bittaker was sent to the California Men's Colony at San Luis Obispo for assault during a robbery. It was at this prison that Bittaker met Roy Norris and discovered that each harbored an aberrant fantasy about raping, torturing, and murdering young girls. They became inseparable in prison and made plans to carry out their deviant fantasies upon release.

Roy Lewis Norris was conceived out of wedlock but his parents married as was the social custom of the day. A younger sister was born shortly after his birth. They lived in a trailer close to other extended family members. Norris' family struggled financially and, reportedly, his mother was addicted to drugs.

His father was a strict disciplinarian and administered corporal punishment when angered. Norris and his sister were placed with foster families several times during their childhood. He always claimed he was ill-treated in most homes, denied adequate care, and was sexually abused in one foster home.

Norris was above average in intelligence, a fair student, but was a shy and introverted child. He especially had a difficult time around girls and was often admonished for inappropriate behavior when interacting with them. In his early teens, he started a consenting incestuous sexual relationship with an older female cousin.

At 17, Norris dropped out of school and joined the Navy. In 1969, he was discharged from the Navy for psychological issues after he was charged with the attempted rape of two women. Shortly after his discharge, he viciously attacked a college co-ed with a rock and repeatedly slammed her head into concrete. She survived and was instrumental in Norris' arrest and conviction. According to Norris, Bittaker saved his life inside the prison, bonding them for life per the inmate code.

OUT OF THE MOUTHS OF THE SERIAL KILLER:

The October 17, 2016 UNEDITED letter below is in response to the author asking **Roy Norris** the simple question, why did you kill?

"Ms. Brett,

Your age Ms. Brett? There are a lot of lies on the net (wikipedia). I have participated in many University investigations or inquiries. And I get many requests for interviews-especially on film or video.

Any other books that you've been involved with?

I unwittingly had my letters (my response to the author's letters, which she didn't publish) put in a book format for download, by Ms. Furio (?)

I erred early on while in jail. I called a Radio Reporter to set something correct. She recorded my statements and that night on the radio….my statements were chopped up and respliced to make it sound like I'd said something else. I have not cooperated with anyone since.

What assurance do I have that you'll not use Creative License to rewrite my words?

Thank you,

Roy Norris 10-17-16"

10-17-16

Mr. Brett,

Your age Ms. Brett? There are a lot of lies on the net (wikipedia). I have participated in many University investigations or inquiries. And I get many requests for interviews - especially on film or video.

Any other books that you've been involved with?

I unwittingly had my letters (my response to the author's letters, which she didn't publish) put in a book format for download, by Ms. Furio (?).

I erred early on while in jail. I called a Radio Reporter to set something correct. She recorded my statements and that night on the radio .... my statements we chopped up and respliced to make it sound like I'd said something else. I have not cooperated with anyone since.

What assurance do I have that you'll not use Creative License to rewrite my words?

Thank you,

Roy Norris
10-17-16

OUT OF THE MOUTHS OF THE SERIAL KILLERS:

"The animals would eat her up, so there wouldn't be any evidence left." Bittaker reportedly said this to Norris after disposing of the body of their first murder victim by throwing the remains over a canyon cliff.

Bittaker wrote that victim 1 *"...displayed a magnificent state of self-control and composed acceptance of the conditions of which she had no control. She shed no tears, offered no resistance and expressed no great concern for her safety ... I guess she knew what was coming."*

Norris said to victim 5: *"Go ahead and scream or I'll make you scream." "What are you sniveling about?"*

Additional Facts:

• Bittaker and Norris abducted, raped, sodomized, tortured, and killed five innocent teenage girls, relishing in affecting intense fear on their faces before they died. Three victims were tape-recorded during their horrific ordeal. One was photographed as she pleaded for her life. Two bodies were never found.

• Bittaker dubbed his and Norris' van, *"Murder Mack,"* inspired by the Hillside Stranglers who also named the vehicle they used to kill.

• Bittaker has never shown nor expressed remorse. While on trial, he penned a book entitled, "The Last Ride", that detailed his and Norris' murder and torture spree.

• Bittaker and Norris' last murder victim was Shirley Lynette Ledfrod. Her torture tape sealed the sexual sadists' fate when it was played in court.

- In 1995, Bittaker filed a nuisance lawsuit against the state of California's DOC claiming to be a victim of cruel and unusual treatment because he was served a broken cookie and crushed sandwiches.

- Bittaker had a near-genius IQ.

DANIEL BLANK " *River Parishes Serial Killer"* 6 Kills

DOB: 1962 LA

SENTENCE: Sentenced to death by lethal injection in 1999 and 2000 (over-turned) plus received two irrevocable life sentences in 2001.

Facility: Louisiana State Penitentiary, Angola, LA INMATE 416437

THE CRIME: A gambling habit and lifestyle that he could not afford started a murder spree that began on 10/17/1996 and ended with Daniel Blank's arrest on 11/14/1997. He beat or stabbed to death six mostly well-to-do elderly people, plus he shot and beat another 66-year-old married couple but they survived the attack and helped lead the police to Blank. All were attacked with objects in their home.

Blank was acquainted with most of his victims and all lived within a 20-mile radius of his family home. He confessed to 6 killings and the additional attempted murders during a 12-hour taped interview with investigators. His live-in girlfriend, Cynthia Bellard, was also arrested on murder charges but agreed to testify against Blank in exchange for having all charges dismissed.

Many locals voiced their opinion that Blank was not capable of planning these crimes on his own and some feel that Bellard was, at the least, equally guilty.

BACKGROUND: Daniel Joseph Blank grew up in abject poverty, He was one of eight children born to a sugar refinery worker. The exact date of his birth was never recorded.

Blank dropped out of school after the eighth grade but reportedly only reads at a third-grade level. His IQ tested 85.

As a teenager, he intentionally burned down a building and was sent to reform school. He had no other run-ins with the law until his arrest for murder at age 35.

He never married but was the father of four children.

OUT OF THE MOUTH OF THE SERIAL KILLER:

"I grabbed it (a trophy) *and then I pushed her and she came back up, and that's when I hit her with it and went out of it."*

...I liked houses with safes in them."

Additional Facts:

- Blank suffered a head injury after being hit by a car at age 12.

- During trial preparation, he was diagnosed with a learning disability that impaired his ability to verbalize well.

- A psychologist testified at trial that Blank had a low IQ and an abnormal personality. He claimed Blank suffers from a schizoid-affective paranoia disorder, causing him to constantly feel anxious and extremely inadequate.

- Acquaintances described Blank as a quiet family man who was a gifted mechanic.

- In December 1998, Blank escaped using a second-floor Donaldsonville courthouse bathroom window. He was quickly recaptured.

- It was estimated in 2016 that it would cost $30,000 to purchase the drugs to execute Daniel Blank. The Finance Committee in Ascension Parish, LA approved the output without objection.

- He favored slots and video poker and frequented many varied gambling facilities.

- Blank was arrested in Texas where he had moved and purchased a mobile home. Prior to his arrest, he had offered $65K in cash to purchase an automobile repair shop.

- Blank was granted a new trial in 2016 due to a clerical error during court procedures in 2000. He entered a guilty plea to first-degree murder for killing a woman in 1997 in exchange for a life sentence, thus taking the death penalty off the table.

- Daniel Blank's six innocent victims: Victor Rossi, 41, Barbara Bourgeois, 58, Lillian Philippe, 71, Sam Arcuri, 76, his wife, Louella, 69, and Joan Brock, 55. (Mrs. Brock was the wife of an employer who fired Blank.)

WILLIAM BONIN *"Freeway Killer"* 21+ Kills

DOB: 1/08/1947 CT

DOD: 2/23/1996, age 49

SENTENCE: DEATH/ LETHAL INJECTION

FACILITY: SAN QUENTIN, CA

THE CRIME: From 8/5/1979 until apprehended on 6/11/1980, William George Bonin is responsible for the deaths of 21 or more southern California children and young men. Bonin lured his victims into his converted Ford Econoline van, then forcefully bound each with handcuffs before he sexually assaulted them. After, he tortured his victims before he routinely strangled or beat his prey to death, although one victim was forced to drink acid, three died from ice picks being driven into their ears, and one child died of shock.

The bodies were callously dumped along California freeways, earning Bonin the diabolical tag, "Freeway Killer." At times, he worked in concert with four accomplices, Vernon Butts and Gregory Miley whom he met in 1979, James Munro, a co-worker and roommate, and William Pugh, a teenage delinquent who became the driving force behind Bonin's capture.

BACKGROUND: William Bonin and his two brothers had it bad. Both parents were alcoholics. His father also had a gambling addiction and a violent temper he regularly unloaded on his wife and sons. The children were severely neglected, frequently going without adequate food or clothing unless a kind neighbor took pity. The boys were often left in the care of a maternal grandfather who was a convicted child molester. He had molested Bonin's mother when she was a child but she was so unconcerned or so uncaring that she proffered up her children to endure the same abuse. The grandfather eagerly complied.

In 1953, six-year-old Bonin and his brothers were placed in an orphanage. The staff ruled with an iron hand and any infraction of the many rules resulted in harsh punishments that included severe beatings and torture. Methods of torture included being made to hold stress positions for lengthy periods of time or having one's head forcefully held underwater in a sink or bucket full of water. Bonin was sexually assaulted by the adolescent boys. He always made the strange request to first have his hands tied behind his back. With this concession granted, he neither fought back nor resisted the assault. The Bonin children were left at this institution of horrors for three years before the parents came for them. As an adult, Bonin bore scars on his head and buttocks as testimony to the abuse he suffered during his time spent in the orphanage and juvenile detention center. He also bore psychological scars.

Bonin was arrested for the first time when he was age 10. He had stolen license plates and was placed in a Connecticut juvenile detention center. There he was regularly sexually assaulted by the older juveniles and one adult male counselor.

As a teenager and young adult, he sexually assaulted young males and later added torture to the attacks if the victim resisted. Quickly, he escalated to murder.

OUT OF THE MOUTH OF THE SERIAL KILLER:

(Said to Vernon Butts regarding a recent kill): *"We* **(James Munro)** *got it in the van; it's a good one. Come on out and see it."*

"I'd still be killing. I couldn't stop killing. It got easier with each one we did."

"I like the sound of kids dying."

(Near the time of execution, when asked if he had any final words for the families of his victims:) *"They feel my death will bring closure, but that's not the case. They're going to find out."*

(Final written statement of Bonin before his execution:) *"I feel the death penalty is not an answer to the problems at hand. I feel it sends the wrong message to the people of this country. Young people act as they see other people acting instead of as people tell them to act. I would advise that when a person has a thought of doing anything serious against the law, that before they did, they should go to a quiet place and think about it seriously."*

ADDITIONAL FACTS...

• Bonin married at an early age trying to curb his preference for young males but both the marriage and effort failed.

• During Bonin's 14-years on death row, he painted, wrote short stories, poems, and an autobiography. He regularly corresponded with individuals, including the family of his victims. Reportedly, Bonin never showed any remorse nor made any apologies. His letters to victims' families were often cruel and crude. *"He was such a screamer."* (Excerpt from an incredulous letter from Bonin to the mother of one of his victims.)

- Before being executed in 1996, Bonin passed time incarcerated playing bridge with fellow death row inmates Randy Kraft, Douglas Clark, and Lawrence Bittaker. All four serial killers were reported to have genius or near-genius IQs.

- No family member nor friend would claim responsibility for William Bonin's remains following his execution. He was cremated in a private ceremony and no family attended the service. Later, his ashes were scattered over the Pacific Ocean by prison personnel.

William Bonin had four accomplices: Vernon Butts, Greg Miley, James Munro, and William Pugh: Butts committed suicide awaiting trial, Miley was killed in 2016 by another inmate while incarcerated, Munro is incarcerated and has repeatedly been denied bail, and Pugh was released from prison in 1985.

GARY RAY BOWLES *"The I-95 Killer"* 7 Kills

DOB: 1/25/1962 VA

DOD: 8/22/2019 FL, age 57 by lethal injection, RAIFORD, FLORIDA

SENTENCE: DEATH PENALTY-TWICE

FACILITY: Union Correctional Institute (Death Row 23 Years)

THE CRIME: Gary Ray Bowles killed six gay men (he claims he killed seven) in a spree starting in 3/1994 and ended with his arrest in 11/1994. His spree spanned three states: Florida, Georgia, and Maryland. He robbed his victims but robbery does not appear to be the motive and each kill was branded as an "over-kill." Some of his victims were found with a cloth, paper, leaves, or a sex toy shoved very deeply into their throats. Bowles hung out in gay bars where he met his likely prospects. He would offer household chores and sex in exchange for a place to stay.

BACKGROUND: Bowles biological father died before he was born from black lung. He, his mother, and his older brother were often violently abused by an alcoholic stepfather. He left home at age 13, after seriously injuring the stepfather with a brick in retaliation. His mother stood by her husband, basically abandoning Gary. He was homeless for a time and immediately started earning money as a prostitute, a profession he continued to engage in for approximately 20 years even though he always professed he was a heterosexual. His first arrest was in 1982 (age 20) for the sexual battery of a girlfriend and he was sentenced to six years. His second offence was for the unarmed robbery of an elderly woman and he was sentenced to four years.

He was described as handsome, charming, manipulative, a liar, the perfect con man.

OUT OF THE MOUTH OF THE SERIAL KILLER: In a first UNEDITED letter to the author, Bowles claimed he killed his first victim because the victim showed him a pornographic video of a young boy with two adult men: *"It shocked me." "I just snapped."* It should be noted that no video tape was found at the crime scene nor any evidence that the victim had been a pedophile. In fact, none of his six known victims had any past arrests or reputations for engaging in sexual acts with a child. *"I guess I am a serial killer but I guess not your average serial killer." "Sad to say, but it's not hard to kill somebody. You can kill someone pretty easy if you have a mind for it." "In my mind they all got what was deserved. I just wanted to kill as many people as I could before they caught me." "I wasn't trying to commit the perfect crime." "I was just, you know, out of my mind with rage and hate." "I felt kinda like a sense of justice. In my mind I thought what I was doing was alright."*

An UNEDITED excerpt from a second letter written by Gary Ray Bowles to the author 4/23/2016:

"Each murder was for different reasons, but when I did the first one I seen something that caused me to remember something from when I was 9 years old, and it caused me to snap and kill for the first time. After the first murder I knew my life was over, and that lead me to kill six more times. The F.B.I. never charged me with the 7th murder but I've proved I did it and they still won't charge me."

Gary Ray Bowles final written statement before execution: *"I'm sorry for all the pain and suffering I have caused. I hope my death eases your pain. I want to tell my mother that I am also so sorry for my actions. Having to deal with your son being called a monster is terrible. I'm so very sorry. I never intended this to be my life. You don't wake up one day and decide to become a serial killer."*

"I was treated with respect for the last 73 days on death watch, and I felt human again." *"I'm sorry to the other families who did not get closure. I've told the FBI everything, no cases left open."* Bowles response when authorities asked about cold cases on their books.

ADDITIONAL FACTS:

• Bowles was placed on the FBI's Most Wanted list while on the run in 1992. Most likely, the violence and over-kill exhibited during his killing spree created the urgency to quickly locate and apprehend him.

• Bowles beat a girlfriend so badly in 1982 that a detective remarked she had seen better looking bodies in the morgue. He was sentenced to six years but received an early release.

• He was the subject of A&E's show, "The Killer Speaks"/ 2014 Season 2, Episode 4.

JERRY BRUDOS *"The Lust Killer"*
"Shoe Fetish Slayer" 4+ Kills

DOB: 1/31/1939 SD

DOD: 3/28/2006 OR

SENTENCE: 3 LIFE TERMS. Died in prison from liver cancer, age 67.

Facility: Oregon State Penitentiary

THE CRIME: Jerome Henry Brudos, married with children, was a sadistic necrophiliac with a life-long shoe fetish who stalked, tortured, raped, and killed four innocent young women in the Portland/ Salem, Oregon area from 1/26/1968 until he was apprehended on 5/25/1969.

He dressed the naked corpse of his first victim in assorted undergarments and took photos. He also took her left foot as a souvenir, kept it in a garage freezer, and masturbated while gazing at the foot wearing high heels from his collection. He kept the garage locked and refused his family entrance.

He hung his second victim in the garage and raped the corpse for several days before disposing of her body. He kept her right breast and made a souvenir paperweight. He kept both breasts of his next victim after hanging her and raping her corpse.

Two intended victims of Brudos escaped and were able to furnish authorities with information that eventually led to his arrest and detailed confession. Brudos told authorities that after he finished with a victim, he put on high-heel shoes and masturbated. He originally pleaded NGRI, Not Guilty by Reason of Insanity, but a few days before his trial was to begin, he changed his plea to guilty. He was sentenced to Life since Oregon did not have a death penalty at that time.

BACKGROUND: Jerome Henry Brudos was the younger of two sons. He always claimed his mother had desperately wanted her second child to be a girl and never forgave him for not being born female. Reportedly, she berated and belittled him his entire life.

Five-year-old Jerry Brudos retrieved a pair of high-heel shoes from a junk yard trash bin and was immediately enamored. He wore them to his prudish mother's complete horror. She ultimately burned the shoes to halt Brudos from continually parading around the house in the heels. He began to steal shoes from nearby homes he broke into and quickly added women's underwear to his take. He enjoyed wearing both and began to use the undergarments and heels to enhance masturbation as he approached puberty.

He was sent to the psychiatric ward of the Oregon State Hospital for evaluation and treatment at 17 after a violent attack on a girl neighbor. There he admitted he was planning to imprison a female who was to become his sex slave, just one of many he intended to eventually capture. For whatever reason, the hospital released Brudos after only nine months even after diagnosing him as exhibiting an extreme hatred towards his mother that translated to all women. He was also labeled borderline schizophrenic.

He joined the army in 1959. After two years, he was discharged early from the service due to mental issues after he confided his sexual fantasies to an army psychologist. In 1961, 22-year-old Brudos married his pregnant 17-year-old girlfriend after a very brief courtship. Both were virgins when they met. Brudos began openly dressing in women's underwear and heels. His wife, replicating his mother's negative reaction from his youth, strongly disapproved.

Intimacy between the couple declined to the point they began to occupy separate bedrooms.

THE VICTIMS: Brudos' four innocent victims. They ranged in age from 19-23:

Linda Kay Slawson, age 19, was selling encyclopedias door-to-door on 1/26/1968 when she unfortunately approached the Brudos' family home. Her body was never recovered, but her left foot was found. It had been cut off and stored in Brudos' shop freezer. He used the dismembered foot to display various shoes in his collection. The sight of it sexually thrilled him and he later admitted that he masturbated while gazing upon this macabre souvenir.

Jan Susan Whitney, age 23, an honor student, was driving home from college on 11/25/1968 when her car broke down. Brudos strangled her to death in his car with a leather strap and then transported her body to his garage. Once there, he hung her corpse from a ceiling hook and had sex with the body for several days before cutting off her right breast and disposing of her body. His crafted a resin mold from the dismembered breast with the intention of creating paperweights.

Karen Elena Sprinkler, age 19, was scheduled to meet her mother for lunch on 3/27/1969. Brudos abducted her from a parking garage at gunpoint and drove her to his garage. He forced her to pose in other women's underwear for photos before hanging her. He raped the corpse then cut off both breasts before dumping the mutilated body in the Long Tom River.

One month later, Brudos abducted **Linda Dawn Salee**, 19, from a shopping center where she had gone to buy birthday gifts for a boyfriend. He strangled her and threw her corpse in the Long Tom River. He admitted during interrogation that he had posed as a police officer to lure her into his car.

OUT OF THE MOUTH OF THE SERIAL KILLER:

"I have no intention of baring my soul." (His reply when asked at a parole hearing why he had killed.)

"I'm more stable now than I ever was out on the streets."
"I think I've got a whole new personality."

"I'm trying to get on with my life."

"...an act of vengeance. This is not over. They cannot remove my legal rights." (*Brudos'* response to the Parole Board's 1995 decision to never grant him a parole.)

"One day's like another in here. I tend to lose track."

"It was a slow Saturday night..." (Laughing response to Portland media personality, Lars Larson, when Larson asked Brudos about the murders he committed.)

Additional Facts:

• In grade school, Brudos tried to steal a teacher's extra pair of high heel shoes she kept in a desk drawer. She embarrassed him in front of the class.

• Brudos mother was vocal and adamant in her confirmed belief that anything sexual was filthy and repulsive. He once told a psychiatrist that he remembered his mother as always wearing sensible shoes.

• Twelve women went missing around Portland while he resided in that city. He is suspected of more kills but has never been charged with any additional crimes. He was only convicted of killing three victims since the body of one victim, Linda Kay Slawson, was never found.

• A neighbor implicated Brudos' wife in the murders but she was cleared of all charges. She divorced her husband in 1971, moved, and changed her name.

She sought and received a court order forbidding her children from having any contact with their father.

• Brudos was said to write to shoe companies ordering catalogues that he hoarded in his cell.

• While incarcerated, Brudos was attacked by fellow prisoners and sexually assaulted.

• Brudos earned two college degrees behind bars: General Science and Counseling. He was working on his master's degree in counseling when he died.

• He is buried in the Oregon State Penitentiary Cemetery. No one claimed his body.

• The Oregon State Hospital that 17-year-old Brudos was sent to in 1956 was the same hospital that "One Flew over the Cuckoo Nest" was filmed starring Jack Nicholson.

• At the time of his death from natural causes at age 67, Brudos was the longest incarcerated inmate in the ODOC. He had been imprisoned for 37 years.

JUDIAS BUENOANO *"The Black Widow"* 3+ Kills

DOB: 4/4/1943 TX

DOD: 3/30/1998/Electric Chair/ Starke, FL

Buenoano was on Death Row for 13 years before being executed.

THE CRIME: On 3/30/1998, Judy Buenoano, 54, became the first woman executed in Florida in 150 years and the first and last woman to die in the state's electric chair, Old Sparky. Florida had not executed a woman since 1848, when a freed slave was hanged for killing her former master. Greed motivated Buenoano to kill her husband of eight years, a boyfriend, her 19-year-old first born son, and to attempt the murder of a fiancé, all for insurance money. She used lethal doses of arsenic to kill both her husband and her boyfriend. Her son survived his 1979 poisoning attempt so she drowned him in a canoe outing in 1980. Before being arrested, she had collected approximately $240,000 in insurance claims from the three deaths and was hoping for a pay out from the anticipated murder of her fiancé. Unfortunately for Buenoano, the botched 1983 bombing of her fiancé's car led authorities to her.

They would soon discover that she had been giving her fiancé "vitamin pills" laced with arsenic and formaldehyde but he was obviously not dying quickly enough to suit her.

Buenoano was on Death Row for 13 years before being executed. She was the first woman executed in Florida in 150 years and the first and last woman to die in the state's electric chair.

(Photo source: www.whatliesbeyond.boards.net)

BACKGROUND: Born Judias Welty into abject poverty, her father was an itinerant farm laborer and her mother died of TB when Judias was young. Grandparents took in Buenoano and her infant brother while two older siblings were sent to an orphanage and placed for adoption.

Her father remarried when she was 12 years-old and retrieved his two children, but Buenoano always claimed her stepmother hated her and she was the brunt of extreme physical abuse from both the stepmother and her father. She was often hungry. At 14, she was sent to an adult jail for violently attacking her parents and throwing hot grease on two stepbrothers.

She claimed that when her two-month sentence was completed, she asked to be placed in a reform school rather than return home. It is more likely she was no longer welcome in the home. She remained in a girls' reformatory until age 16. She never reconciled with her family nor with any family member.

In 1961, she gave birth to an illegitimate son, the child she would end up murdering for insurance money when he was only 19.

She married in 1962, and gave birth to two children, a second son and a daughter. She murdered her husband of nine years in 1971 and cashed in several life insurance policies. Less than a year later, she collected an additional $90,000 when her house burned to the ground. The fire was of a suspicious nature but no charges were brought.

OUT OF THE MOUTH OF THE SERIAL KILLER:

"...defamation, assassination of character... to make me into a vile monster."

"I think they just didn't have any other leads whatsoever. They never investigated anybody else." "Why, why did you single me out?"

"Possibly, I am a different person. But I was a Christian when I came here. I was a devout Catholic. I've not changed in that."

"I would have found myself guilty if I were the jury."

"I have eternal security and I know that when I die I will go straight to heaven and I will see Jesus," "I'm ready to go home."

When asked if she had any final words: "No, sir." Reportedly, she had planned to say "vaya con Dios" that translates to "go with God."

Additional Facts:

- Women compose less than two percent of the death row population in the United States. Our society has always been reluctant to sentence a woman to death except in extreme cases.

• Buenoano's husband had only been back from fighting in Vietnam for three months when she poisoned him in 1971. *"He came home from Vietnam ill and he never got well. It had nothing to do with me, I was not in Vietnam."*

• The Widow Goodyear changed her last name to "Buenoano" meaning "good year" in broken Spanish.

• Her oldest son proved to be a problem for his mother in school so she placed him in foster care where he received free psychiatric care rather than pay for his treatment from insurance funds. That son survived the attempted poisoning but, as a result, was left partially paralyzed and required leg braces. When his mother pitched him out of the canoe, he had no way to survive in the water with the heavy braces pulling him down. She would have watched as he struggled for his life. Four out of five of the life insurance policies Buenoano had on her son were double indemnity polices in the case of accidental death. On the stand, she shouted out to the prosecuting attorney: *"You don't know what happened in that canoe. You weren't there."* Her younger son was also on the boat but he claimed he was knocked out and remembered nothing.

• Buenoano had changed the life insurance policy on her last victim, a fiancé, from $50,000 to $500,000 without his knowledge. She told him she was pregnant and sent him out for celebratory champagne. His car blew up when he started the engine, almost killing him. Buenoano was not pregnant. In 1975, she had opted to be surgically sterilized. It was later discovered that Buenoano had booked a world cruise for herself and two children but had not included the victim, her fiancé, in the reservation.

• Police had a strong suspicion that Buenoano had an accomplice in the failed car bombing. Her 16-year-old younger son was a prime suspect. He was tried but subsequently acquitted of the charges.

• In 1990, she received a stay when, "Old Sparky", Florida's electric chair, malfunctioned during an execution. Electrocutions were temporarily halted pending an investigation.

• Buenoanos' daughter adamantly defended her mother, always believing in her innocence. Had she been successful in her hard-fought appeals through the Florida court system, Colorado would have most likely tried her for capital murder.

• In the past, she operated her own nail salon and day care center. She was a Licensed Practical Nurse.

• Ironically, she was executed on her murdered son's 37th birthday. She never admitted to any guilt, she never showed remorse.

• Judias Buenoano always boasted that she would never be executed. Witnesses say she went to her death looking like a frail and frightened old woman, all her previous bravado obviously missing.

TED BUNDY 36+ Kill

DOB: 11/24/1946 VT

DOD: 1/24/1989, age 42

SENTENCE: DEATH by Electrocution

FACILITY: Raiford Prison, Starke, FL

The term "Serial Killer" was first used to describe Ted Bundy in an attempt to understand his mindset.

THE CRIME: Theodore Robert Cowell Nelson Bundy killed women and female children in 7 or more states from 1974-1978, possibly starting prior to 1974. He was handsome, intelligent, educated, well-liked by peers, and successful. He was also an organized killer. All these factors added to his ability to escape detection for many years. Most of his victims were young, classically attractive women with long dark hair parted in the middle leading to the speculation that his choice of victims mirrored a long-time girlfriend of a like description. Bundy always dismissed this theory. His last victim was a 12-year-old girl, the age at the time of his girlfriend's only child, a daughter.

His usual MO was to openly approach his victim and pretend to need their help. When alone, he would bludgeon them, strangle the victim to death, then have sex with the dead body. At times, he would return to the crime scene and have sex with the decomposing, rotting corpses. He decapitated at least 12 known victims and kept some of the severed heads at his residence as souvenirs. ***"Then I cut her head off with a hacksaw and I took it home with me."***

A secondary, earlier MO was to break into a residence late at night and bludgeon the sleeping residents to death.

Background: His Mother, Eleanor Louise Cowell, gave birth to Bundy in a facility for unwed mothers. His maternal grandparents portrayed themselves to both Bundy and the community as his parents while Louise pretended to be his sister. The identity of his father was never established. Bundy held a strong resentment, almost hatred, towards his mother for her deception.

She married in 1951 and Ted took the surname of his stepfather, Bundy. He was an honor student in high school, active in his Methodist Church, and a boy scout. In spite of this, he was arrested for shoplifting twice as a juvenile. In an interview held hours before his execution, Bundy was adamant that his family bore no blame for his actions. *"I grew up in a wonderful home." "A fine, solid Christian home."*

OUT OF THE MOUTH OF THE SERIAL KILLER:

Most mental professionals have labeled Bundy a sociopath or a psychopath. Both mental conditions allow the individuals to readily distinguish right from wrong but block feelings of guilt and remorse. This makes it easy to ignore established rules and laws. A quote from Bundy in 1981: *"Guilt doesn't solve anything, really. It hurts you. I guess I am in the enviable position of not having to deal with guilt."*

Speaking of himself, *"...the most cold-hearted son of a bitch you'll ever meet."*

Towards the end, it appears Bundy was searching for a valid excuse as to why he killed: *"I've met a lot of men who were motivated to commit violence just like me. And without exception, without question, every one of them was deeply involved in pornography." "Well-meaning, decent people will condemn the behavior of a Ted Bundy, while they're walking past a magazine rack full of the very kinds of things that send young kids down the road to be Ted Bundys." "There lots of other kids playing in streets around this country today who are going to be dead tomorrow, and the next day, and the next day and month, because other young people are reading the kinds of things and seeing the kinds of things that are available in the media today."* According to researchers and interviewers, Bundy was always blaming someone or something else, from the police who he said planted evidence to the victims themselves, claiming their look of vulnerability lead to their demise.

Concerning his background: *"I'm not an animal, and I'm not crazy and I'm not a split personality. That's all there is to it. People refuse to believe that. That's their problem. There's nothing in my background, I swear to God, and I know it: I've analyzed my own background and I know there's no doubt." "...no one factor or collection of factors that would explain or would otherwise lead one to believe that I was capable of murder."*

Speaking to his pattern of revisiting the crime scenes to relive the experience and have sex with the decomposing corpses. *"When you work hard to do something right you don't want to forget it."* As the time of his inevitable execution approached, he pleaded that he could help authorities solve many cold cases if he was allowed to live. 36 hours before his 1989 execution, he confessed to killing Debra Kent, a 17-year-old Utah high school student. He told authorities where he left her body and offered to help police to solve other open cases if not executed. DNA testing had previously confirmed that remains found were that of Debra but her murder had gone unsolved. *"I don't wanna die, I'm not gonna lie to you. I admit that and I'm not asking for clemency, I'm not asking for forgiveness,*

I'm not asking for sympathy. I know they're gonna kill me sooner or later. You don't need to worry about that but there's a lot of crimes I can solve if the state can just see fit to make me live two or three years longer, I mean look, I know I'm not like other people, I know I can't feel sympathy for other people but I'm still human." His ploy failed and a large crowd outside Raiford Prison cheered when he was pronounced dead.

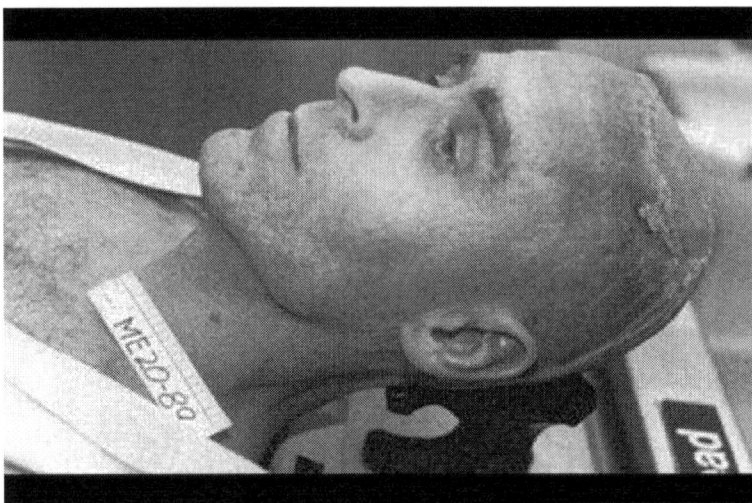

Photo of prolific Serial Killer, Ted Bundy, after Florida execution 1/24/1989. As the time of his execution approached, he pleaded that he could help authorities solve many cold cases if he was allowed to live. His ploy failed and a large crowd outside Raiford Prison in Florida cheered as he was put to death.

(Photo source: Pinterest)

Bundy confessed to 36 killings, but he is strongly suspected of more. Truth or bravado, he suggested that the authorities **"add a digit, then you'll have it."** It is likely that Bundy did not remember how many he killed nor the exact details of each crime. Bundy's last victim was a 12-year-old Florida schoolgirl he abducted on her way home from school in broad daylight.

Additional Facts:

• Bundy was first incarcerated in 1975 in Utah for kidnapping and assault. Authorities in several states began to suspect him in connection with unsolved murders. In 1977, he masterminded two escapes in Colorado before being recaptured in Florida in 1978. It is believed he killed at least 3 more victims during this time on the run, including his last victim, a 12-year-old child.

• While acting as his own lawyer in his 1980 murder trial, he proposed marriage to his then-girlfriend Carole Ann Boone who was testifying on the stand in his defense. She accepted but divorced Bundy before his execution. Supposedly a daughter was conceived while Bundy was on death row but that claim has never been substantiated.

DAVID CARPENTER *"The Trailside Killer"* 10+ Kills

DOB: 5/06/30 CA

SENTENCE: Death

Facility: San Quentin, CA INMATE C-96500

THE CRIME: Between 8/19/1979 and 5/2/1981, David Joseph Carpenter, a convicted sexual predator dubbed "The Trailside Killer" by the media, attacked hikers along remote trails in Santa Cruz and Marin counties. In his wake, he left behind 10 or more victims shot to death. Others he raped or attempted to kill or rape.

Authorities were able to link one gun, a .38-caliber Rossi special revolver, to all shooting crimes in both counties. A friend of Carpenter's testified that she purchased that gun for him, at his request, prior to the first attack. Authorities tied a pair of shoes recently purchased by Carpenter to shoe prints left behind at a crime scene. This was before DNA science, but semen linked Carpenter to victim's Anne Alderson's rape, plus he was identified in a line-up by the lone survivor, Steven Haertle.

In 2010, DNA tied Carpenter to the 10/21/1979 murder of Mary Frances Bennett, 23. She had been jogging near the Palace of the Legion of Honor at Lands' End in San Francisco when she was savagely attacked with a knife, raped, and killed. Her body bore over 20 stab wounds. Carpenter had buried Bennett in a shallow grave and covered the mound with branches.

Carpenter remains a suspect in four additional kills. He has always maintained he is innocent of all crimes.

BACKGROUND: David Carpenter had an unhappy childhood. Reportedly, he was harshly disciplined by both his alcoholic father and his demanding mother. He developed a pronounced stutter early in life and continued to wet the bed late into puberty. Carpenter was unpopular with classmates and was the brunt of cruel teasing due to the stuttering and the extravagant, almost feminine manner in which his mother forced him to dress. She also forced him to take violin lessons and ballet classes that caused an even wider gap to develop between himself and his peers.

By age 17, he was convicted of sexually abusing two younger female cousins, ages 8 and 3. He was committed to the California Youth Authority. He was released after one year.

In 11/1955, Carpenter married his 19-year-old wife. She divorced him in March 1962, while he was incarcerated. The couple had 3 children: a son and two daughters. His wife complained that her husband insisted upon having sexual intercourse three times a day and had an insatiable sex drive. She also claimed Carpenter had a volatile temper.

In 1960, 30-year-old Carpenter was charged and convicted of attempted murder for attacking a woman with a knife and hammer. He served a little more than half of his 14-year-sentence and was paroled on 4/7/1969. While incarcerated, he was diagnosed by a prison psychiatrist as having a sociopathic personality disorder.

On 8/8/1969 Carpenter married his second wife. In 5/1970, he was sent back to prison and served 9 years on kidnapping, robbery, and parole violation charges. His second wife divorced him while he was imprisoned. Carpenter was released in 5/1979, to a halfway house. On 8/19/1979, Carpenter is suspected of killing Edna Kane, 44. Her naked body was found in the Mt. Tamalpais State Park. She was in a kneeling position and had been shot in the head. He was never charged with her murder.

On 9/6/79, Carpenter was released from the halfway house. This 49-year-old middle-aged, divorced man, with gray thinning hair, glasses, and a pronounced stutter moved back to his parents' home and continued to kill.

OUT OF THE MOUTH OF THE SERIAL KILLER:

"Please don't hurt me." **(When told by authorities he was under arrest.)**

"I have a funny quirk." (Spoken to his 1960 survivor he attacked with a knife and hammer.)

"There are many [court] *cases to research and staying up with laws pertaining to my case is essential to my ongoing appeal."*

"Despite my age. I'm relatively healthy. My medical issues are minor in comparison to others here [on Death Row] *and I have them under control."*

"They claimed I was the logical suspect. By then, everyone believed I was the Trailside Killer. It began because I was supposed to pick up Heather Scaggs on May 2, 1981, but I did not. That is why I became the logical suspect,"

"I was the logical suspect. Everyone was convinced I was the trailside killer long before I was charged with any of those murders. Even the investigators knew I was innocent."

"Investigators said that if I did not have an alibi, then I must be guilty. I produced credible alibis and they knew it. But even where there wasn't an alibi, that does not make someone guilty."

"I was convicted by the media long before I was even found guilty of a crime."

Additional Facts:

• His 1960 attack survivor claimed that Carpenter lost his stutter when he was attacking her and angry.

• Carpenter took the stand in his own defense and professed complete innocence. He testified for seven days.

• He remains a devout Catholic. As of 2020, Carpenter is the oldest CADOC inmate.

DEAN CARTER 5 Kills

DOB: 8/30/1955 AK

SENTENCE: 2 DEATH SENTENCES, PLUS 78 YEARS FOR RAPE & BURGLARY AGAINST TWO VICTIMS NOT KILLED

Facility: San Quentin, CA INMATE C-97919

THE CRIME: Some people handle rejection better than others.

Dean Phillip Carter was a tall, handsome, quiet young man but there was just something strange about him. Most called Carter "odd" and few women were attracted to him. One night he snapped. He had been rebuffed the previous day by two women he knew, one of whom he had half-jokingly proposed to after knowing her only a few weeks. Carter was still feeling the sting of rejection when he attended a party on 3/25/1984. He became infuriated when he discovered another "girlfriend" had gone on vacation without notifying him nor including him as previously planned. That night, he broke into her San Diego residence and raped her housemate at knifepoint, then stole money from the home.

On 3/27, a woman awoke to find Carter standing over her bed in her Ventura County, CA apartment holding a knife. She had previously met Carter at the party and spurned his awkward advances. The 22-year-old woman was sodomized, repeatedly raped, and strangled so brutally that she passed out several times. She lived by pretending to be attracted to Carter. After he left the following morning, she immediately called the police. He never left behind a live witness again.

Carter's murder spree spanned from approximately 4/10/1984 to 4/12/1984. In its wake, he killed five innocent women, all known to him. Each was sexually assaulted, robbed, and brutally strangled.

On 4/17/1984, police pulled over Carter in Ashford, Arizona for suspected drunk driving. He was arrested and a search of the vehicle he was driving proffered personal items from all five of his murder victims. DNA later connected Carter to three kills plus his fingerprints were found at one crime scene. Dean Carter has always claimed to be innocent of all charges.

BACKGROUND: Carter was put up for adoption by his unmarried mother, an Eskimo native. He never knew his biological father. He was adopted by a Nome, Alaska family. His father was the fire and police chief of the town. If we judge the success of Carter's adoption by his juvenile record, then we can assume the placement did not go well.

By age 12, he was sent to a youth ranch for delinquent boys. He ran away three times. Upon his release, his adoptive parents placed him into foster care and basically turned their back on the child. Carter fared no better in his new situation. He continued to steal and burglarize homes throughout his teens and by age 18, he graduated to adult prison. He served time in Alaska for auto theft and was imprisoned in Oregon on burglary charges.

Carter was released from prison in the early 1980s and moved to Anchorage AK. There he secured a job as a cameraman with a local TV station. He left that job after a dispute with management and moved to Seattle. An unfavorable reference from his previous employer, coupled with a criminal record, made it difficult for Carter to secure another position. He decided to try his hand at freelancing. He struggled both financially and emotionally.

In 3/1984, 28-year-old Dean Carter headed to California for a fresh beginning.

OUT OF THE MOUTH OF THE SERIAL KILLER: In a letter to the author written 10/3/2016:

Dear Mary,

I received your letter and since you sent a SASE I am sending you a note to thank you for your interest, but I don't see how anything like what you propose would help me at all. I am sure you have written to others on the Row and I hope you will have some success with them.

Best Wishes,

Dean Carter

(Unedited excerpts from DeadmanTalking.com/Column 1) DeadManTalking.com is a website with featured columns by Carter proclaiming his innocence and commenting on the ills of the justice system. It is hosted by a friend.

"There is the sense that people on Death Row are slobbering animals that should be kept in a cage and executed as soon as can be arranged. I have even heard on talk shows where people have advocated an electric chair right in the courtroom, and as soon as the verdict is rendered, strap the person in and cook them. Never mind that the system makes mistakes, what are a few innocent people being killed, as long as you can get rid of the others in the process. But most of the people on Death Row are fairly normal. Sure, there are the ones here that I would never turn my back on. There are some people here that would make Hannibal Lechter seems like a nice guy. But as I said, most guys here are not slobbering lunatics or

cold blooded killers - but there are some here that could be put in that category."

(Unedited excerpts from Dean Carter in Column 27 regarding the families of the victims): *"Since I'm on the topic of victims and families, I would like to talk about another group of families who are also victims. The forgotten victims. These are the families, friends and loved ones of those who are killed by the government. The families of those on death row haven't done anything wrong, yet they also suffer the loss of someone they love. Not only do they lose a loved one, but they also are subjected to the hate and anger of the victims' rights groups. They also have to deal with a prison system that treats them like second class citizens because they have a loved one sitting on death row. I have seen the faces of the loved ones of someone who is about to be executed and I know their pain is as deep and horrible as any other family who has lost a loved one. Not only do they suffer the loss of their loved one, but in many cases, they are also there standing by helplessly and watching in horror as their loved one is being killed I can't help but wonder how these people will be able to find closure. That is all I have to say about that topic, so I will move on to other things."*

Additional Facts:

- One of two survivors of Carter's murder spree claimed the more terrified she acted, the more violent he became.

- *"He wanted to make love to her,"* said Jim Grunert, a deputy district attorney in Ventura, CA. *"She said no."*

- Carter abused alcohol and drugs from an early age.

- He is the father of twin sons.

DOUG CLARK 6 Kills (with CAROL BUNDY) 2+ Kills *"Sunset Strip Killers"*

DOB: 3/10/1948 PA

SENTENCE: Clark: Sentenced to death in 1983

Facility: San Quentin State Prison, CA INMATE C-63000

(Carol Bundy: Sentenced to life but she died in prison in 2003 from a heart condition at age 51.)

THE CRIME: In 6/1980, Douglas Daniel Clark picked up two teenage girls along the Sunset Strip in California, forced them both to perform oral sex, then shot them in the head. He took their bodies to an abandoned garage and had sex with the bodies. Later, he dumped them near a freeway. The bodies were discovered within 24 hours.

Clark shared the gory details with Carol Bundy, his lover, bragging about his killings. She became nervous when the media reported the sensationalized story and called the police, most likely to protect herself should Clark be arrested, but she did not give the police enough information to lead them to Clark.

Within two weeks, Clark again killed two women after luring them into his car and made no effort to conceal their dumped bodies. This time he took the head of one woman as a trophy. When he brought it home, Bundy put make-up on the head before Clark performed his sexual acts. The head was later dumped in an alley.

In total, Clark is charged with killing six women and was arrested after Bundy confessed to police in detail about her and Clark's crimes. Some doubts arise from Bundy's confessions that contained inconsistencies. Both Clark and Bundy had purchased guns, same caliber, at a local pawn shop in Bundy's name they called "their toys."

By testifying, Bundy avoided the death penalty. She was subsequently charged with two murders, but it is possible or even probable that she was equally guilty in other killings.

BACKGROUND: Doug Clark comes from a somewhat privileged background. His father was a high-ranking officer in the Navy and the family traveled the world, moving often.

Clark attended an exclusive international school in Geneva. He also attended Culver Military Academy, a college prep boarding school in Indiana, but was expelled. He was drafted in 1967, entered the Air Force instead of attending college, and was honorably discharged in 1971.

He spent almost a decade moving around the country, working a series of blue-collar jobs. He settled in Los Angeles and it was there he met Carol Bundy in a local bar she frequented to watch her married lover perform. Clark and Bundy quickly discovered they shared a common interest: violent sex, S&M, and other dark desires including rape, torture, murder, and necrophilia. Clark and Bundy were also pedophiles.

They soon moved in together and started bringing prostitutes home to share sexually. Clark was described as handsome, but Bundy was older, over-weight, not attractive, and wore thick glasses. She had reportedly been sexually molested and beaten by her violent, alcoholic father as a child and was in and out of several abusive marriages.

At the time she and Clark met, Bundy was having an affair with her married building manager. She was upset and often angry because he would not leave his wife. Bundy would eventually kill him in his van after luring him inside on the pretense of having sex. She also decapitated him. Bundy had previously told her lover details of crimes she and Clark had committed and she began to worry he would go to the authorities. The police would discover brain matter in the van and a spent shell casing. Their investigation was made easier when Bundy confessed to co-workers. In custody, she quickly turned on Clark and told the police everything. Clark defended himself at trial and basically blamed Bundy for most of the murders. In a letter to the author from Doug Clark, he claimed Carol Bundy **"added 8 murders. (before 6-14-80)."**

OUT OF THE MOUTH OF THE SERIAL KILLER: From statements written in a rambling, *sometime illegible* seven-page letter from Clark dated 4/27/2016:

"Carol Bundy is the Xerox Copy Cat of Ted Bundy...his nastiest & bloodiest fan?" June 1, 1974 T.B. Killed

June 1, 1980 C. B. Killed

June 11, 1974 T.B. Killed

June 11, 1980 C. B. Killed (Two)

June 14, 1974 T. B. Killed & Decapped (#1)

T.B. Killed & Didn't Decap (#2) T.B. tried for 3'd

June 23, 1980 "Ditto,"

C.B.(1-2-3)" She's the least known "master manipulator".

While Clark was very willing to discuss Carol Bundy's guilt in great lengths and the guilt of others, **"...if you're still interested in discussing this & about 20 other SK cases I am very conversant upon_____"**

Doug Clark never mentioned his part in any of the killings nor gave insight as to why he killed.

ADDITIONAL FACTS:

- Clark acted as his own lawyer which might explain why the insanity plea was not proffered.

- According to acquaintances; he was handsome, overly self-assured, and a narcissist with a high IQ.

- He was remarkably successful with women and most found him attractive with a highly developed sex drive.

DEAN CORLL "Candy Man"
"Pied Piper" 28+ Kills

DOB: 12/24/1939 IN

DOD: 8/8/1973 TX, age 34

Killed by accomplice before apprehended

THE CRIME: If you are going to embark upon a life of crime, be careful when picking your partners. That choice could come back to bite you. Or in the case of Dean Arnold Corll, *kill you.*

Seventeen-year-old Wayne Henley did just that on 8/8/1973 when he shot Corll three times, killing him. Henley, along with another teenager, David Brooks, had spent almost three years procuring adolescent boys for Corll, mostly from the low-income Houston Heights neighborhood in Houston, Texas. Sardonically, many of the boys were their friends and acquaintances. They would lure young boys to Corll's home, knowing that once there, the victims would be handcuffed, raped, tortured, and killed.

Police called to the scene of Corll's murder worked through the layers of Henley's confession to uncover an even more horrific crime. Eventually authorities would locate 17 bodies of young males buried in Corll's boat shed and more bodies scattered around Houston and outlying areas. The remains bore signs indicating they had been strangled or shot. All had been sodomized. One interred body had been mutilated with the penis cut away. Police searched the Corll family's cabin and discovered a room that had been turned into a torture chamber, complete with a board outfitted with ropes, a large dildo, handcuffs, and petroleum jelly. Plastic sheeting protected the carpet. Also found in a nearby van was a crude wooden coffin-like box with air holes cut into the top, bags of lime, and shovels. Henley and Brooks had been paid $200 for each life sacrificed.

From 1970 to 1973, Corll is known to have killed 28 boys. Authorities believe that the number is higher, suspecting he most likely also killed boys from 1965 to 1970. Those were the years between his discharge from the Army and his witnessed first kill.

BACKGROUND: Dean Corll was the older of two sons born to married parents who divorced and married other spouses, but both biological parents maintained an active part in their sons' lives. His father was an electrician and his mother a homemaker. She started a cottage industry making candy that developed into the Corll Candy Company. In 1964, Corll, age 25, was named Vice President of the company. He had worked in the family business before and after school.

Corll was withdrawn as a child, very shy, and slow to make friends. Ironically, he was reportedly overly sensitive to others and showed concern for their well-being. In 1950, a heart murmur was detected and his parents were advised to stop their son's sports and physical activities. He was also not permitted to take Physical Education classes at school. This set Corll apart even further from his peers and isolated the boy from other pre-adolescent and adolescent males.

In 8/1964, Corll was drafted into the Army. He claimed he realized he was homosexual while he was serving. He received an early "hardship" discharge in 1965, citing he was gravely needed in his family business. The Army may have granted Corll a quick release for another reason. "Hardship" was one of numerous covert reasons used by America's service branches at that time to dismiss gays.

In 1970, 30-year-old Corll had been enjoying a three-year consensual sexual relationship with David Brooks, age 15. Brooks was not homosexual, but he hung out with Corll as one of his young sexual partners for financial gain. He introduced Corll to 14-year-old Wayne Henley in 1971, and the three quickly formed a repulsive and sordid business partnership. From 1970-1973, first Brooks, then Brooks and Henley knowingly brought Corll young victims to be tortured, raped, and shot or strangled to death solely for the $200 they were paid per child.

On 8/8/1973, Henley brought a girl to the home along with a 19-year-old boy. It infuriated Corll that Henley would dare bring a female into the home. The three teenagers passed out from drugs only to awaken to find themselves now potential victims. Henley appeased Corll by assuring him that he would willingly assist him in killing the other two if freed. Corll relented and released Henley. Henley ultimately picked up a nearby gun and shot the naked 33-year-old Corll to death.

Wayne Henley was convicted and given six consecutive life terms. David Brooks was sentenced to life imprisonment for four murders. Henley was never charged in Corll's death. That killing was ruled a justified homicide.

After being secured by handcuffs, the victims were strapped to the so-called "torture board" as it was sadistically nicknamed by Dean Corll, Wayne Henley, and David Brooks.

(Photo Source: www.Murderpedia.org)

Wayne Henley (L) and David Brooks (R) in handcuffs aiding authorities who are digging in search of the remains of victims. The duo was paid $200 for each boy delivered to Corll to be tortured to death.

(Photo source: www.Murderpedia.org)

OUT OF THE MOUTH OF THE SERIAL KILLER:

"I need to do a new boy." (Wayne Henley claimed this was his and David Brooks' signal to procure another victim for Corll.)

"Kill me, Wayne! You won't do it!" (Corll's last words.)

ADDITIONAL FACTS:

- Corll received the neighborhood nickname of "Candy Man" and "Pied Piper" because he was known to freely hand out samples from his family's candy business to children and particularly to teen-age boys. He also plied the adolescent boys with drugs and alcohol.

- Some victims were kept and tortured over a period of a few days.

- Corll occasionally dated girls in school and before being drafted into the Army. He had a two-year relationship with a girl in Indiana from 1960-1962 but declined her suggestion of marriage.

- A Houston art gallery once hosted an exhibit of Wayne Henley's paintings that were offered for sale.

- David Owen Brooks is Inmate 00248288 at Terrel Unit in Rosharon, Texas. Wayne Henley is inmate 00241618 at Michael Unit in Tennessee Colony, Texas. It is unlikely either will be paroled.

JUAN VALLEJO CORONA *"The Machete Murderer"* 25+ Kills

DOB: 1934 MEXICO

DOD: 3/4/2019 CA age 85

DIED FROM NATURAL CAUSES

SENTENCED: 25 CONSECUTIVE LIFE SENTENCES SINCE CA DID NOT HAVE THE DEATH PENALTY AT THIS TIME

Facility: Corcoran State Prison, Corcoran, CA

THE CRIME: Going to work for The Juan Corona Migrant Employment Agency might seem like a good thing at first but unfortunately the job would likely be short-lived. Literally. Included with housing and transportation to the job site was a free burial service, albeit brief and without ceremony.

By 1962, Juan Corona, once a migrant worker, was now a licensed labor contractor. He brokered the workforce for local farms and controlled wages paid his hands. On 5/26/1971, Juan Corona was charged with the rape and murder of 25 male migrant and itinerant farm laborers he had slain for homosexual gratification and/or financial gain. Corona never confessed so it is not clear when the killings began nor the actual number of men he slaughtered.

His killing ground was around Yuba City, California. The bodies of his victims were found buried in shallow graves, scattered among local fruit groves. The men had perished from gun shots, stabbing, or from being bludgeoned to death. Most were found with their shirts pulled up over their heads and their pants pulled down. Many had been hacked about the head with a machete. Corona chose victims who were alcoholics, homeless, transients, or immigrants, all without families. He correctly understood that their disappearance would not cause much alarm, especially in an industry that employed short-term, transitory labor. Most victims had been slain shortly before they were due their earnings.

BACKGROUND: Juan Corona was born sometime in 1934 to impoverished parents who never bothered to record his birth. He was the third of three sons, one brother was a half-brother. In 1950, 16-year-old Corona illegally came to America and began working as a migrant farm laborer. His brother and half-brother had immigrated to America earlier, settling in Marysville, CA across the Feather River from Yuba City. In 1953, Corona moved to that area to be near family.

In 1/1956, his half-brother had him committed to a state hospital where Corona was diagnosed as "schizophrenic reaction, paranoid type." In the month prior, the Feather River had experienced a flood of biblical proportions. It was deemed the most destructive and deadly flood in the recorded history of northern California. Thirty-eight people lost their lives and hundreds lost their homes and everything they owned. Corona was not directly touched by the flood, but inexplicably he was so shaken by this natural disaster that he had a complete mental breakdown. He was tormented by the devastation he saw in his town. He began to hallucinate and saw ghosts. He obsessively read the bible and quoted scripture. While consigned to the hospital, he received over 20 shock treatments. That therapy would be considered barbaric by today's psychiatric standards but shock treatments were typical for the times.

From 1958 until 1962, he worked his way through the ranks until the former migrant worker was the boss of many migrant workers. He brokered their services to farms and ranches needing cheap labor and put single and homeless men into bleak barrack-like housing for a fee. He provided transportation to and from job sites as well as food, again for a fee. Corona had a reputation for being a harsh man to work for and was known to have a quick temper. In 1970, he again sought and received treatment at a mental hospital.

OUT OF THE MOUTH OF THE SERIAL KILLER:

"I killed them because they were trespassing." "(They) were winos."

"Not even a single person has family here." (Corona stated to parole board in 2003 indicating no one cared about his victims. Sadly, 14 bodies were never claimed and 4 deceased remain identified to this day as only "John Doe.")

"They were all ready to go to the next world."

Additional Facts:

- In prison, Corona was considered a loner. Reportedly, he was always unpopular with fellow inmates who shunned him.

- In December 1973, Corona was stabbed repeatedly for failure to say "excuse me" when bumping into a fellow inmate. He lost his left eye. In 2016, he was reported as almost blind, plus he suffered from dementia and mental illness.

- Corona professed to hold deep resentment towards gay men. His half-brother, Natividad, was gay and they eventually parted ways. Natividad died of syphilis and diabetes in 1973.

- Corona was repeatedly denied parole.

- A store receipt for purchased meat found at a grave site led authorities to Corona.

He was married and divorced twice. His second wife divorced him while he was incarcerated. He is the father of four daughters.

CHARLES CULLEN *"Killer Nurse"* 29+ Kills

DOB: 2/22/1960 NJ

SENTENCE: Sentenced to 15 consecutive life terms on 3/1/2006 in New Jersey. Sentenced to seven life sentences for seven murders in Pennsylvania. He was additionally sentenced to three counts of attempted murder. Cullen is eligible for parole June 10, 2388, give or take a day or two.

Facility: New Jersey State Prison, Trenton, NJ INMATE: 000153648D

THE CRIME: Charles Edmund Cullen is the most prolific serial killer in the history of New Jersey. Even he does not know how many people he killed as a nurse, preying on helpless elderly and ill patients.

His Modius Operandi (MO) was to kill the patient by administering a lethal overdose of medicine, usually in an lV bag. He worked in numerous hospitals in both New Jersey and Pennsylvania and, by his best guess, he murdered at least 40 innocent people from 1988 until his arrest on 12/12/2003.Some authorities have estimated the count could be in the 100's. He confessed in court to 29 murders.

He evaded being caught for 15 years by changing hospitals when the cloud of suspicion fell upon him concerning unexplained deaths, missing drugs, contaminated lV bags, or Cullen's involvement with patients not his own. The national shortage of nurses helped make it easy for Cullen to quickly gain new employment. Also in his favor, were the many hospital authorities who were extremely reluctant to alert the public to the possibility of a killer on their staff. They often looked the other way if Cullen was willing to resign and move on, unfortunately to another unsuspecting hospital.

He was finally stopped due to a diligent co-worker who alerted authorities.

BACKGROUND: Cullen was the youngest of eight children. His father passed away when Cullen was seven-months-old and his mother was killed in an automobile accident when Cullen was age 17.

His mother raised her children in a strict Catholic household and Cullen always claimed his childhood was miserable. She never remarried and the death of his father was a constant theme shadowing his early life.

He tried to kill himself when he was nine by deliberately drinking what he thought was a poisonous liquid he had concocted using ingredients from his childhood chemistry set. This would be one of many suicide attempts.

Cullen was an extremely introverted child and was ostracized in school well into high school. He retaliated against peers once when he was, 17, by lacing drinks at a party with rat poison. Several were sickened but no one died. No charges were ever brought.

He experienced an even deeper depression with the loss of his mother. Shortly after her death, Cullen dropped out of school and joined the US Navy. Life was no better for him in the service. He was very unpopular with fellow crew members who constantly harassed the loner. He was given the unflattering nickname, "Fish Belly." In March 1984, he received an early discharge for medical reasons.

Later that year he enrolled in nursing school. He graduated in 1987 with honors and married one month after graduation. A daughter was born 10 months later. He killed his first known victim, a 72-year-old male, just two months after the birth of his child.

The marriage quickly disintegrated. His wife claimed he would turn off the heat in winter to control her and began to psychologically punish her and the child. He abused the family pets. Shortly after the second daughter was born in 1992, his wife lobbied for a domestic violence charge against Cullen and requested a restraining order. In 1/1993, she filed for divorce and again requested a restraining order. She stated that she sensed Cullen would harm her and her children with medication readily available to him at his workplace.

Later that year, Cullen began stalking a co-worker and even broke into her apartment as she and her child slept. He pled guilty to trespassing and received a year of probation. Cullen was in and out of treatment centers for attempting suicide, all the while killing helpless patients, ironically ending countless lives but failing to end his own.

At the time of his arrest in 2003, he was living with a girlfriend and they were expecting a child. His girlfriend was a nurse.

OUT OF THE MOUTH OF THE SERIAL KILLER:

"I just couldn't stop. I couldn't stop it."

(Did you know it was wrong?) *"Yes. At the time and later. But like I said I don't know if I would have stopped."*

"I tried to kill myself throughout my life, because I never really liked being who I was. I didn't feel I was worthy of anything."

Additional Facts:

- An older brother died in 1987 from a drug overdose.

- Cullen was the only male student in his nursing program. One year he was elected president of his class but even this long-desired acceptance by his peers in the profession of his choice did not stop him from eventually killing.

- Those close to the case said it was as simple as Cullen killed because he could.

- He preferred to work the less active night shift in the ICU ward when most patients were asleep. This gave him cover and more control.

- In 12/2005, Cullen reportedly wanted to donate a kidney to a relative of an ex-girlfriend.

- "The Good Nurse; A True Story of Medicine, Madness, and Murder", is a book by author, Charles Graeber, about Amy Loughren, the nurse who stopped Cullen's killings by alerting authorities.

JEFFREY DAHMER *"Milwaukee Cannibal"* 17 Kills

DOB: 5/21/1960 WI

DOD: 11/28/ 1994, age 34, Columbia Correctional Inst., WI/ killed by an inmate-beaten to death

SENTENCE: Sentenced to 16 life sentences

The Crime: From 1978-1991, Jeffrey Lionel Dahmer drugged, raped, murdered, dismembered, and at times ate 17 men and male children in Milwaukee, WI.

He killed his first victim in 6/1978 when he was only 18-years-old. He took a young hitchhiker home to his parents' empty house where they both consumed alcohol. When the man tried to leave, Dahmer hit him with a barbell, strangled him, cut up the corpse, bagged the parts, and buried the bags and murder weapon in the woods behind the home. Dahmer was not connected to another murder for nine years.

He dismembered his victims, at times keeping body parts as mementos, and he repeatedly had sex with the dead, decomposing bodies. He would often photograph his victims at different stages of death so he could relive the experience.

He experimented with crude lobotomies by drilling holes into a few victims' skulls while they were still alive so he could inject them with a solution of muriatic acid. He claimed he was trying to turn them into zombies so they would stay with him forever and be completely under his control.

Towards the end of his murdering reign, he also ate parts of some of his victims, claiming *"...it was a means to keep them with me always."*

BACKGROUND: Dahmer was born into a middle class, two parent family. He was the older of two sons. When Dahmer was six, his family relocated to Ohio due to his father's career change. Growing up, his mother exhibited signs of anxiety and depression to the extent that her children were neglected. His parents' marriage ended in a bitter divorce when Dahmer was a teenager.

His few close classmates describe him as shy, quiet, polite to teachers, but having a radical sense of humor, "the class clown". He had a reputation for drinking alcohol to excess as a young teenager, often showing up to class drunk. Dahmer had also started to secretly kill and mutilate animals.

He left college after one semester. Alcohol was cited as the problem. He joined the army at his father's urging and was stationed in Germany. However, the army honorably discharged him early for alcoholism in 1981.

He returned home to Ohio, but soon moved to Wisconsin to live with his grandmother after being arrested on a minor charge while drunk. His first real run-in with the law occurred in September 1986, when he was arrested for indecent exposure. He was sentenced to one-year of probation.

He soon had another run-in with police regarding young boys resulting in a child molestation charge. Dahmer received a one-year jail term with the stipulation that he could work during the day but was required to return to jail at night. It was during this incarceration period that his father wrote the courts requesting help for his son's drinking problems. Dahmer was released early after serving 10 months of his sentence. No program was ever offered.

OUT OF THE MOUTH OF THE SERIAL KILLER:

"I know society will never be able to forgive me. I know the families of the victims will never be able to forgive me for what I have done. I promise I will pray each day to ask for their forgiveness when the hurt goes away, if ever. I have seen their tears, and if I could give my life right now to bring their loved ones bock, l would do it."

"I feel so bad for what I did to those poor families, and I understand their rightful hate."

"l take all the blame for what I did." "l do not blame the police, the courts or the probation system. I failed the system, it did not fail me." Regarding his parents: *"...totally innocent." "They had no knowledge of it." "l wanted to find out just what it was that caused me to be so bad and evil."*

"The subtleties of social life were beyond my grasp. When children liked me, I did not know why. Nor could I formulate a plan for winning their affection. I simply didn't know how things worked with other people ...And try as I might, I couldn't make other people seem less strange and unknowable."

"It was not a case of hating them. It was just the only way I knew of to keep them there and keep them with me."

"It gave me a sense of total control and increased the sexual thrill, I guess, knowing I had total control of them and that I could do with them as I wished."

"It's hard for me to believe a human being could do what I have done, but I know I did it."

Probably most telling: *"The only motive that there ever was to completely control a person, a person I found physically attractive, and to keep them with me as long as possible, even if it meant just keeping a part of them with me."*

Additional Facts:

- As a young child, Dahmer was fascinated by dead animals. Upon request, his father taught him how to bleach and preserve animal bones thinking his son had a learning tendency geared towards science. *"I wanted to see what the inside of these animals looked like." "It became a compulsion...it was exciting to see."*

- Dahmer went from dismembering animals found dead to killing animals and dismembering them. He claimed as a teenager his fantasies escalated to vivid mental scenes of killing males. *"I acted on my fantasies and that's where everything went wrong" "It just escalated slowly but surely." "...it felt like it was out of control." "I suppose it could have turned into a normal hobby like taxidermy."*

- Dahmer was a true practitioner of necrophilia. He only wanted sex with the comatose or dead.

- Dahmer used his grandmother's basement, without her knowledge, and later his own two apartments to kill and dismember most of his victims. Other residents of Dahmer's second apartment building often complained of foul smells permeating the halls. Inside could only be described as a hellish nightmare, including the refrigerator that contained human remains ready to be cooked.

- On 5/27/1981 police were called to investigate a young boy running naked in the streets. The boy was incoherent and could not make a statement. Dahmer met the police and stated it was just a lover's spat. The police believed Dahmer's explanation and escorted the two back to Dahmer's apartment. They did not make a detail investigation of the premise. After the police left, Dahmer strangled the 14-year-old, his 13th victim. Ironically, Dahmer's 12th victim was dead and decomposing in the bedroom.

• He first pled not guilty, then changed his plea to guilty but insane. However, it only took the jurors 5 hours to return a guilty verdict, rejecting the insanity plea.

• Dahmer was segregated from other inmates in prison until he convinced officials to allow him the freedom to socially mingle. On 11/28/1994, Dahmer was assigned to a work detail with Jesse Anderson, a white supremacist, and Christopher Scarver, a black convicted murderer. Scarver beat both Dahmer and Anderson to death with a metal bar. In an interview with the New York Post decades later, Scarver claimed the guards allowed the killings. He also claimed that Dahmer felt no remorse: *"Some people who are in prison are repentant but he was not one of them."*

• In 1995, the City of Milwaukee raised over $400,000 to purchase Dahmer's possessions to keep them from being sold to curiosity seekers. The effects were incinerated.

• Authorities were convinced none of Dahmer's relatives had any knowledge of his crimes.

Inmate, Christopher Scarver, who beat Dahmer and another white inmate to death in prison in 1994. (Photo sources: Pinterest)

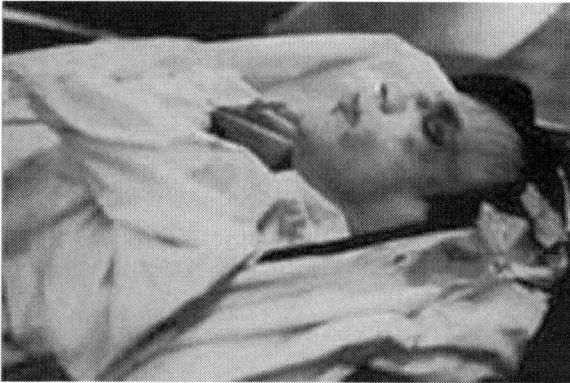

Death Scene. (Photo sources: Pinterest)

JAMES DAVEGGIO & MICHELLE MICHAUD 4+ Kills

JAMES DAVEGGIO

DOB:7/27/1960 CA

SENTENCE: DEATH 9/25/2002 and is on Death Row awaiting execution.

Facility: San Quentin, CA INMATE T-68062

MICHELLE MICHAUD

DOB: 11/7/1958 CA

SENTENCE: Death penalty

FACILITY: Central California women's Facility (CCWF) INMATE W96070

THE CRIME: On12/2/1997, James Anthony Daveggio and his sexual partner, Michelle Lyn Michaud, abducted 22-year-old Pleasanton, CA college coed, Vanessa Lei Samson, while she was walking to work early that morning. She was forced into the couple's converted green Dodge Caravan, tied up, and tortured before being raped and finally strangled to death.

The back seat of the van was removed and the inside was rigged with a mirror, ropes, hooks, and torture instruments. Evidence and confessions revealed that the victim had a rubber ball gag inserted into her mouth and that she had been additionally raped by Michaud using two altered curling irons.

Vanessa was later taken to a motel room where the brutal torture continued before she was forced back into the van, strangled to death, and her body dumped down a snowy embankment along a deserted road.

Daveggio and Michaud were arrested separately the next day on unrelated charges. Eventually authorities would discover the extent of their crimes, including other murders and brutal rapes, including the two vicious rapes of both Daveggio's and Michaud's own young daughters.

All totaled, James Daveggio brutally raped at least 17 victims and killed four, possibly more. Working with his prostitute partner, Michelle Michaud, the two sexually sadistic assailants brutally raped at least four victims before killing Vanessa Samson. Five years after Vanessa Samson's death, both killers were themselves sentenced to death.

FBI profilers consider this one of the first cases in which both male and female partners equally participated in the sex crimes.

BACKGROUND: James Daveggio's was the second of three children. His parents divorced when he was five. His father would remarry several times and had adulterous affairs with numerous girlfriends.

From an early age, Daveggio was in trouble with authorities. He continually got into fights at school, often skipped classes, and stole from local stores. When he was 16, he was sent to a juvenile facility. He joined the marines in 1978 but a foot injury during basic training afforded him an honorable discharge.

Shortly after his release, he robbed a gas station, committed numerous burglaries, was charged with drinking while operating a motor vehicle, and raped his first victim but was never incarcerated. Between 1978 and 1989, Daveggio married and divorced three times and fathered five children, one illegitimately. When he was age 33, he got a vasectomy. He claimed he was tired of paying child support.

In 1984, he was arrested for forcing a woman to perform oral sex at gunpoint but all charges were dropped. In 1985, Daveggio worked with a partner, Jonathan Huffstetler, to again force a woman to perform oral sex but this time he was charged. He was sentenced to a one-year prison term and five years of probation. He was placed into the Sex Offender data base but routinely failed to notify officials of his constant moves.

OUT OF THE MOUTHS OF THE SERIAL KILLERS: Unedited letter to the author dated June 23, 2016:

Dear Mary,

I am not really sure why I have decided to write you back, other than you included a 5.A.5.E. As you should know there have been two books written about me and both cases I did write to either of those writers. (I believe that Daveggio meant to say "did NOT" write to either of those writers.)

I have never understood those who commit crimes and later try to get justification by trying to explain why they did it, like that would make it all okay. No one cares why a person killed someone. No matter what you say it can never be right.

I am sorry that it made me laugh that society would care what I have to say.

In closing, Yes, all who take a life should share the same guilt!!

Sorry, I could not be more help.

Sincerely, James A. Daveggio

Michaud described each vicious assault as *"an adventure."* Daveggio referred to them as *"huntings."*

Daveggio: *"I, in fact, did not kill Ms. Samson. By law I am as guilty of her death as Michelle is. Do I care or feel for Ms. Samson? Yes, watching your family, unfortunately, I have never seen love as you all have for her. Yes, I think of it every day."*

Daveggio in a phone call to his mother: *"Mom, I swear to you, I did not kill anybody."*

From Michaud's site on: www.writeaprisoner.com: *"Sometimes it feels the whole world has forgotten me. It would be nice to hear my name at mail call. I look forward to hearing from you soon. Thank you, Michelle"*

Additional Facts:

• Daveggio was nicknamed "Froggie" because of his scratchy voice.

• He joined the marines when he was 17 after dropping out of high school but was injured in a basic training maneuver and was honorably discharged. At 21, he joined the army but received a medical discharge within a few months.

• He was proud of being placed in the Sex Offender data base and boasted about it to acquaintances.

• Daveggio was briefly a member of a motorcycle gang, "The Devil's Horsemen". He dyed his hair purple to match his motorcycle. A newspaper story alleged that he once stole $1,500 from the club.

• He completed a course in the diesel engine program at the Sequoia Institute in Freemont, CA and reportedly made good grades.

• Daveggio was chronically unemployed due to his quick temper on the job. He and Michaud were both unemployed at the time of their final arrest and living out of the van they killed in.

- They were both addicted to methamphetamines

- Daveggio and Michaud met in a bar in 1996. A year later, they were converting Michaud's van into a torture chamber and began their three-month crime spree.

- Michaud often bragged that she made $1,000 a night as a high-priced prostitute and call girl. She was arrested for prostitution in 1991.

- Reportedly, she was a kept woman and the van in which she and Daveggio killed was registered in the names of both herself and her benefactor.

- She always claimed that she hated sex with men and preferred women.

- She delved into witchcraft.

- Newspaper accounts after her arrest report she did volunteer work at a Catholic church and was a school crossing guard where her daughter attended Catholic school. In her profile on www.writeaprisoner.com she claims her religion preference is Jewish.

- She is the mother of a son and a daughter. She and Daveggio savagely raped the daughter.

- Michaud told friends that she and Daveggio rarely had sex unless a third party, a female, was involved. They often paid prostitutes to join them sexually during their first months together.

- At trial, it was brought out that Daveggio and Michaud were influenced by the 1970s "sex slave murders" of Gerald and Charlene Gallego.

PAUL DUROUSSEAU *"The Jacksonville, FL Serial Killer"* 7+ Kills

DOB: 8/11/1970 TX

SENTENCE: DEATH BY LETHAL INJECTION

Facility: Union Correctional Institution, Raiford, FL INMATE J19087

THE CRIME: The science of DNA testing is an amazing tool used in solving crimes. Paul Durousseau raped and strangled a 26-year old Fort Benning, Georgia woman to death on 9/7/1997. Her case would go cold and unsolved for six years until advanced DNA techniques linked him to the rape and murder.

Typically, Durousseau would befriend a woman or charm his way into a woman's residence without force. Once inside, he would bind and rape his victim, then brutally strangle the woman to death. He also robbed them.

Durousseau killed seven or more young black women during his six-year-killing span that ended when he was apprehended on 6/17/2003. Two of the women were pregnant. The victims ranged in age from 17 to 26. He was tried and convicted for the murder of Tyresa Mack, a 24-year-old single mother of three small children.

It is strongly suspected that Durousseau killed women in Germany while stationed there in the early 1990s but he has never been charged with any German murder.

Paul Durousseau has never confessed to any killing, nor shown remorse.

BACKGROUND: Paul Durousseau is the younger of two boys. He was born in Beaumont, TX but moved with his unwed mother and half-brother to Los Angeles when he was one-year-old to be near his mother's family. He only saw his biological father a few times after the move.

In 11/1992, 22-year-old Durousseau enlisted in the Army and was stationed in Germany. He enlisted to avoid marrying a woman he impregnated. There he met his wife, also a soldier stationed in Germany. They were married in October 1995, and in 1996, Durousseau reenlisted and was stationed at Fort Benning, Georgia. On 3/13/1997, he was arrested for kidnapping and raping a woman in Georgia but all charges were dropped. One month after being acquitted on that charge, he raped and murdered his first victim.

In 1997, his wife moved from Georgia back to her hometown of Jacksonville, Florida citing domestic violence at the hands of her husband. Durousseau followed her after he received a dishonorable discharge from the Army and they reconciled. He had been court-martialed for being in possession of stolen goods.

The marriage was rocky due to Durousseau's violent temper and physical attacks upon his wife, coupled with his adulterous behavior. In 9/2001, Durousseau was sentenced to a short jail term for domestic battery. His wife escaped with her life. During most of their marriage, her husband was stalking, attacking, and killing innocent young women.

OUT OF THE MOUTH OF THE SERIAL KILLER: Paul Durousseau has never admitted guilt nor shown remorse.

"They already made up their minds, that I was the one, that I was guilty. Nothing I could say would have changed anything. So I lied." (Testifying at trial admitting he lied to police about knowing the slain women.)

Additional Facts:

- Neighbors and friends described him as being sexually suggestive and crude around women as young as 13.

- Durousseau, a convicted felon, was able to obtain a variety of positions including school bus driver, auto mechanic, animal control officer, and eventually cab driver. That job gave him the ability to hide in plain sight in various neighborhoods where he stalked his prey.

- Defense presented DNA evidence that linked Durousseau to Tyresa Mack's murder in addition to two other killings where his DNA was present and the MO was consistent with the Mack slaying. He took the stand in his own defense against council's advice. Durousseau admitted he had sex with all three women before their death, but claimed he was not their killer.

- Durousseau used a unique type of slipknot and extension or coaxial cable cords to strangle his victims.

WAYNE FORD 4-6 Kills

DOB: 12/3/1961 CA

SENTENCE: DEATH PENALTY 8/1/2006

Facility: San Quentin, CA INMATE F65748

THE CRIME: Wayne Adam Ford made it easy for the police. On 11/4/1998, he walked into a Sheriffs' Department in Eureka, California with a woman's dismembered breast in his shirt pocket. It was contained in a plastic baggie.

Ford stated that he had brought the sliced off breast with him so law officials would be convinced of his guilt. Those present when Ford turned himself in said he seemed remorseful and fully ready to unburden his dark secret. He claimed that he had killed women to keep from killing his wife, an act that would have left his son an orphan.

Ford confessed to the murder of four women, but it is strongly believed he killed at least two others.

From 10/14/1997, until his last kill on 11/3/1998, Ford, a cross-country trucker, preyed on prostitutes and hitchhikers. He bound and sexually assaulted his murder victims, strangled them to death, then dismembered two of the bodies. His first victim was so mutilated that her identity has never been confirmed.

Ford stored some body parts in his freezer and reportedly had attempted to cook some. A coffee can with solidifying human fat was also found. During a taped interview at the time of his arrest, he described how he engaged in erotic asphyxiation with as many as 50 women but stated that only four died. He claimed he was simply not able to revive them.

In 2006, Ford was finally tried and found guilty after lengthy legal delays. He received the death sentence later that same year.

BACKGROUND: Ford's parents divorced when he was nine. His mother was a German immigrant and his father was an American. Ford, the second born son, was shuffled back and forth between parents and became a problem in his father's home after the father remarried when Ford was 15.

He lived briefly with a family friend and an uncle until he quit high school and joined the Marines when he was 17. At that time, he already had a juvenile record going back to his early years.

When he was 19, he was hit by a drunk driver. Friends and family claimed they noticed a definite personality change after the accident.

He eloped with his first wife in 1981 and forced her to have an abortion when he discovered she was pregnant. While still married, he was arrested for the attempted rape of a 15-year-old female. His wife left him and filed for divorce in 1983.

In 1985, he was honorably discharged from the Marine Corps even though he had been demoted and cited for several rule infractions. The official release forms stated, "character and behavior disorders." While in service, military hospital professionals had diagnosed Ford on three separate occasions with a borderline personality disorder, once stating he exhibited homicidal thoughts.

During the next decade of his life, he worked a series of jobs, most involving driving. He never kept a job long because of his attitude and anger issues. He was arrested twice for animal cruelty, had an off-and-on-again intimate relationship with a male roommate, and married his second wife. She left him after two years and took their infant son.

At trial, a prostitute tearfully described how, in 1998, Ford bound and beat her, strangled her during sex, revived her with CPR, then assaulted her again and again. She testified afterwards he exhibited remorse, cried, and showed her pictures of his ex-wife and child. Another victim claimed Ford had a reputation among prostitutes for erotic asphyxiation. Several of Ford's girlfriends made the same accusation.

OUT OF THE MOUTH OF THE SERIAL KILLER:

…*"(I) hurt a lot of people." "I hurt people. That's why you guys just have to keep me."*

When asked about the severed breast during interrogation: **"(It's)** *just the tip of the iceberg."*

"There was no struggling and no pain inflicted upon the victims. All acts and activities were consensual. Anything that might have appeared to be painful or torturous was done post-mortem."

"Most serial killers are proud of their work. Not me."

Additional Facts:

• His mother tried to commit suicide twice, once before and once after her two children were born.

• Ford was a long-haul trucker. Authorities believe he probably killed more than he confessed to since his MO was to pick up prostitutes and hitchhikers for sex.

• He blamed his horrific behavior, in part, on a 1980 traffic accident that resulted in a brain injury. Ford also blamed his murder spree on his inability to visit his child after his divorce. His second wife testified in court that she never kept her son from his father. She claimed that her ex-husband had never showed interest in the child.

• When Ford turned himself in, he was not a suspect in any of the murders.

• In later years, Ford claimed that he should have only been charged with the accidental death of his four victims since he vowed they all died during rough, consensual sex. He also claimed he tried in vain to resuscitate each.

• His first victim had almost 30 stab wounds in her torso. There were possibly more stab wounds on her body, but the torso was the only body part ever found.

• It was the severed breast of Patricia Ann Tamez that Wayne Ford carried into the police station on 11/4/1998. Her nude body had been found floating in the California Aqueduct in San Bernardino County in 10/1998. She had been strangled and one of her breasts removed. He had not been a suspect in her murder.

• It took six years to bring Wayne Ford to trial. Ford's case was the first in California to be tried under a serial killer law that allowed multiple murders in multiple jurisdictions to be consolidated and tried together in one court of law. His trial was delayed years while that law was hashed out in the legal system before being passed and instated. In 2006 Ford was convicted and sentenced to death.

• Ford often sits naked and ranting in his San Quentin maximum security cell. His appearance has radically changed. His hair and beard are long, dirty, and unkempt.

KENDALL FRANCOIS 8 Kills

DOB: 7/26/1971 NY

DOD: 9/11/2014 Ny (In Prison Of Natural Causes, Age 43)

Sentence: 8 Life Terms, No Parole (He Pled Guilty To Avoid The Death Penalty)

THE CRIME: Many people let their house get a little messy at times, but the Francois' family home was totally out of control.

Police were alerted by a woman who escaped after Francois picked her up then attacked her in his car. When police arrived at 99 Fulton Avenue in Poughkeepsie, NY on 9/2/1998 to serve a search warrant, they were confronted with a garbage-filled, rat-infested, filthy residence and overcome by the rancid odors and squalor. They also found a dead body in the attic that had been kept under Kendall's bed for days before being relocated.

Eventually, seven more bodies would be recovered from the home, five located in the attic stuffed into plastic bags, and three buried in shallow graves in the basement crawl space. In custody was Kendall Francois. He had confessed to killing the women, seven of whom were listed as missing persons by family members or friends. The house smelled so horrific from decades of accumulated garbage that his mother, father, and sister lived in the house unaware of the rotting flesh that permeated their living space.

In time, Francois, age 27, confessed to killing eight women from October 1996 until his arrest on 9/2/1998. He originally pled not guilty but changed his plea to guilty to avoid the death penalty. Possibly it had been tediously explained to him how hard it would be to justify all those dead bodies in his home.

BACKGROUND: Not much is known about Kendall Francois' early life. Certainly, nothing that would explain him growing up to become a serial killer. Francois was born into a two-parent household and grew up on Fulton Street in the home his parents owned. He had an older brother and two younger sisters. His father was a factory worker and his mother was a nurse. The only thing out of the ordinary was the fact the home was hoarded and disgustingly filthy.

Francois was teased in grade school because of his size. By age 14, he was over six feet tall and weighed almost 250 pounds. By high school, however, his size worked for him. He became a star football player and was on the wrestling team. He graduated in 1989. In 1990, he joined the army and was stationed in Oklahoma and Hawaii. In 1994, he received an honorable discharge, returned home, and took classes at a local community college but did not graduate even though he sporadically attended the school until 1998.

He worked from 1996 through 1997 at a local middle school as a custodian and hall monitor. He was not popular with the students because of his poor hygiene habits. They gave Francois the unflattering nickname, "Stinky". He was verbally reprimanded for his inappropriate manner with the female students. Teachers complained to the administration that they had noticed Francois touching girls' hair and making sexual offensive comments but he was never written up. In 1997, he went to work at another school but was quickly fired for the same unprofessional offenses.

OUT OF THE MOUTH OF THE SERIAL KILLER:

"I Killed them...I'm not sure about those." (When authorities showed him photos of missing prostitutes going back to 1993.)

Additional Facts:

• Francois victims were mostly Caucasian women of petite stature with brown hair. All were prostitutes or drug addicts, ages 25 to 51.

• Francois had been diagnosed HIV-positive in 1995.

• The crime scene investigation at the Francois residence lasted 29 days. Those participating in the search complained they could not get the stench of the house off their clothes even though they were covered from head to toe in sterile suits. Investigators remarked they had never seen people living in such deplorable living conditions. Rodent and roach infestation was rampant and animal and human waste was abundantly present. Ironically, it was Francois' habit to bathe the corpse before discarding his strangled victim in the attic or basement.

• His mother was a registered nurse at a psychiatric center. No family members were ever considered suspects in any murder.

JOHN WAYNE GACY *"Killer Clown"* 33-35 Kills

DOB: 3/17/1942 IL

DOD: 5/10/1994 IL, age 52

SENTENCE: Death/ Executed by lethal injection

Facility: Executed at Statesville Correctional Center, IL/14 years on death row at Menard Correctional Center, IL

THE CRIME: John Wayne Gacy, Jr. raped, sexually assaulted, and murdered teenage boys and young men from 1972 until he was apprehended in 1978. He was charged with 33 kills but authorities suspect him in the death of at least 2 more victims.

He would lure his victims to his home or kidnap them by force. Once there, he would restrain them with handcuffs or rope, rape them, then either asphyxiate or strangle his victims to death. This was his MO except for his first victim whom he stabbed to death. Authorities speculate he preferred a cleaner crime scene after his first kill.

Gacy buried 27 bodies in the crawl space of his home he shared with his second wife, her children, and his widowed mother, buried two under his garage and in his yard, plus discarded four victims in the river when either the stench in his home became too noticeably offensive or he had run out of room in the crawl space. *"The lime was used to cover the smell."*

BACKGROUND: Gacy had a loving relationship with his mother and two sisters, but was never close to his father, an abusive and violent alcoholic who missed no opportunity to belittle his son. His mother often tried to shield her son from the husband but this only enraged the father more. He would taunt his son with insults such as "sissy" or "queer."

Gacy was overweight as a child, clumsy, shy, and did not interact successfully with most of his peers. He was diagnosed with a congenital heart condition and suffered blackouts. He was hospitalized for a burst appendix when a teen. His father often accused his son on faking illnesses for attention and would not allow his mother to seek medical attention for Gacy for the appendix attack until it had almost been fatal.

His father's abusive behavior finally led Gacy to flee the home at age 19. He moved to Las Vegas and worked for an ambulance service and then as a mortuary night janitor before returning home a few months later. While a mortuary janitor, Gacy later admitted he had lain beside and caressed a deceased male teenager.

He never graduated from high school but in spite of this fact, he graduated from a business college in 1963. He was hired as a management trainee for a shoe company in 1964 and transferred to Springfield, IL. In Springfield that same year, he met and married his first wife and went to work for his new, wealthy father-in-law in the fast-food industry. Gacy also became involved with the Jaycees, a leadership training and civic organization for people between the ages of 18 and 40. He volunteered numerous hours with this organization. It was during 1954 as a newlywed that he had his second homosexual experience, this time with an older man, claiming he was drunk when the man seduced him.

In 1966, Gacy's father-in-law promoted him to a high-paying position in Waterloo. His wife gave birth to a daughter that same year and a son in 1967.

Gacy's father visited the couple in their home in 1966 and finally gave his son the acclamation he always sought, plus he sincerely apologized to his son for his abusive behavior throughout Gacy's childhood. John Wayne Gacy Jr. should have finally been happy and content with life. Instead, he became enamored with the alternative lifestyle of some members of the local Jaycees that involved drugs, prostitution, and pornography.

He opened what he called "a club" in the basement of his home where he allowed teenage workers of his to socialize, play pool, and drink. Gacy was known to only socialize with the young males. In 8/1967, Gacy committed his first known sexual assault upon a teenage boy.

In 1968, he was arrested on the felony charge of sexual assault of two teenage boys. He pled guilty to two counts of sodomy and was sentenced to 10 years, serving only 18 months. His wife divorced him in 1969 while he was serving time and all contact between his wife and two children were severed. Upon release from jail, divorced, and out of a job, he moved back home and lived with his recently widowed mother. She helped him financially get back on his feet. Gacy went to work for a construction company, and soon started his own construction business. He was a born salesman and an excellent businessman.

He married his second wife in 1972, a divorced woman with two daughters. The marriage would end in divorce in 1976 due to Gacy's habit of staying out all night and his stash of homosexual materials that he continually brought into the home.

On 1/2/1972, Gacy killed his first victim. He picked up 15-year-old Timothy Jack McCoy from Chicago's Greyhound bus terminal and killed him, stabbing him to death. He buried him in his crawl space and covered his grave with concrete.

OUT OF THE MOUTH OF THE SERIAL KILLER:

"That's when I realized that death was the ultimate thrill."

'There is not one of them that didn't, didn't die, that I am aware of, that didn't die through their own hands or through their own wrong doing." 3/16/1979

"There's been 11 hardback books on me, 31 paperback, two screenplays, one movie, one off-Broadway play, five songs, and over 5,000 articles. What can I say about it?" "I have no ego for any of this garbage."

"... if Jeffery Dahmer doesn't meet the requirements for insanity then I'd hate like hell to run into the guy that does."

"I should never have been convicted of anything more serious than running a cemetery without a license."

"Vengeance is mine sayeth the Lord because they will be executing somebody who didn't commit the crime."

Gacy's reportedly last words before execution on 5/10/94: *"Kiss my ass."*

Additional Facts:

• Gacy called himself, *"Pogo the Clown."* He performed at many charitable events and fundraisers as this persona and enjoyed the admiration of the community for his good deeds. He was also a popular entertainer at children's parties.

• In 1955, he was named the third most outstanding Jaycee within the State of Illinois.

• As a Democratic Precinct Captain, he was important enough in the Democratic Party to have his picture taken with then-First Lady Rosalyn Carter.

• Gacy revoked his guilty plea before trial and entered an insanity plea. It only took the jurors less than two hours to reach a guilty verdict and another two hours to recommend death.

• Gacy sold many pieces of his artwork through the mail while incarcerated earning thousands of dollars.

• Gacy funded a 900-phone line where anyone could call in and listen to his recorded claims of innocence.

• In 1970, a prison psychiatrist warned against Gacy's release from jail on his two sodomy charges, calling him a sexual sadist who would be dangerous his entire life. He was released anyway after only serving 18 months of a 10-year -sentence.

• After the execution had begun, the lethal chemicals injecting into Gacy's arm unexpectedly solidified and clogged the tube. The execution took 18 minutes

GERALD ARMOND GALLEGO Jr. and CHARLENE ADELLE WILLIAMS GALLEGO *"The Sex Slave Murders"* 10 Kills and 1 Fetus

GERALD GALLEGO:

DOB: 7/17/1946 CA

DOD: 7/18/2002 NY, age 56

SENTECNE: 2 Death sentences: Nevada and California

FACILITY: Ely State Prison, Ely, NV

Died at a Nevada DOC's medical center. Colon Cancer

CHARLENE WILLIAMS

DOB: 10/10/1956 CA

RELEASED 7/17/1997

THE CRIME: It is usually a good thing when a married couple shares the same interest and hobbies. That is unless you are Charlene and Gerald Gallego. Their shared interest constituted hunting innocent young female victims to be used as sex slaves to satisfy the couples' sadistic sexual desires.

From 9/12/1978 until they were apprehended on 11/17/1980, the deadly duo abducted, bound, repeatedly raped, sodomized, and then killed nine innocent women and one man in three states: California, Nevada, and Oregon.

Most victims were shot or beaten to death with a tire iron, shovel, or hammer. Two were strangled. Many had bite marks on their breasts and buttocks. The bodies were callously dumped or buried in remote locations. A pregnant 21-year-old victim was buried alive.

The Gallegos plucked their prey from public places like malls and county fairs. Ritually, Charlene, a bi-sexual, would lure the unsuspecting victims into the couples' van or car. Once inside, Gerald would subdue them at gunpoint. The couple had a penchant for kidnapping two victims at a time to fulfill their perverted fantasies. After each abduction and kill, it was Charlene who would thoroughly clean the vehicle to eliminate all traces of the crime.

On 11/2/1980, Gerald and Charlene spotted a young California college couple outside a fraternity dance. He approached them with a gun and forced both into his vehicle. Friends of the couple were close by and reported the incident and license plate number to police. This information ultimately led to their apprehension on 11/17/1980, but sadly not before both young people had been slain. They had been driven to a remote location where Gerald shot the male in the head and dumped his body. They then took the female back to the couples' apartment where Gerald and Charlene repeatedly raped her before driving the victim to a second desolate location where Gerald shot her to death.

Charlene eventually turned on her husband in 1982 to save herself. In a plea bargain, she agreed to testify against Gerald in exchange for a lighter sentence. Authorities were shocked to learn of the extent of the couple's murder spree. Charlene broke down and revealed the identity of all their victims and agreed to take authorities to several burying grounds to reclaim bodies.

She pled guilty to two counts of first-degree murder in California and one count of second-degree murder in

Nevada. She was given a 16-year, eight-month sentence in both states, the sentences to run concurrently.

BACKGROUND: GERARMOND GALLEGO, JR: It is said that the apple never falls too far from the tree. In Gerald's case, the entire family tree was filled with bad apples on both sides. Gerald's mother was a prostitute, working the mean streets. She hired out her young son to pimps to use as their runner between johns and the street whores. A series of men moved in and out of his mother's life. Gerald was beat often by his mother, plus she allowed her various boyfriends and Gerald's two stepfathers to physically abuse him and his two half-brothers.

As a child, his mother had been shuffled back and forth between various relatives, many of whom were well known to law enforcement. Her caregivers had served jail time for serious crimes such as armed robbery, murder, and child molestation.

Gerald Gallego, Sr. awaited the birth of his son, Gerald, Jr., while sitting in a cell in San Quentin. Junior never met his father so he was probably not all that upset when his father made history in 1955 by becoming the first person to die in Mississippi's gas chamber. Gallego, Sr. had gunned down two policemen while trying to flee the scene of crimes. That was the same year that Gallego, Jr. started amassing his own impressive rap sheet, including a stint in a juvenile detention center when he was, 13, for trying to rape a six-year-old girl. He was released in 1951.

In 1962, 15-year-old Gerald returned to juvenile prison for one year on a conviction for armed robbery.

By his early 30s, he had been arrested for incest, rape, and sodomy. Most likely, bigamy could have been added to the list since he had married at least six women but failed to divorce most. He married his first wife in 1963 when he was 16 and she was 21.

In 1959, he and an older half-brother were arrested for armed robbery. He was sentenced to five years in prison and released on parole in 1974.

In 9/1977 he met Charlene Williams. They were introduced to one another by friends and there was an immediate attraction. A match made in hell. They moved in together within a few weeks and the two wed a year later even though Gerald was still legally married to another wife. Charlene once said in an interview that Gerald was initially a complete gentleman and brought her flowers after their first date. *"I thought he was a very nice, clean-cut fellow."* That quickly changed. Often Gerald could not achieve nor maintain an erection and blamed Charlene. He became very abusive, both physically and emotionally. In 1978, he found her in bed with another woman, a girlfriend of his, and violently beat both. On 9/12/1978, their two-year murder and rape spree began. Gerald always claimed it was Charlene's idea to capture a woman to use as a sex slave forced to please both.

BACKGROUND: CHARLENE WILLIAMS, an only child, could not have had a more traditional and pampered childhood. Her father was a successful businessman who provided his family a lovely upper middle-class home in an affluent suburb of Sacramento. As a child, she was given music lessons and proved to be a gifted violin player. At school, she was remembered as a quiet, well-behaved student that excelled. The only clue that the Williams' family life was not Beaver Cleaver perfect was the fact that the interior of the home was hoarded and ill-kept.

Charlene's behavior changed for the worse when she started junior high school. She became involved with drugs and alcohol by age 12. By 15, she was sexually active and bragged to friends she was involved with a black man. Her parents refused to acknowledge the warning signals and turned a blind eye to their daughter's rebellious lifestyle.

Her grades plummeted to the point that she almost did not graduate from high school. Her parents encouraged her to go to college, but she quickly flunked out within one semester.

Charlene quickly married and divorced twice, then had an affair with a married man that ended when she suggested a threesome that included his wife. In 9/1977, 19-year-old Charlene was introduced to 29-year-old Gerald through friends and there was an immediate attraction. They married on 9/30/1978 in Reno, Nevada.

OUT OF THE MOUTHS OF THE SERIAL KILLERS:

(Charlene speaking in 2013 during an interview about the 10 victims:) *"I did not kill any of them. "No, for God's sake, no. No, I never did. I wouldn't be sitting here right now if I did."*

"He is just one sick bastard, he was. I would've done anything I could if I could've stopped him. I know I couldn't have stopped him; I tried to stop him."

"I put him on death row. Am I proud of that? Yes I am."

"When I first went to prison, I truly believed I deserved the death penalty even though there was no evidence against me. I knew somebody had to take responsibility for everything, and I knew he wouldn't."

"He portrayed to my parents that he was a super family guy. But soon it was like being in the middle of a mud puddle. You can't see your way out because he eliminated things in my life piece by piece, person by person, until all I had around me were members of his family, and they're all like him, every one of them. Prison was freedom compared to being with him."

"There were victims who died and there were victims who lived. It's taken me a hell of a longtime to realize that I'm one of the ones who lived."

(Charlene speaking of the crimes) *"I see it every day. I always see it; it never goes away. There isn't one more than the other. They're all horrible, horrible memories, every single one."*

"You know I tried; I tried to save some of their lives."

(In describing one victim being killed by a shovel swung by Gerald) *"...a loud splat like a flat rock hitting mud, and the girl sank to her knees and slowly toppled over on her face."*

"I tried to get away. I tried, and people, especially women, will say, 'well, if you want to get away you can always get away.' It's not that easy; it's not that easy at all. I don't know (why Gerald did not murder me) *because he sure tried."*

(Speaking of her life after prison) *"It might be a word, a scent carried on o breeze, happening upon a certain location, and everything comes back. I hove days when it takes all morning to get it together. The memories will be with me the rest of my life."*

(Speaking of her life after prison doing charity work) *"It isn't so much that I really changed, it's just so much that I was finally able to be myself."*

(Gerald speaking to Charlene before the two went hunting for victims) *"I'm getting that feeling."*

Additional Facts:

- Gerald Gallego's mother had three sons by three different fathers. Gerald was the middle child.

- Gerald fathered at least two children in earlier marriages, both daughters. He sexually molested one daughter starting at the age of six.

- Charlene was impregnated by Gerald twice. She aborted the first fetus in July 1978, and gave birth to the second child, a son, born in prison three months after her arrest. He was raised by maternal relatives and died in combat.

- Charlene stole a relative's birth certificate to allow Gerald to use the alias, "Stephen Feil."

- Gerald was employed at various times as a bartender and a truck driver.

- Charlene was fond of forcing two victims to perform sexual acts on each other as she watched. She also forced some victims to gratify her sexually.

- Two of their victims, 14-year-old Brenda Judd and 13-year-old Sandra Colley, were classified as runaways for four years until Charlene confessed to their abduction in 1982. She was unable to lead authorities to their burial site. The girls' bodies, buried together, were not found until 1999. They had gone missing after attending a county fair in Nevada.

- Gerald's trial was delayed due to Nevada's budget problems. The public in Lovelock, Nevada raised over $20,000 earmarked to be used to prosecute him.

- Gerald acted as his own attorney in his first trial in California. He cross-examined Charlene on the stand for six days. *"Mrs. Gallego, isn't the bottom line of your deal to blame both these murders on me to save yourself?"* He also foolishly took the stand in his own defense. The prosecution gave him *"a legal licking"* during their interrogation but in his closing, Gerald begged the jury to believe his testimony *"on faith, if nothing else."* They did not.

• On 6/21/1983, he was sentenced to death in California for his last two kills, Craig Miller and Mary Beth Sowers.

• During his second trial in Nevada, he opted for a public defender. However, the outcome was much the same and the Nevada jury also sentenced him to death. Charlene again was a star witness for the prosecution.

• Gerald became one of the few American criminals to be simultaneously put on death row in two states.

• Gerald's father became the first man to die in the Mississippi gas chamber in 1955 for the slaying of two police officers in separate incidents. He had vowed to kill any policeman who attempted to arrest him and send him back to prison

ED GEIN 2+ Kills

DOB: 8/27/1906 WI

DOD: 7/26/1984 WI, age 77

SENTENCE: GUILTY OF FIRST-DEGREE MURDER, later changed to guilty by reason of insanity.

Facilities: (1) Central State Hospital for the Criminally Insane, later renamed the Dodge Correctional Institution, Waupun, WI (2) Mendota State Hospital in Madison, WI. Here he died from complications of cancer.

THE CRIME: Edward Theodore Gein shot and killed two neighbors, both middle-aged Caucasian women and both business owners. The first victim was killed on 12/8/1954 and the second known victim was murdered on 11/16/1957. He is also strongly suspected of killing his older brother.

He was a grave robber and most likely practiced necrophilia and cannibalism although he always denied these accusations. He made articles from the deceased's bones, body parts, and skin to either keep as trophies, for companionship, to punish the women, or to simply use as utilitarian and decorative objects around the house. He never explained his compulsion to surround himself with the dead and decomposing body parts.

His last victim's body was found in Gein's shed the day after she was reported missing. She was hanging upside down, gutted, and decapitated. Her anus and vulva were also cut away. Her head and the head of his first victim were found in his home.

BACKGROUND: From the very beginning of the parents' marriage, there were bitter feelings and resentments that surfaced continually, manifesting themselves in contemptuous bickering and vicious arguments. The stern, overly devout, and domineering mother was in the habit of constantly belittling her heavy-drinking husband who was unable or unwilling to keep steady employment. She was also extremely strict on both of her sons, admonishing them to turn out better than their father. Divorce was not considered because of the couples' strict religious roots.

His mother worked a small grocery store in La Crosse owned by her husband but the business was sold to purchase a small farm on the outskirts of Plainfield, WI, a tiny town with a population of less than 700 residents. Here she kept her two sons isolated from civilization, allowing them to leave the homestead only to attend school. They were never allowed to make friends and their time away from school was spent mostly doing chores. She warned them to avoid the sins of the world, including women who were all evil whores in her eyes.

She read daily to them from the Bible, mostly passages of hate, fire, and brimstone. Both boys were severely disciplined if they faltered from the course their mother set for them. When Gein was 34, his father died. He and his brother were still living at home, working the farm, but now picked up odd jobs in town for extra money.

The brother died under suspicious circumstances in 1944, leaving Gein alone and mentally dependent on his mother, his only companion. His mother died in 1945. Gein, a 39-year-old socially inapt, shy, friendless, middle-aged man, was left totally alone in the isolated world that his irrational, unstable, and fanatical mother had created for him.

He began to create a woman costume from the skin of dead women so he could slip it on to become his mother.

OUT OF THE MOUTH OF THE SERIAL KILLER:

"I like this place, everybody treats me nice, some of them are a little crazy, though."

When asked if he often wore the masks made of human skin at home: *"Not too long. I had other things to do."*

Regarding Bernice Worden's murderer when questioned by police: *"It must have been someone pretty cold-blooded."*

Listeners thought Gein joking when said of the missing Mary Hogan, his first victim: *"She isn't missing. She's at the farm right now."*

When told that his home had mysteriously burned down before it could be auctioned off: (Arson was suspected but the brief investigation into the cause of the fire yielded no arrests.) *"Just as well."*

Additional Facts:

• Even though Ed Gein did not kill as many victims as other serial killers or have even enough proven kills to technically be classified as such, his mode of killing and horrific deeds were so gruesome that he inspired several unforgettable and nightmarish fictional film characters: "Leatherface" from The Texas Chainsaw Massacre, "Norman Bates" from *Psycho,* and both "Hannibal Lecter" and "Buffalo Bill" from The Silence of the Lambs.

• He was an average student but his slight frame, effeminate mannerisms, inappropriate reactions to situations, and poor social skills made him a target among peers. He stopped school after the seventh grade.

• Before his older brother's suspicious death in a fire on 5/16/1944, the brother had begun to shun his mother's strict warnings about people outside the family unit and to talk ill of the mother to Gein.

• His mother died on 12/29/1945 leaving her only remaining son isolated and totally alone in the world.

• Gein only robbed graves of middle-aged white women he knew had a strong resemblance to his dead mother. These bodies he would carry home.

• Because of Gein's slight frame and frail appearance, police were at first dubious that he was physically capable of robbing a grave and carrying off a fresh corpse.

• Both brothers worked as hired handymen for neighbors as adults and were considered both trustworthy and dependable by their town customers. He often babysat the children of neighbors.

• Neighbors later mentioned that Gein was in the habit of bringing them fresh venison. However, he told authorities he had never hunted deer. The heart of his last victim was found near the wood stove used for cooking.

• He was paid a farm subsidy from the government so he allowed the fields to go to seed and stopped working his farm.

• Gein would not admit to either necrophilia or cannibalism even though authorities and mental health professionals were certain he was guilty of both. *"They smelled bad."*

• He was diagnosed with schizophrenia.

• After his mother's death, Gein boarded up her bedroom and parlors and never altered those areas, keeping them as a shrine to her memory. He only lived in one room of the house and in a shed off the kitchen. The rest of the house was left to decay and rot. Gein did not have electricity nor indoor plumbing and he was described as living in extreme chaotic squalor.

• Among the grotesque items found in his residence: a belt made from female nipples, displayed masks made from skinned women's faces, bowls made from the top of female skulls, four noses, a window shade drawstring made from lips, human skin covering several chair seats, and skulls on his bedposts.

• He was buried in a Plainfield, WI cemetery next to his mother. Vandals and souvenir hunters broke off portions of his tombstone and desecrated the gravesite. His tombstone was finally stolen but recovered in Seattle a year later. It is now housed in a Waushara County museum.

• A carnival sideshow owner purchased Gein's car for $760 at a public auction in 1958. He charged his customers a quarter to see the car in which Gein hauled off the bodies of his victims.

Ed Gein's tombstone was finally stolen after vandals and souvenir hunters broke off hunks of the marker and desecrated his gravesite. A portion of the remaining stone was recovered in Seattle and is now housed in a Waushara County museum. Note the faint 666 mark of the devil incised on the stone by a vandal. The Gein family home suspiciously burned to the ground. (Photo source: www.cultofweird.com)

KRISTEN GILBERT *"Angel of Death"* 40-100+ Kills

DOB: 11/13/1967 MA

SENTENCE: 3/14/2001, 4 consecutive life sentences without parole, plus 20 years

Facility: Federal Medical Center, Carwell, Fort Worth, TX INMATE 90371-038

THE CRIME: If you are a doctor working in a hospital and you tell a nurse to never again administer to one of your patients because you do not trust her, shouldn't you pass that information along to someone in authority?

A doctor said just that to nurse, Kristen Heather Strickland Gilbert, in 1990, but she was not investigated until 2/1996 when three nurses working with the "social butterfly of Ward C" alerted authorities to their suspicions. In seven years, there were 350 deaths on Gilbert's shift, an inconceivable statistic by hospital standards and impossible to be chalked up to being merely a coincidence. In 1996 alone, hospital records showed that Gilbert was present or on duty for 37 deaths. Authorities determined there was less than an one percent likelihood of that being a statistical possibility.

In 3/1989, Kristen Gilbert began work as a RN at the Veterans Affairs Medical Center in Northampton, MA, Ward C, where it is suspected that she killed 40-100 or more patients, many relatively healthy men. She used epinephrine, a drug that causes cardiac arrest. She administered the drug through a needle. Epinephrine was not a controlled substance at the time, but co-workers started to notice that bottles of the drug went missing after Gilbert's shifts. Her first known kill was on 8/21/1995, a 66-year-old Caucasian male.

Gilbert's trail started on 11/20/2000. Her ex-boyfriend took the stand in favor of the prosecution. Testifying under oath, he claimed that Gilbert confessed her guilt to him over the phone in 7/1996. Her ex-husband also testified that Kristen had confessed the murders to him. It was noted that both men had, at some point in time, sought and obtained a restraining order to protect themselves from Gilbert.

She was charged with three counts of first-degree murder, one count of second-degree murder, and two counts of attempted murder. In 3/2001, 33-year-old Gilbert was sentenced to life without parole.

Gilbert has never confessed to any murders and still maintains her innocence. Prosecutors proffered two theories at trial for the possible motives: 1) she enjoyed coming to the rescue of patients in an emergency, life-or-death situation and being praised by staff for her calm and efficient response and/or 2) a medical emergency on her ward was a way to see her boyfriend who was required to rush to all medical codes and, in turn, have him see her performing well under fire. After all, the attention seeking, narcissist Gilbert was not just killing. She was also saving the lives of some victims, the ones who did not succumb to the dangerous drug she had just given them.

BACKGROUND: Kristen Heather Strickland was the oldest of two daughters born into a middle-class, two parent home. Her father was an engineer and her mother was a substitute teacher for a local school. Her sister was seven years younger and Kristen always believed that her sister was her father's favorite child. Kristen would later contend her mother abused alcohol and beat her, but that claim was never substantiated. In fact, many of Kristen's claims proved to be without merit. She was a born liar. She lived in a fantasy world of her own making, and often preferred homespun fiction to fact. This trait continued throughout her school years and into adulthood.

Kristen was an excellent student and earned high marks. She accelerated through school and graduated at age 16. Her only run-ins with school authorities were the result of her lying and overly aggressive verbal and physical abuse of boys. Kristen did not respond well to many males. She was known to fake suicide attempts if she felt a relationship was going the wrong way. She was also known to tamper with a boyfriend's car if angered or attack him, hitting, scratching, and screaming. She tormented many ex-boyfriends, as well, long after the relationship had ended.

Kristen attended several community colleges and eventually earned a Certified Nursing Assistant (CNA) certificate. Her first position was as a visiting home health aide. In 1987, she scalded a young mentally disabled boy over 60% of his body by submerging him in extremely hot bath water. She was not prosecuted but she was terminated.

In 1988, she received her RN degree from Greenfield Community College. In 1989, she went to work as a RN at the Veterans Affairs Medical Hospital in Northampton, MA, Ward C, where she was considered bright, compassionate, highly skilled, and a very social, well-liked co-worker. Most likely her popularity on the ward allowed her the cover needed to kill for such an extended period without detection.

In 1/1988, 21-year-old Kristen eloped and married Glenn Gilbert. They had two sons but divorced in 1995.

In 1994, Kristen began an adulterous relationship with James Perrault, a security guard at the hospital where she worked. When their relationship ended in 1996, Kristen called in a series of three bomb threats to the VA hospital.

At the time, she was also under investigation for murder. She was originally indicted on a federal charge for the bomb threats but while behind bars, authorities began to piece together a case against her for murder.

Kristen went on trial 1/7/1998 for her bomb threats and was sentenced to 15 months in jail. On 11/24/1998, she was indicted for murder. On 11/20/2000, her murder trial began.

OUT OF THE MOUTH OF THE SERIAL KILLER:

"If my patient dies, can I leave early?"

"This is my last call. In 25 minutes, I'll see you in hell." (First bomb threat called into ex-boyfriend, hospital security guard, James Perrault 9/26/1996.)

Additional Facts:

• In 2/1988, Glen Gilbert claimed Kristen chased him around the house brandishing a butcher knife after an argument. They had been married one month at the time.

• She is the mother of two sons, one born in 1991 and the other, 1993.

• By 1990, staff were jokingly calling Gilbert an *"Angel of Death"* due to the number of patients who expired while she was on duty.

• Her ex-husband called authorities to his home in 8/1996. He had discovered a book on poisons that belonged to Gilbert in the pantry. A month later she arrived on his doorstep and tried to attack him.

• The police traced one of the bomb threat calls to a phone booth. Gilbert's fingerprints were found on the receiver.

• For reasons known only to her, Kristen often erroneously bragged about being related to the infamous Lizzie Borden of ax fame even though no ancestoral connection existed.

LORENZO GILYARD *"The Kansas City Strangler* 13+ Kills

DOB: 5/24/1950 MO

SENTENCE: On 3/16/2007 LIFE WITHOUT PAROLE

Facility: Crossroads Correctional Center, MO INMATE 44287

THE CRIME: Lorenzo Jerome Gilyard, Jr. is accused of murdering 13 women: 12 prostitutes and one mentally ill woman from 1977 to 1993 in the Kansas City, MO area. He was sentenced for the murder of six.

It was his MO to strangle his victims, raping 11. The nude or partially nude bodies were all found in secluded local locations. The bodies showed ligature marks on the neck and obvious signs of struggle. His used wire, nylon hose, and shoestrings. All victims were missing their shoes and most had cloth stuffed in their mouths. Some bodies were posed.

Gilyard first came under police radar when he was questioned in the murder of a prostitute in 1987. He provided authorities with a blood sample. That sample eventually linked him to that prostitute's murder and the murder of 12 other women through semen and his DNA. He was arrested in 4/2004. Forensic evidence indicated all women fought desperately for their lives.

He pled not guilty and still claims he is innocent. *"Their scientists against my scientists."* Gilyard avoided the death penalty by agreeing to a trial before a judge with no jury. Presiding Judge John O'Malley said at Gilyard's sentencing, *"He's forfeited any right to live here among the rest of us. That's the comfort we can derive."*

BACKGROUND: Gilyard's father was convicted of assault and rape in 1970, his younger brother is in prison for life without parole for a drug-related murder, and a younger half-sister was convicted of murdering one of her customers while working as a prostitute. She was also charged but not convicted of killing another prostitute.

He was a poor student when he bothered to attend classes. As a teen-ager, he already had a reputation for violence towards women.

Gilyard served nine months in prison in 1974 for child molestation involving a 13-year-old girl. He was suspected of several other rapes (1969-1974) but was never convicted.

In 1981, he was sentenced to four years for assault and burglary but he was released early. In 1983, he was sentenced to four years for making a bomb threat.

At the time of his arrest, he was a manager for a trash collecting company and married. His wife divorced him after his arrest.

OUT OF THE MOUTH OF THE SERIAL KILLER: In an undated and UNEDITED 2016 letter to the author:

Thank you

Got your letter, but only thing I can say was that I was railroad. "Im Innocent." Im working on trying to prove it. I started to send you my prove. But decided not to waste my time. Youve already formed your opinion of me. So thanks but no thanks.

God Bless

4384 days

arrested 4-16-04

Your letter arrive 4-16-16

"That's strange"

Additional Facts:

- At the time of his arrest, Missouri's most prolific serial killer was married and living in a modest home in a quiet neighborhood. Neighbors professed shock that this mild-mannered man was capable of such violence.

- Gilyard married and divorced three times. He had at least eleven children with his wives and girlfriends.

DAVID GORE and FRED WATERFIELD
"Killing Cousins" 6 Kills

DAVID GORE

DOB: 8/21/1953 FL

DOD: 4/12/2012 FL, age 58

SENTENCE: DEATH BY LETHAL INJECTION

Facility: FL State Prison, Raiford, FL

FRED WATERFIELD

DOB: 9/29/1952 NJ SENTENCE: TWO LIFE SENTENCES

Facility: Hardee Correctional Institution

Bowling Green, FL INMATE 096510

THE CRIME: From 1981 through 1983, David Alan Gore and his older cousin, Fred Waterfield, picked up women and teenage girls in Vero Beach and Indian River County, Florida and took them to private locations for the sole purpose of raping and murdering their victims. On 7/26/1983, Gore and his cousin picked up two teenage hitchhikers, handcuffed them together after brandishing a handgun, and drove them back to his parents' empty house where Gore secured them in separate rooms before violently raping each. Left alone, one girl escaped and was running down the home's driveway, naked, with her hands tied behind her back when Gore panicked and shot her twice in the head. A young boy on a bicycle witnessed the horrific event and called police. Gore was apprehended after a brief stand-off with police and the second young girl was rescued. After his arrest, Gore admitted to killing five other women and led authorities to the bodies of four of the victims.

For whatever reason, Fred Waterfield had left the scene on 7/26 before Gore's attacks so he was not at the home when police responded. However, Gore's incriminating testimony against Waterfield during interrogation led to Fred Waterfield being arrested, tried, and convicted for two of their previous rapes, murders, and dismemberments. Gore testified against his cousin and always claimed that his cousin was equally guilty in all crimes.

Background: David Alan Gore was raised in a seemingly normal, middle-class family. He was raised by both parents, neither of them addicted to alcohol or drugs. He was the older of two children. Gore's early obsessions in life were said to be females and firearms but he was awkward around girls and had a hard time carrying on a conversation with them. To make matters worse, he was overweight, not attractive, unpopular, and socially inept. He was fired from an early job because he was caught watching ladies using the gas station restroom where he worked through a hole he had drilled in the bathroom wall. In 1980, Gore was sentenced to prison for five years for armed trespassing of a vehicle when he was found hiding in the back seat of a woman's car with a gun. He served one year. He was married three times, marrying one wife twice. All ended in divorce.

Frederick Levin Waterfield's father was absent from the home often due to his job with NASA. Waterfield credited David Gore's father, his uncle, for raising him. Waterfield was handsome, smart, a star football player in school, and popular among his peers. However, he was a sexual predator from an early age. He sexually assaulted a child who was a friend of the family when he was 10 and the girl was eight. He raped his cousin, Gore's sister, with Gore's help when she was 15 and he was 19. He married several times and fathered three daughters, plus an illegitimate child. Waterfield spent a lot of time at the Gore residence and he and Gore reportedly spent hours fantasizing about bonding and raping women before they acted out on their dark desires.

OUT OF THE MOUTH OF SERIAL KILLER FRED WATERFIELD: An UNEDITED letter written to the Author dated 6/17/2016

Dear Mary:

I'm in receipt of your May 25th letter and I pray this finds you and yours well. It has been on my mind just how to respond to your request. May I suggest that you look into the study made by Samuel ( ), Ph.D,.M.D. and Stanton E. ( ), Ph.D compiled in their "The Criminal Personality" Vol. 1-3. I'm not sure if Dr. ( ), from the U. Florida, published any of his research in this field, but if you would, see what you can find. Before he passed away he left quite a bit of his research with the Fla. D.O.C.'s prisoners for us to develope (sic) treatment programs.

You are far from the first research writer to broach this subject with me. I can not tell you how much documentation that has been sent to them and the profound disbelief of how these events could have unfolded without the truth finally coming out of the bag. For what ever (sic) reason they decided not to write the story. It didn't surprise me because they realized I have absolutely no insight into the criminal events of David Gore based on the testimony of eye and victim witnesses. That testimony is supported with physical evidence along with the sworn testimony of both State Prosecutors Robert ( ) & James ( ).

If you would like to examine some of this material please send me your email address and I'll have it forwarded to you. I only pray that you can figure out how to use this information to contribute important clarification to the public.

Mary, may I ask you if you have a close personal relationship with our Father who is in heaven, Jehovah God? The reason I asked this question is you may not be able to understand the depth of my beliefs based on Scripture as the conclusion of the system of things progresses. Nothing a man has to say is beneficial in disclosing the truth or the heart of the matter.

I have come to understand that no man or woman can defend themselves. It is only through the testimony of the people who are material witnesses or actual physical evidence that defends us. But, what happens when this information is withheld from disclosure to the actual fact finding jurors? The defendant is nailed to the stake just like Jesus Christ was. Please think about that if you decide to go forward with any research in this matter.

Sincerely, Fred

OUT OF THE MOUTH OF SERIAL KILLER DAVID GORE:

"I started dragging her back and she was trying, like, resisting, fighting me, so I throwed (sic) her to the ground. That's when I shot her in the head." "…reflex, just to shut her up."

When speaking of the disposal of his third victim: *"…fed her to the alligators."*

His last statement in writing and spoken before execution: *"I would like to say to Mr. and Mrs. Elliott that I am truly sorry for my part in the death of your daughter. I wish above all else my death could bring her back. I am not the same man today that I was 28 years ago. When I accepted*

Jesus Christ as my Saviour (sic) *I became a New Creature in Christ and I know God has truly forgiven me for my past sins. I am able to face today because I know Christ lives in me. The Apostle Paul said "for to die is to gain". So I do not fear today but truly look forward to spending Eternity in Christ. Mr. and Mrs. Elliott, I have prayed for you both and pray y'all can find the peace that only Christ can give. Last, I just want to say I have had a tremendous amount of remorse and pray you and your family can forgive me. God bless all of y'all."*

The Victims: The six innocent victims of Serial Killers David Gore and Fred Waterfield: Angelica Lavallee, 14, Lynn Carol Elliott, 17, Hisang Huang Ling, 48, Ying Hua Ling, 17, Judith Kaye Daley, 35, and Barbara Ann Byer, 14.

Additional Facts:

- The cousins turned on each other. Gore incriminated Waterfield in all crimes and testified against him but Waterfield was convicted in only two of the rapes, murders, and dismemberments.

- To this day, Waterfield claims he is innocent of all crimes. David Gore was executed in 2012 and read from a written statement accepting responsibility for his actions and asking for forgiveness. He claimed he found Jesus.

ROBERT HANSEN *"Butcher Baker"* 17-30 Kills

DOB: 2/15/1939 IA

DOD: 8/21/2014 AK: NATURAL CAUSES, age75

SENTENCE: 461 YEARS WITH NO CHANCE OF PAROLE

Facility: Spring Creek Correctional, Spring Creek, AK

THE CRIME: Everyone needs a hobby and Robert Christian Hansen's hobby was hunting. Unfortunately, Hansen enjoyed hunting a specific two-legged species: mostly topless dancers and prostitutes from the rough downtown Anchorage AK area known as the Tenderloin District.

From 1973 until his capture in 1983, he is suspected of killing 17 or more women that he lured with the promise of money. Once in his vehicle, the victim was forcefully bound and driven or flown to a remote site, then raped. At times, he enjoyed the deadly game of stalking the stripped naked women as prey, then killing them with a hunting knife or high-power rifle after demanding they run for their lives. This punishment was reserved for women who dared to resist, fought back, failed to sexually please Hansen, or demanded payment for sex.

He got sloppy in 1983. He sent his wife and two children on a European vacation. An empty house provided Hansen with an easier, more convenient place to bring his victims.

In June 1983, Hansen picked up a 17-year-old prostitute, immediately handcuffed her at gunpoint, and drove her to his home. There he raped, tortured, blindfolded, and chained her, then slept. The next morning, he was in the process of transporting her to his plane when she escaped, still handcuffed, and ran for her life. Hansen chased after her, but she was able to flag down a truck. Eventually, she led authorities to Hansen's doorstep.

Authorities and possibly even Hansen do not know the exact number of women he killed, many victims used as human prey in his diabolical hunting game. (Photo source: Pinterest)

BACKGROUND: Robert Christian Hansen was born to a Danish immigrant and his wife. He was their only child. His father was a baker in the small town of Estherville, Iowa. Reportedly, Hansen's father was strict, cold, and distant. Hansen tried vainly his entire life to please his father, even following in his footsteps and becoming a baker as an adult. His mother was devoutly religious and frugal. From age 10, Hansen was expected to work in his father's shop. Long work hours and little pocket money further isolated Hansen from peers.

Hansen was slight, shy, and had a pronounced stutter. As a teen-ager, he developed an acute case of acne that made him even more withdrawn. He longed to ask out a pretty, popular girl, but was too intimidated to try. That inferiority complex first felt in the presence of his father was now intensified amid classmates, especially female classmates. Soon those repressed feelings of lowliness turned to rage and Hansen found himself fantasizing about getting even and being in control. He started hunting and developed an early passion for the sport.

He graduated from high school in 1957. That same year, he joined the Army Reserve and was stationed at Fort Dix, NJ. There 18-year-old Hansen had his first sexual encounter with a prostitute. He continued to visit prostitutes regularly for the next two years. In 1959, he returned home and went back to work in his father's shop.

In 1960, he married his first wife after a brief courtship. That same year, while serving as a volunteer fireman, he and a 16-year-old employee of his father's bakery set fire to a school bus garage and were caught when the youth confessed. Hansen was sentenced to three years on an arson charge. His wife divorced him while he was incarcerated. Hansen continued to have run-ins with the law.

In 1963, Hansen married his second wife after another very brief courtship. In 1967, the couple moved to Alaska. He had been an enthusiastic hunter since adolescence, but Hansen became an avid hunter after moving to Alaska and quickly mastered the bow and arrow. A few of his kills were impressive enough to be included in Pope & Young's World Record Books.

In 1971, Hansen was arrested on one count of an armed attempted rape and one count of armed rape and assault. The courts were lenient and he was released to a halfway house on work release after only serving three months in jail. His first known kill was in 1973.

OUT OF THE MOUTH OF THE SERIAL KILLER:

"You can't rape a prostitute, can you?" (I would never kill) *"a good girl."*

"You know if you go to a motel or something with it, it's more or less like a prostitution deal. I'm going and, or I'd — I guess I'm trying to even convince myself maybe I wasn't really buying sex, it was being given to me, in the aspect that I was good enough that it was being given to me. Uh, if I can explain that a little bit better, gentlemen. Going back in my life, way back to my high school days and so forth, I was, I guess what you might call very frustrated, upset all the time. I would see my friends and so forth going out on dates and so forth and had a tremendous desire to do the same thing. From the scars and so forth on my face you can probably see, I could see why girls wouldn't want to get close to me and when I'm nervous and upset like this here; if I, I'll try to demonstrate if I can think about exactly what I'm going to say and if I talk slow I can keep myself from stuttering. But at the time during my junior high or high school days I could not control my speech at all. I was always so embarrassed and upset with it from people making fun of me that I hated the word school, I guess this is why I burned down the bus way back in Iowa . . . I can remember going up and talking to someone, man or woman, classmate or whatever and start to say something and start to stutter so badly that especially in the younger years I would run away crying, run off someplace and hide for a day or so. The worst there was that I was the rebuttal of all the girls around the school and so forth. The jokes. If I could have faced it, I know now if I could have faced it and laughed along with them it would have stopped but I couldn't at the time and it just, it got so it controlled me, I didn't control it. I didn't start to hate all women, as a matter of fact I would venture to say I started to fall in love with

every one of them. Every one of them become so precious to me 'cause I wanted their — I wanted their friendship . . . I wanted them to like me so much. On top of things that have happened, I don't want to, I'm not saying that I hate all women, I don't. Quite to the contrary, if, I guess in my own mind what I'm classifying is a good woman, not a prostitute. I'd do everything in my power, any way, shape or form to do anything for her and to see that no harm ever came to her, but I guess prostitutes are women I'm putting down as lower than myself. I don't know if I'm making sense or not. And you know, when this started to happen I wanted —you know . . . It happened the first time there, you know, and I went home and I was literally sick to my stomach . . . Over the years I've gone in many many topless and bottomless bars in town and so forth and never, never touched one of the girls in there in any way, shape, or form until they asked. It's like, it's like it was a game — they had to pitch the ball before I could bat. They had to approach me first saying about I get off at a certain time, we could go out and have a good time, or something like this here. If they don't, we weren't playing the game right. They had to approach me. I've talked to, I suppose I made it a point to try to talk to, every girl in there. Sometimes if I thought there was a possibility that she didn't say it the first time but she might come back and say it again, now I've invited two or three table dances with her and comment to her how nice she looked and everything else and I try to keep it in a joking tone, "Gosh you know, you sure would be something, you know, for later on," but that's as far as it would go until she, then she had to make, I guess play out my fantasy. She had to come out and say we could do it but it's going to cost you some money. Then she was no longer—I guess what you might call a decent girl. I didn't look down at the girls dancing, what the hell they're just trying to make a buck."

Additional Facts:

- The FBI Profiler Unit at Quantico, VA was consulted in the Hansen case. It set a legal precedent in 1983 when psychological profiling was used as the main basis for issuing search warrants on Hansen's property.

- Authorities and possibly even Hansen do not know the exact number of women he murdered, and many of his victims were used as human prey in his diabolical hunting game.

- Although the Pope and Young Club initially stated that Hansen's crimes did not invalidate his bow hunting records, they have since removed his name from their record books.

WILLIAM GEORGE HEIRENS
"The Lipstick Killer" 3 Kills

DOB; 11/15/1928 IL

DOD: 3/5/2013 IL, age 84

SENTENCE: Three consecutive life sentences for murder, one life sentence for burglary

Facility: Vienna Correctional Center and Dixon Correctional Center, Dixon, IL Inmate C06103

Died: University of Illinois Medical Center, Chicago, IL of natural causes.

THE CRIME: Three murders shook the very core of postwar Chicago, IL. *"A city that never locked its doors was changed forever, their collective innocence lost" (Chicago Tribune).*

On 6/5/1945, Josephine Ross, 43, was found stabbed to death in her home. On 12/10, 33-year-old Frances Brown was shot twice and stabbed to death in her apartment. Written on a bedroom wall in lipstick was the ominous message: ***"For heaven's sake catch me before I kill more. I cannot control myself."*** The killer had lingered at both crime scenes long enough to wash his victims. He closed the first victim's wounds with masking tape. Neither woman was sexually assaulted.

On 1/7/1946, six-year-old Suzanne Degnan was abducted from her bedroom as she slept and strangled to death. Her decapitated head and five other severed body parts were located scattered about the city's sewer system resembling a gruesome scavenger hunt. A ransom note had been left behind demanding $20,000. The child had not been sexually assaulted.

On 6/26/1946, Heirens was caught burglarizing a home in the Degnan neighborhood. He turned a gun on apprehending police, but the weapon jammed and failed to fire. After a month in custody, he confessed to all three murders. His fingerprints matched a print on the ransom note and prints found at the crime scenes. A hand-writing expert stated Heirens was the author of the ransom note.

Heirens appeared in court on7/30/1946. When asked for his plea, he stunned both the prosecution and defense by claiming he was not guilty. Heirens was adamant that he confessed guilt only because during interrogation he had been beaten, forcefully injected with the truth serum (sodium pentothal), and had been threatened with the death penalty.

Eventually he accepted his lawyer's and parents' advice and reversed his not guilty plea but he always claimed he had done so because he believed he would never have received a fair trial, plus the possibility of the death penalty had again been factored back into the charges. On 9/ 5/1946, 17-year-old William Heirens was imprisoned. He was never tried in a court of law. He was sentenced based solely upon his confession.

Heirens was one of Illinois' longest incarcerated inmates. He always maintained his innocence. He was denied parole and clemency on several occasions even though he had a growing number of supporters expressing belief in his false imprisonment. The family of Suzanne Degnan, however, never doubted Heirens' guilt and her brother and sister attended each parole hearing for decades to voice their opposition to his release. Jim Degnan noted that Heirens' supporters had over six decades to prove his innocence but had failed to do so. Even after his death, the debate continues: Lipstick Killer vs. Convenient Scape Goat.

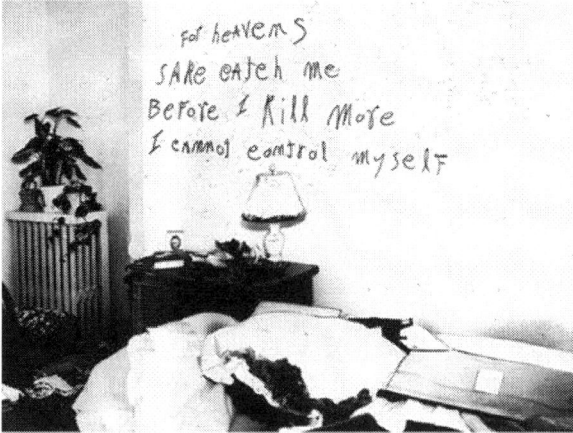

Crime scene photo showing a disturbing bedroom wall message written in lipstick. (Photo sources: Pinterest)

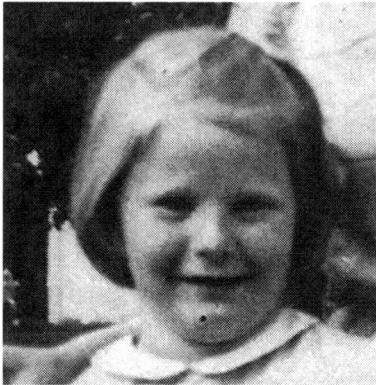

Heiren's youngest victim was only 6-years-old. She was dismembered, her body parts scattered around Chicago. (Photo sources: Pinterest)

BACKGROUND: Heirens was born into a turbulent household. His alcoholic father was a florist with a failed business and the family often went without necessities even when his father took a job with a local newspaper. The parents fought bitterly and Heirens said he would stay away from home as much as possible to avoid the hostilities.

His Catholic mother was devoutly religious and worked to instill her harsh views on her two sons, especially her rigid views on sex as being disgusting and dirty. Heirens claimed that on the few occasions he kissed a girl, he would become so ashamed that he would later cry and even vomit.

At age 13, Heirens was arrested for possessing a loaded gun. Subsequently, other weapons and stolen articles were discovered at his residence and he was sent to the Gibault School for wayward boys in Terre Haute, IN. Although already showing signs of being a loner, he made good grades and participated in team wrestling. He was released nine months later and returned home only to be quickly arrested on suspicion of trespassing with the intent to burglarize. He was sent to St. Bede's Academy in Peru, IL, a juvenile detention center run by Benedictine Monks. While incarcerated, staff discovered he was very bright and encouraged him in his studies.

Heirens was a compulsive serial thief. He continued to steal after his release from St. Bede's and began burglarizing homes in order to purchase items his parents could not afford to give him. He enjoyed handling women's undergarments and would often fondle pieces of lingerie found in houses he robbed. He admitted that he often masturbated while burglarizing.

At age 16, Heirens was admitted to the University of Chicago with plans to major in engineering. He worked part time jobs but could not afford many things he needed or wanted. His parents were still not financially able to help. He continued to break into homes to steal. His final arrest for burglary in 6/1946, and the subsequent three murder charges levied, would drastically and irrevocably alter Heirens' young life.

OUT OF THE MOUTH OF THE SERIAL KILLER:

"I confessed to live."

"It had to be solved and I don't think they cared how it was solved so if it wasn't me it would have been someone else."

"Back in '46, I buckled under. When the pressure is on you, you go the way they want you to go."

"Once you come to prison you don't have many friends, especially outside friends, they kinda fall away. You have inside friends, prisoner friends, but they can't do much for you."

(When asked if he ever heard from any prison acquaintances after their release.) *"Most of them, you hear for a little while, and then they kind of fade out. Usually when they get out, they try to forget they were ever in."*

"I'd just like to take a walk around the block or whatever."

Additional Facts:

• After Heirens was arrested, his parents and younger brother changed their last name to "Hill" due to negative publicity and threats upon their lives.

• The ransom note read: *"Get $20,000 ready & waite (sic) for word do not notify FBI or police bills in 5's and 10's."*

• Heirens attempted suicide once while incarcerated.

• In 1954, the Illinois Supreme Court agreed that while there may have been flagrant abuse of Heirens' Constitutional Rights, none were material to the outcome of the case and did not influence his conviction. A new trial was denied.

- Heirens became the first prisoner ln Illinois to earn a degree from a four-year college. He enjoyed painting and was considered an accomplished artist.

- In later years, Heirens used a wheelchair and suffered from diabetes that affected his eyesight.

- His remains were cremated and prison officials scattered his ashes in a prison garden. While incarcerated, he had spent many years managing the prison garden.

KEITH JESPERSON *"Happy Face Killer"* 8+ Kills

DOB: 4/6/1955 Chilliwack, British Columbia

SENTENCE: 3 Life Terms, Earliest Release Date Is 3/1/2063

Facility: Oregon State Prison, Salem Inmate 11620304

THE CRIME: Strangulation was Jesperson's preferred method of killing. He was a long-distance trucker and preyed mostly on prostitutes and transient women in many states and jurisdictions, people he considered throw-away individuals whose disappearance would not muster much attention.

He was arrested in 1995 for the murder of his long-time girlfriend. This would be his last murder and most likely he would not have been detected for years had he continued to beat, kill, and rape virtual strangers, his MO.

Jesperson has eight known kills, but he is suspected of more. He once claimed to have killed as many as 160 people but later recanted that statement.

BACKGROUND: For whatever reason, Keith Hunter Jesperson was treated more severely by his violent, alcoholic father than his siblings. He was an unusually large child, shy, and clumsy. His older brothers gave him the nickname, Igor, and that negative label stuck with him throughout his school years. He was a loner and had a hard time making friends and maintaining relationships. He was often in trouble when he was young and on two occasions attempted to murder another child.

At a young age, Jesperson violently abused and killed animals and he continued that behavior throughout adulthood. He also set fires.

He married once, was the father of three, but divorced after 15 years of marriage when his wife left with the children after suspecting her husband of having affairs. It was often his custom to openly leer at women, flirt, and make obscene remarks both to them and about them.

His first known victim was Taunja Bennett in 1/1990, shortly after his marriage ended. When others took credit for this killing, Jesperson was so enraged that he wrote an anonymous confession on the bathroom wall of a truck stop many miles away. *"Jan 21 Killed Tanya [sic] Bennett In Portland Two People got The Blame So I can Kill again cut Buttons off Jeans Proof."* He signed that confession with a smiley face. He began to taunt the media and law enforcement officials with letters signed with the smiley face and relished reading about himself in the newspapers and hearing of his deeds on the news.

OUT OF THE MOUTH OF THE SERIAL KILLER:

In an UNEDITED letter from Keith Jesperson dated 4/25/2016 when posed the simple question "Why Did You Kill?":

"Dear M. R. Brett

Fourth Book? Have your publisher send me your first three books so I can read how you write. You are not the first writer to request this kind of thing. I can receive books from book stores, Amazon.com, your publisher. You cannot send it personally. Rules. I'll let you think/ know how I like how you write. If I'm interested. Take care Ken"

In an UNEDITED letter from Keith Jesperson dated 5/22/2017:

"M. R. Brett Check at my book @ Dangerous Ground My Friendship with a Serial Killer by M. William Phelps Let me know what you think of it. Ken"

Additional Facts:

- His life's goal was to become a Royal Canadian Mounted Police but he was so severely injured during a training accident that he was deemed physically unfit for the job. He returned to his original work as a long-distance truck driver, enabling him to kill undetected in many states and police jurisdictions.

- Jesperson described his victims as *"piles of garbage."* In 1995, he tied one of his victims to the underside of his truck and dragged her face down *"to grind off her face and prints."*

- Melissa Moore, Jesperson's grown daughter, has made it a mission to communicate with children and other innocent relatives of Serial Killers. She no longer communicates with her father.

VINCENT JOHNSON *"The Brooklyn Strangler" "The Williamsburg Strangler"* 5+ Kills

DOB: 1/6/1969 NY

SENTENCE: LIFE WITH NO CHANCE OF PAROLE

Facility: Clinton Correctional Facility, Dannemora, NY INMATE 01A2526

THE CRIME: Someone should have taught young Vincent not to spit on the sidewalks. Between 8/26/1999 and his apprehension on 8/5/2000, 31-year-old Vincent Johnson, a small, homeless, crack-addicted, sadomasochistic sexual offender stalked and strangled to death five Brooklyn women, all with arrest records for either prostitution or drug use. He was arrested when the DNA obtained from his spit on a sidewalk matched DNA from four crime scenes.

Johnson's killing fields were the Bedford-Stuyvesant and Williamsburg neighborhoods of Brooklyn, NY. He strangled his victims with any ligature readily available and left their bodies at the scene of the crime. Authorities suspect he raped at least three of his victims. Their nude or partially nude bodies had all been bound. The victims ranged in age from 21 to 28.

Another homeless man, originally charged with the murders but cleared by DNA testing, alerted authorities to Johnson. At first, Johnson denied murdering the women when questioned by police and had previously refused to submit to a DNA test. Eventually, however, he confessed to five of the suspected six slayings. Prior to his known year-long murder spree, he only had a rap sheet for minor offenses: drugs, subway fare fraud, and criminal trespassing.

BACKGROUND: Not much is known of Vincent Johnson's early years. He was born to an unwed mother and never knew his biological father. No one cared enough about this newborn to even bother to give the infant a middle name. His mother was reportedly a prostitute that also abused drugs. The first days of the infant's life were spent suffering agonizing drug withdrawals.

Around the age of six, he was awarded to the court system due to neglect. Neighbors claim the child was often left alone in their tenement apartment without food for long periods of time. Social services placed Vincent into the foster care program. Unfortunately, his foster mother viewed the child as a paycheck and afforded him minimum care and little or no affection. He grew up hating women.

He claimed he killed his victims on Thursdays because that was the only day of the week his foster mother was at home the entire day. As a child, he had learned to loath her presence.

In 1990, he began a long-term relationship with a live-in girlfriend. Johnson originally sold crack on the streets but soon he and his girlfriend became addicted to the drug. His girlfriend left him in 1995 due to their violent, drug-propelled physical fights.

When arrested, he was getting by on the streets by panhandling. Johnson was homeless and slept on the streets. He murdered most of his victims where he slept and coldly walked away leaving the body behind.

OUT OF THE MOUTH OF THE SERIAL KILLER:

"I didn't see strangling her as doing something wrong at the time."

(Spoken to the homeless man that ultimately led to Johnson's arrest:) *"I want that girl."* *"You could leave if you don't want to do that."* (Suggesting he help tie the woman's hands behind her back and then rape her.)

"The thoughts of my childhood and foster care and mom came into my mind." (Before killing a victim)

(In an anonymous written apology to the family of his first victim:) *"I'm sorry I did it. I hope this brings closure. I need help."*

Additional Facts:

• He is the father of a daughter by a long-time, live-in girlfriend.

• He is 5 feet 3 inches tall and weighed 130 pounds at the time of his arrest.

• He claimed he never had enough to eat during his entire childhood and was always hungry.

• in three slayings, Johnson used articles belonging to his victims to strangle them: Tennis shoelaces were used in two killing and a drawstring from sweatpants was used in one murder. One victim also had her throat slit.

• Another homeless man was originally charged with the murders but was cleared by DNA testing. He alerted the authorities to Johnson. Johnson had once tried to enlist his help in binding a homeless woman he raped and killed.

GENENE JONES *"Angel of Death"* 11-60 Kills

DOB: 7/13/1950 TX

SENTENCE: 99 YEARS AND 60 YEARS TO RUN CONCURRENTLY

Facility: Dr. Lane Murray Unit Gatesville, TX INMATE 00380650

THE CRIME: Imagine you are in such need of attention that you will harm and even kill innocent babies placed in your care just to get it.

From 1978 until her indictment on 5/25/1983, Genene Anne Jones injected helpless infants on her Texas hospital ICU unit and later at a pediatric clinic with powerful paralytic muscle relaxers so she could revive the child and save the day. Sadly, the infants did not always pull through.

The drugs she used caused hemorrhaging or paralyzed the skeletal muscles of the tiny babies, including the muscles that kept their hearts beating. It will never be known how many children Jones unleashed her dark obsession upon, but it is estimated that she is responsible for the death of 11 to 60 infants, ages four weeks to 15-months-old, but she was only originally convicted of one death and one attempted murder.

Jones has always maintained her innocence.

BACKGROUND: Genene Jones was adopted by a night club owner and his wife. She was one of four children adopted. The parents fought continuously. Her mother drank heavily and her father was a professional gambler and womanizer who was often absent from the home. He opened a nightclub with a large dance floor and pool area he named, The Kit Kat Swim Club. Jones craved attention from both parents but was especially attached to her father. *"We just had a ball together."*

Genene was an over-weight child who bossed her peers and continually tried to draw attention from her teachers and parents by faking illnesses. Even as an adult, most co-workers described her as loud, coarse, confrontational, and always ready with an off-color joke or to start a conversation about sex. She strove to be the focus of each work and social setting. Still Jones was considered by many who worked with her to be one of the most competent nurses at the hospital.

Jones lost one brother to cancer in 1967 and another brother blew himself up that same year while constructing a pipe bomb. A year later, her father died from cancer at age 56. Genene became irrationally mesmerized by death, funerals, and the attentive response paid to the survivors by consoling friends and family. At the same time, she became irritated that her grieving mother temporarily closed herself off. Genene resented her mother for not being there for her in her time of need.

In 1968, 18-year-old Genene married her high school sweetheart after falsely claiming she was pregnant. They divorced in 1974 but reconciled for a short time in 1977. The union produced a son born in 1972, and a daughter born in 1978. In the divorce proceedings, Jones claimed her husband was physically abusive, a claim he always vehemently denied. *"...a man of violent and ungovernable temper and passion." "...struck me with great force."* Genene had worked as a beautician but with two children to support, she needed a better income. She went to nursing school and received her Licensed Vocational Nursing (LCV) certificate.

Jones' first job was at Methodist Hospital, but within 8 months she was fired. *"I had a conflict with a doctor. It was a lack of feeling on the physician's part toward the patient, and I stood up for the patient and he didn't like it. They asked me to resign."* She next accepted a position at South Texas Medical Center complex, working in the obstetrics-gynecology ward at Community Hospital. However, after three months she resigned citing medical reasons.

On 10/30/1978, she began working as a Licensed Vocational Nurse in the pediatric intensive care unit of San Antonio's Bexar County Hospital, now called Medical Center Hospital. *"The first baby I ever took care of was a preemie with a dying gut. I picked that kid up and I knew I was going to stay there."*

In 1981, a staff member alerted hospital administration of her suspicions surrounding Jones and the unusual number of infants inexplicitly dying under her watch. An internal probe concluded 10 children died of sudden and unexplained complications while Jones was attending them, but hospital officials did not notify authorities. Instead, all nurses on the pediatric ICU were repositioned, including Jones, and the unit was re-staffed by Registered Nurses. Jones resigned in 3/1982 under a cloud of suspicion.

In 8/1982, Jones was hired to work in a newly opened pediatric clinic in Kerrville, TX. Within one month, seven children who had been brought in with minor illnesses or for a routine check-up had experienced life-threatening emergencies after being placed in Jones' care. Chelsea McClellan, a 15-month-old infant girl, died. The death was originally attributed to SIDS, Sudden Infant Death Syndrome.

Kerrville is a much smaller town than San Antonio and the activities at the clinic did not go unnoticed. A group of Kerrville doctors alerted authorities and eventually an investigation showed traces of succinylcholine in the embalmed tissue of Chelsea's body. On 5/25/1983, Jones was indicted for the death of one child and for causing injury to 7 additional children. Later, she was also charged with the injury of one child at the Medical Center Hospital.

On 2/16/1984, Jones was convicted of the murder of Chelsea McClellan and sentenced to 99 years in prison. It took the jury less than three hours to reach a verdict. On 10/24/1984, she was sentenced to an additional 60 years for the attempted murder of an infant at Medical Center Hospital.

OUT OF THE MOUTH OF THE SERIAL KILLER:

"I'm sick and tired of being crucified alive and having people think I'm a baby killer. I haven't killed a damn soul."

"I always cry when babies die. You can almost explain away an adult death. When you look at an adult die, at least you can say they've had a full life. When a baby dies, they've been cheated. They've been cheated out of a hell of a lot."

"I've been in nursing since 1977, and Bexar County's the only place I've been killing people?"

"If you're going to sit there and say that I killed babies, you're going to have to tell me that a doctor ordered me to do it."

"My mouth got me into this, and my mouth's going to get me out of it."

"I would bathe the children, and I would sing to them while I bathed them. If that sounds insane, tough shit. If you can't die with dignity, why live with dignity? We talked to them even after death. We're not God. We don't

know when the spirit leaves the body." (Referring to the procedure after the death of a child in Pediatric ICU.)

"Why do babies always die when I'm around?"

"They're out to hang me." "This unit is my life. If you try to take me away from this unit, I have my black book with the name of every kid who's died in the unit and the doctor who caused the death." (Spoken to her supervisor.)

Suicide note Jones, 33, wrote to her 19-year-old husband before taking an overdose of pills on 9/27/83:

"There isn't any way to explain to you why things are going to change. Sometimes, as wrong as it may seem, you have to except what life dishes out. When your older, and I know your tired of hearing that, but you will be able to understand why, why I have to go away. It doesn't mean I don't love you. Please believe that. No amount of money or worldly goods could ever buy my love. It is so deep & strong. it will last for all eternity.

Please explain if you can to Heather & Michael how much I love them. It's such a strong love, I can't put it on paper. I know I'm asking alot, but I really feel your (sic) the only one who could do it.

I'm not guilty of murder, & I hope you believe that. But Daddy's way is right. It takes all the pressure off you and the seven people, whose life I have altered. No one can hurt me with my Daddy. He'll straighten this whole thing out & then we'll go home & everything will be alright. No more problems for you, no more nightmares for me.

Please make sure Michael and Heather are not separated. I know how my mother feels about Heather, but I also know how she feels about Michael. If Debbie or you can't take them together, please be sure whoever does are good people. People with lots of love. Please don't be angry. I'm going with Daddy because I miss him and I want to be with him. He'll take care of both of us.

You'll be fine. Please believe that.

I love you,

Genene

Additional Facts:

• It has been alleged that Medical Center Hospital where Jones worked destroyed records to keep from being embarrassed, shamed, or sued after her crimes came to light. With no records to consult, the exact number of children Jones killed or injured will never be known.

• On 4/24/1983, 33-year-old Jones married a 19-year-old nursing home aid. He filed for divorce in December 1983. Her false claims of being pregnant did not alter her new husband's decision to seek a divorce.

• THE 1977 MANDATORY SUPERVISION TEXAS LAW (amended in 1987) was put into law to aid in over-crowding in Texas jails. It was in effect when Jones was sentenced and would have meant that Jones would have been released in 2018 unless the state charged her with another murder. Texas re-indicted her for five murders to stop that mandatory release.

PATRICK KEARNEY *"The Freeway Killer" "Trash Bag Murderer"* 21-43 Kills

DOB: 9/24/1939 CA

SENTENCE: 21 LIFE SENTENCES

Facility: Mule Creek State Prison Ione, CA INMATE B88913

THE CRIME: Patrick Wayne Kearney mastered the art of the kill by becoming an accomplished multi-tasker. Kearney, a bespectacled man of small stature, would pick up a potential young male victim in his vehicle, immediately shoot his prey in the head without warning, then drive his car home, careful to obey the posted legal speed limit with the dead body slumped in the front seat. Conveniently, Kearney was also a necrophiliac.

After having sexual intercourse with his many victims' dead bodies, Kearney would often dismember them in his home bathtub then discard the remains in various remote places. The severed parts were usually stuffed into industrial trash bags. He drained the blood from many bodies to keep the decomposing odor to a minimum. He was also known to wash body parts to remove fingerprints. If a victim resembled a known person from his past he bore animosity towards, he claimed he would beat the dead body to both vent anger and feel empowered.

Kearney's killing grounds were in Southern California and Mexico. He claims he committed his first three murders in 1962 when he was age 23. He is suspected of killing 21 to 43 men and boys, ages five to 28, before he was apprehended in 1977. Most were hitchhiking,

A 17-year-old victim's murder would eventually lead authorities to Kearney who was arrested on 7/1/1977. Kearney had killed the adolescent on 3/13/1977 when the boy arrived at his home looking for Kearney's long-time lover, David Hill, who was away at the time. Kearney invited the adolescent inside and quickly shot the boy without provocation. He had sex with the corpse, dismembered the body, and discarded those remains in the desert. A witness directed authorities to Kearney through Hill in connection to the 17-year-old's vanishing. Kearney was already under police radar for the death of an eight-year-old boy.

BACKGROUND: Kearney was the oldest of three sons born to married, middle income parents. His mother was a homemaker and his father was a police officer with the Los Angeles Police Department. By most accounts, his family life was stable.

Sadly, his life at school was not. Reportedly, Kearney was a sickly, slight, shy child that was the brunt of constant peer taunting. This derisive behavior escalated through junior high. Adolescent Kearney was constantly goaded with homosexual slurs. These cruel and negative childhood memories were apparently a major influence in creating the malicious, immoral adult that Kearney would eventually become. He claimed by the eight, he had fantasies centered around revenge killings.

After graduating from high school, Kearney joined the Air Force and was stationed in Texas. There he met David Hill. They became friends and lovers in spite of the fact that Hill was married. The relationship lasted two years before Hill rekindled his relationship with his estranged wife.

After Kearney was honorably discharged from the service, he briefly attended California State University at Long

Beach. In 1962, he killed three victims. That was the same year that David Hill and Kearney reconnected and moved in together. They were still a couple when they were arrested on 7/1/1977. Ultimately, Kearney avoided a trial by pleading guilty. Kearney took full responsibility for the murders and cleared Hill. David Hill claimed no knowledge of Kearney's crimes and was never charged.

OUT OF THE MOUTH OF THE SERIAL KILLER:

"Yeah, I made a mistake in befriending this kid. Letting him know where I live. And I shot him before we ever went anywhere. Didn't go anywhere for the weekend. . .I disposed of the body. . .. You aren't going to find him." **(Victim, Michael Craig McGhee)**

"...because they did not bleed much when shot there." (Referring to shooting many victims with a .22-caliber behind the ear.)

"(Killing) excited me and gave me a feeling of dominance."

Additional Facts:

• Supposedly, Kearney has a genius level IQ of 180. He was fluent in Spanish and French. Reportedly, he also spoke Chinese.

• He worked as an engineer for Hughes Aircraft and was described as a model employee. He quit right before being arrested.

• David Hill was the complete opposite of Kearney in appearance. Hill was over six feet tall and muscular. Kearney preferred manly appearing males, a trait that could have proved problematic for him when trying to subdue a non-cooperative victim.

• David Hill was married, divorced, and the father of a child. He and Kearney had an on-again, off-again love relationship. It is possible Hill was bi-sexual or that Hill, who could never maintain steady and gainful employment, financially used Kearney. Kearney made an excellent salary and owned his own home.

• In 1974, Kearney began to shoot his prey behind the left ear without warning, thus lessening the chances of himself being hurt, over-taken, or drawing unwanted attention from witnesses or police. He also claimed the victim did not bleed as much if shot behind the ear so less to clean up.

• Because Kearney's crimes were committed before California reinstated the death penalty in 1978, the maximum sentencing allowed under law was 21 life sentences even though Kearney fully confessed to 21 murders, rapes, and dismemberments.

• The murder of 17-year-old John Lamay would eventually result in Kearney's arrest and conviction. He had told friends he was going to hang out with "Pat and Dave".

• Two other serial killers, William Bonin and Randy Kraft, are also known as "The Freeway Killer."

EDMUND KEMPER *"Co-Ed Killer"* *"Co-Ed Butcher"* 10 Kills

DOB: 12/18/1948 CA

SENTENCE: Eight counts of life to run concurrently, with the possibility of parole (70 years to life) CA had abolished the death penalty when he committed his adult crimes.

Facility: California Medical Facility (CMF) Vacaville, CA INMATE B52453

THE CRIME: What could go wrong if you are a guy, standing 6 feet 9 inches tall, weigh a fit 285, are considered handsome by women, and have a near genius IQ? A lot if by age 15, you have slaughtered your grandparents, are incarcerated in a mental hospital, and authorities have branded you a criminally insane juvenile. A lot more can go wrong if you are released from juvenile detention at age 21, pronounced cured, then go on to become known as the "Co-Ed Butcher", a necrophiliac, rapist, and murderer who is responsible for the death of young women whose only crime was to be at the wrong place at the wrong time.

From 5/7/1972 until his arrest on 4/24/1973, Edmund Emil Kemper III, picked up six young Santa Cruz women, easily over-powered them, strangled, shot, or stabbed them to death, then took their bodies to his apartment or his mother's home to rape the corpses before and after mutilating the remains. He especially enjoyed decapitating his prey. His mother was his ninth kill. He bludgeoned her to death with a hammer as she slept, decapitated her, then used her head for oral sex and as a dart board. He cut out her vocal cords.

Kemper later invited his mother's best friend to the home and strangled her.

At trial, Kemper's attorney pled "not guilty by reason of insanity" (NGRI). He was found sane and sentenced to eight counts of first-degree murder. He is eligible for parole but, to date, has not been released.

BACKGROUND: Edmund Emil Kemper III was born into a two-parent home, the only son and middle child. The household was in constant turmoil. His docile father, whom Edmund adored, was the target of his mother's unrelenting rage. Reportedly, she was a controlling, critical, and high-strung woman who was never satisfied even though her husband worked hard and provided well for his family.

His father took advantage of every opportunity to be away from the home. He finally left his wife in 1957, and moved out of state, leaving his children in the care of the mother. Her anger and criticism quickly turned towards her son. *"I was a reminder of my father and her failed marriage."* Shortly after the father left, his mother moved her 10-year-old son's room to the basement. She claimed his size and abnormal actions made him a threat to both herself and her two daughters.

At school, Kemper's grades were average, he never caused problems, but he was branded a loner. His large size and most likely peculiar ways set him apart from his peers. He enjoyed tearing the heads and arms off his sisters' dolls. He progressed to killing cats and dogs. Kemper once buried the family cat alive, then dug the body up and kept it in his room, cutting off the head.

When he was 15, his mother sent him to live with his father and new wife, saying she was tired of her son's "weirdo ways." The reunion did not go well. After only one month, Kemper was sent back to his mother. She did not welcome him home, but instead sent Kemper to live with his paternal grandparents on a remote mountain ranch. He walked up behind his grandmother in her kitchen on 8/27/1964, and unprovoked, shot her three times in the head with a rifle. He then repeatedly stabbed her for good measure. He always maintained that his grandmother was just like his mother. *"She was constantly emancipating me and my grandfather."* When his kindly and *"senile"* grandfather returned to the home, he shot him in the head, then phoned his mother to ask for guidance. She told him to *"call the sheriff"*. He promptly obeyed. Kemper then patiently waited on the front porch for the police to arrive.

A juvenile, 15-year-old Kemper was committed by the California Youth Authority to Atascadero State Mental Hospital. While there, he was given a barrage of tests. His IQ tested 136, a score that is near genius level. He was also diagnosed a psychotic and a paranoid schizophrenic. By age 21, he was declared sane and, against all doctor's recommendations, released back into the custody of his mother and, woefully, onto society.

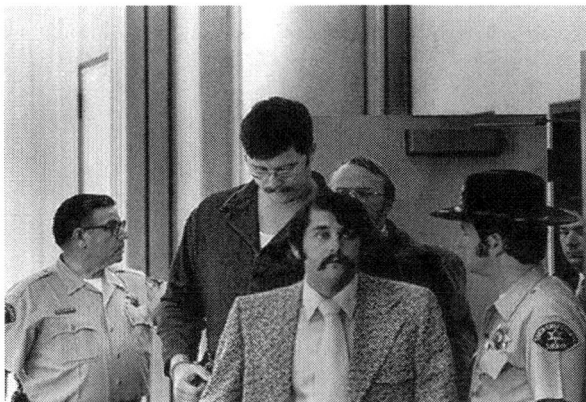

Ed Kemper in custody in 1973. At 21, Kemper had yearned to join the police department. However, his size disqualified him as a candidate. He hung out regularly at a bar called the "Jury Room" where many police, lawyers, and even judges frequented. He was known by many as "Big Ed" and he was considered a heavy-drinking, gentle giant.

(Photo source: www.Murderpedia.org)

OUT OF THE MOUTH OF THE SERIAL KILLER:

"Then I began killings dogs and cats."

"I just wanted to see what it felt like to shoot Grandma." (In custody after killing his grandparents.)

"I ended up trying to take care of my little vicious world myself at Atascadero. I didn't dare say anything about it. They didn't bring it up, they didn't discover it." "Some of those things in the tests, some of the drawings and things, directly pertained to, ah, my feelings, to my little world so I had to disguise that." "I learned everything right there in that department." (He later claimed he had the doctors eating out of his hands.)

"My mother was a sick angry hungry and very sad woman. I hated her." "The monster in my life, the devil in my life was Mom."

"When they got me away from Mom's, when they got me away from Grandma, they said, hey, you're a person, you're a human being, you're intelligent and I said, oh, and everybody tells me how stupid I am."

"I had finally, for the first time in my life, scraped up a small measure of respect for myself in spite of her." (Regarding his mother when he was returned to her custody upon release from Atascadero at age 21.)

"I'm not an expert, I'm not an authority. I have been a killer for almost 20 years. It would be a guess but far more than 35." (1984 interview when asked how many serial killers he guessed were presently at large in America.) *"I was raging inside."*

"Can you imagine the victory, or the coup, that if I had wanted to stop would have been if I said, Mom, I killed those girls, you know, your son killed the co-eds. What do you think of that? And you did it, and we did it, I did it, we did it together."

"I wasn't impotent but emotionally I was impotent. I was scared to death of failing in male female relationships."

"It was scary to go out and dispose of body parts…I had some close calls."

Kemper attended a final mandatory meeting with his parole officer. Unknown to the parole officer, Kemper's 15-year-old victim's severed head and hands were in the trunk of his car. Kemper appeared normal enough to avoid arousing any suspicion and was released from parole. *"I was maintaining a normal livelihood at the same time. Dr. Jekyll Mr. Hyde completely I mean because even my own mother didn't suspect."*

Additional Facts:

• Kemper lived for a time with his mother and sisters in Helena, Montana.

• He was opposed to the counter-culture liberal actions of college students and people his own age. He was considered *"square." "These kids were like aliens to me."*

• He bought a car that resembled an unmarked police car. He later bought a police scanner to listen to police broadcasts.

• He hung out regularly at a bar called the "Jury Room" where many police, lawyers, and even judges frequented. He was known by many as "Big Ed" and he was considered a heavy-drinking, gentle giant.

• Kemper's murdered grandmother had been a free-lance writer for *Boy's Life* magazine.

• At 21, Kemper began to collect knives and guns.

• Local and Santa Cruz campus police advised co-eds to never accept a ride from a stranger unless the car showed a campus sticker. Ironically, Kemper's car bore a sticker due to his mother's campus job. *"I was also involved in killing co-eds because my mother was associated with college work, college co-eds, women, and had had a very strong and violently outspoken position on men for much of my upbringing."* (Kemper's mother worked for the University of California at Santa Cruz. She was an administrative assistant.)

• Kemper was killing in the same area, at the same time, and with much the same MO as another serial killer, Herbert Mullin, who killed 13 victims believing their deaths would prevent an earthquake.

• In 1974, while incarcerated, Kemper requested a lobotomy. *"The surgery would break the conditioning. It would give me a chance. It wouldn't eradicate the condition. It would not do it. It would put a brake in it."* The state refused saying it was too dangerous.

• In prison as an adult, his IQ tested 145.

• Kemper is a model prisoner and does well with the structure jail presents. He spends a great deal of time recording books on tape for the blind. He also teaches computer science to inmates. It is conceivable but highly unlikely that these activities could positively impact Kemper's being granted a parole in the future.

ANTHONY KIRKLAND 5 Kills

DOB: 9/13/1968 OH

SENTENCE: Received two death sentences and two life sentences on 3/3/31/2010; In May 2016, he was granted a resentencing hearing by the Ohio Supreme Court. He again received the death penalty in 2018.

Facility: Ohio State Penitentiary INMATE A626-893

THE CRIME: In 1987, 18-year-old Anthony Kirkland beat and choked his uncle's 27-year-old girlfriend unconscious and set her body on fire while she was still alive. He had become enraged and killed her when she had refused his sexual advances.

He served 16 of his seven to 25-year sentence on voluntary manslaughter charges and was released from prison in 2003 and from parole in 2004.

In 2005, he was arrested and tried for the armed rape of a neighbor but was found not guilty. From 12/22/2006 until his arrest on 3/7/2009, he sexually assaulted, murdered, and burned the bodies of two women and two young girls in the Cincinnati area.

His last victim was a 13-year-old seventh grader who was jogging near her home when she was kidnapped and attacked. She had been strangled and the lower portion of her body was set on fire. Kirkland was apprehended sleeping near the scene of the crime with the child's watch and iPod in his possession.

BACKGROUND: Anthony Kirkland has a brother and two sisters. When he was nine-years-old, he claims he watched his father beat and rape his mother, an act that imprinted on his memory. He also claimed that abuse was a constant factor in the home and that his mother hated him and made that fact well known.

He never married but he is the father of a son. He threatened his son's life in 2007 when the child was 18-months-old. A SWAT team surrounded his residence in a standoff as he held the child hostage. He received a sentence of less than 4 months for unlawful restraint of a minor and was allowed unsupervised visitation with the child.

Four of the five innocent victims of Anthony Kirkland. At the time of his arrest, he had three outstanding warrants.

(Photo source: www.Murderpedia.org)

OUT OF THE MOUTH OF THE SERIAL KILLER: From an UNEDITED letter to the author May, 2015 when simply asked why he killed:

"HELP ME WITH WHAT I WANT, I HELP YOU TO WHAT YOU WANT...GET THIS FOR ME, WE CAN HELP EACH OTHER...IT'S YOUR DECISION..."

(Attached was a form to purchase Kirkland $240.99 worth of TV equipment.)

The following quotes were from a prepared statement Kirkland read at his sentencing hearing:

"I am responsible for the death of those 4 young ladies. I do not even know why I did it. I get so angry and cannot stop myself."

"I don't deserve forgiveness."

"I cannot believe how horrible I am."

"I will never forget or rest or be at peace, nor should I."

"I could not stop the rage and the anger and make the bad Anthony go away,"

"I could not tell the police why t did it because I don't know why. They say I am evil and a monster and they are right. Ever since I was little, everyone said I was bad. Even my mom hated me but I don't blame her, I even hated me."

"I do not blame you if you kill me. I don't deserve to live but please spare my life."

Additional Facts:

- Kirkland confessed to police all crimes but he only pled guilty in court to the murders of the two adult women. He pled not guilty to all charges involving the 13 and 14-year-old girls. He was trying to avoid receiving the death sentence.

- He burned all his victims' bodies in isolated areas. At trial, Kirkland claimed he burned them in a purification ritual. The prosecution countered he burned the bodies to conceal evidence.

- Police brought Kirkland in for questioning in 2006 after the badly burned bodies of two of his victims were found. They released him without charges.

- He was a convicted sex offender and was required to register as such. He was sentenced to a year in jail in 2008 for sexually propositioning a girlfriend's 13-year-old daughter. He served seven months and was released to a halfway house.

- On 2/27/2009, just days before his last kill, he had been kicked out of his halfway house for attacking another resident. The halfway house failed to notify officials that he had been turned out.

- Two of Kirkland's victims were prostitutes and three were innocents at the wrong place at the wrong time.

- *"If we as people, as believers of law and justice, are going to have the death penalty imposed on the worst of the worst...then if not you, Anthony Kirkland, who?"* Quote from Judge Patrick Dinkelacker handing down the death sentence to Kirkland 8/28/2018. His scheduled execution date was set for 3/7/2019. He was not executed on that date.

- Kirkland earned a college degree in prison and is said to be "bright".

RANDY KRAFT *"Scorecard Killer"* *"The Freeway Killer"* 37-62+ Kills

DOB: 3/19/1945 CA

SENTENCE: 11/29/1989 Death

Facility: San Quentin State Prison, San Quentin, CA INMATE E38700

THE CRIME: There just must be a place better suited to stashing a dead body than the car you are driving.

During the early morning hours of 5/14/1983, Orange County highway patrol officers pulled an inebriated Randy Steven Kraft over for erratic driving. Slumped in the passenger seat was the body of a dead man with his pants pulled down to his knees. A bloody knife was beside Kraft and blood stained the passenger seat. A lot of blood.

A further search of Kraft's car revealed 47 photos of men, several who appeared to be either unconscious or dead. Some were nude. A coded notebook page was discovered in a briefcase in the trunk.

Kraft was arrested and taken in for interrogation. A search of his residence proffered additional incriminating evidence: three photos of men from cold case files (one photo was of the dead body positioned on Kraft's couch), fibers matching those found on the body of a fourth victim, a jacket belonging to a fifth victim from Michigan, and a shaving kit belonging to a murdered sixth victim, an Oregon hitchhiker.

Eventually the 61 encrypted codes were broken and many pointed to murdered victims. From 1970 until his arrest in

1983, authorities believe Kraft could be responsible for as many as 62 kills or more. Due to his extensive job-related travels to Oregon and Michigan between 6/1980 and 1/1983, he remains a suspect in cold cases in those states as well as in California. His victims were drugged with Valium or other sedatives dissolved in alcohol, sodomized, tortured, mutilated, then strangled. Some bodies were found with their head, hands, or other limbs severed. Forensic evidence showed several victims were mutilated while still alive. Examples include such atrocities as a nipple burned with a cigarette lighter, castrations, or eyelids cut off so the victim would not have been able to close his eyes. Objects such as tree branches, a sock, a surveyor's stake, and a rock were found shoved into rectums and various innate objects such as a swizzle stick were forced into penises. Most bodies bore bite marks. At Kraft's sentencing, Superior Court Judge, Donald A. McCartin proclaimed, *"I can't imagine doing those things in scientific experiments on a dead person much less someone alive."*

Kraft still proclaims his innocence and shuns all publicity. He has refused to aid authorities in their efforts to close cases and locate bodies of victims. He currently sits on death row in San Quentin.

Inside Kraft's car. When he was stopped by 2 highway patrolmen, there was a dead body in the passenger seat, a large bloody knife, and a lot of blood on the floorboard and passenger seat. More evidence was uncovered in the trunk, including photos of dead men, one positioned on Kraft's living room couch. He still claims to this day that he is innocent.

BACKGROUND: Randy Steven Kraft was born into a two-parent, blue-collar family and grew up in a safe, comfortable, but modest home. He was the youngest of four children and the only son. His mother and sisters doted on him, but his reserved father was cold and distant. Randy constantly tried in vain to gain his father's approval.

In school, he was considered one of the brainy kids but was well-liked by both teachers and peers. The only problems arose from his inability to follow established rules. He graduated 10th out of a class of 390 and his academic achievements won him a scholarship to the prestigious Claremont McKenna College where he majored in economics.

Kraft was a political conservative. He campaigned for Barry Goldwater during his 1964 run for president and supported America's involvement in the Vietnam War, mimicking his father's conservative views. It was also about this time that Kraft realized he was homosexual and had his first sexual relation with a black male. He started taking Valium and abusing alcohol. He tried to seduce an off-duty policeman but was let off with a warning.

Kraft began to neglect his studies during his senior year of college. He was drinking heavily, gambling, taking drugs, and cutting classes on a regular basis. He was due to graduate in 5/1967 but was forced to repeat classes. He graduated mid-term in 2/1968.

It was also in 1968 that Kraft switched his political allegiance to the left and campaigned for Robert Kennedy. He joined the Air Force but was discharged on "medical grounds" in 1969 when he reported to superiors that he was gay. He confessed his sexual persuasion to his parents and was met with disapproval, especially from his outraged father who condemned his son's homosexuality on moral and religious grounds. Kraft started taking methamphetamines and distanced himself from his family. He became more open about his homosexuality and worked for a short period of time at a gay bar.

In 3/1970, Kraft lured a 13-year-old runaway to his residence. There he plied the child with drugs and alcohol, then raped the lethargic, comatose boy. Police became involved, but no charges were brought since the boy admitted to going with Kraft without restraint and freely accepting the alcohol and drugs. He did not tell police he was raped. That would be a secret he kept until 1983 when he testified at Kraft's trial for the prosecution.

In 1971, Kraft began a relationship with a 22-year-old college student from Minnesota, Jeff Graves. They became roommates. In 10/1971, authorities believe 26-year-old Kraft killed his first victim, a 30-year-old gay bartender. Prosecutors claimed he was the first entry in Kraft's encrypted notebook, "Stable." The victim had worked at a gay bar named "Stables" that was close to the gay bar where Kraft had worked called, "Boy Shed." At the time of his arrest in 1983, Kraft was a well-paid, respected Long Beach computer consultant. He was considered a brilliant workaholic.

OUT OF THE MOUTH OF THE SERIAL KILLER: *"I hove not murdered anyone and I believe a reasonable review of the record will show that. That's all I have to say."* (Possibly an unexplained dead body in your car could be viewed as concrete evidence.)

(ln a 1983 letter to one of his sisters:) *"I was just thinking that I could look at this as being away at some sort of school, toking some class I never signed up for."*

(Posted by Kraft on the Canadian Coalition Against the Death Penalty's website, written in the third person:) *"Randy was convicted on hysteria, innuendo and common prejudice against gay persons such as himself. There never was any real evidence against him. There is none today. Instead, the prosecutor lied to make up for no evidence, and hid evidence helpful to Randy. The police also hid helpful evidence at critical times. And the trial judge looked the other way, a Marine Corps veteran prejudiced against gay persons."*

(Profile posted by Kraft on a site that solicits pen pals for inmates:) *"I'm not an old fogey, I like to read all sorts of things and listen to most kinds of music. I enjoy and am pretty good at crossword puzzles and Sudoku and I like to write. ...I am friendly, low-key and sincere. I'm beginning to wonder if there are any sincere people out there."*

Additional Facts:

- Kraft's IQ is 129, near genius level.

- A notepad was found inside a briefcase located in his car's trunk during a search by authorities. On the first page was a handwritten list of 61 notations such as the first entry, "Stable", plus "Airplane Hill", "Jail Out", "New Year's Eve","2 in 1 Hitch", "Parking Lot", and the last entry, "What You Got." Prosecutors called it a death list and contended that each entry represented a victim.

• Forensic pathologists believed that Kraft kept some of his victims drugged and bound so he could torture them for days before strangling them to death.

• Psychologists theorize that by cutting off the male genitals of his victims, Kraft was turning them into sexual females. They suggest Kraft had not come to terms with his homosexuality and his father's rage and the disgust regarding his son's sexual preference.

• Kraft's trial lasted a little over 11 months. The jury was composed of 10 women and two men.

• A fair estimate of the cost to California taxpayers for the trial to convict Kraft and to legally address the appeals that are still being filed would be approximately $15M. California estimates it costs $90K a year to keep an inmate on death row.

• Kraft's preferred victim: young Marine hitchhikers, his ideal of the perfect masculine male.

• Many jurors claimed to be traumatized by the graphic testimony given in court even after the trial ended. The horrific details surrounding the deaths of each victim were meticulously presented, but the most gruesome of the murders detailed was the 1/1976 savage killing of a 22-year-old man. His body was discovered in Cleveland National Forest near San Juan Capistrano. His face, nipples, chest, and genitals bore burn marks from a cigarette lighter. A knife had been used to gouge his legs and castrate him, his genitals then stuffed into his anal cavity. While alive, his bladder had been punctured by a swizzle stick being violently shoved into his penis and his eyelids had been removed to force him to watch his own mutilations.

• A popular speculation is that Kraft acted in concert with an accomplice, his onetime roommate and lover, Jeff Graves. Graves died from AIDS before he could be questioned by authorities so the team theory was not brought up by either side during trial.

• At the time Kraft was killing, William Bonin and Patrick Kearney were also independently killing men along the same interstates. All three serial killers were dubbed "The Freeway Killer" by the media. Bonin was executed on 2/23/1996 at San Quentin and Kearney is incarcerated in California with no possibility of parole. Kearney was arrested on 7/1/1977 and Bonin was apprehended on 6/11/1980. Authorities expected the killing of young men to cease after Bonin's arrest, but it soon became apparent there was a third serial killer at large.

• Kraft sued the author and publisher of "Angel of Darkness" for millions claiming the book wrongly slandered his reputation and limited his future employment opportunities. A judge dismissed the suit as being frivolous citing obvious case flaws.

TIMOTHY KRAJCIR 9 Kills

DOB: 11/28/1944 PA

SENTENCE: Two 40-year terms, plus 13 consecutive life sentences.

Facility: Pontiac Correctional Center, IL INMATE C96201

THE CRIME: Timothy Wayne Krajcir literally got away with murder for three decades until the advancing new technology of DNA fingerprinting finally caught up with him.

He started committing serious crimes by the age of 18. In his first known attacks, he brutally raped two women and attempted to stab one to death with 10-inch scissors while she held her child in her arms. He was sentenced to 25 to 50 years in 1963 for rape and attempted murder but was released after serving only 13 years. The condition of that 1976 early release required Krajcir to attend college. Ironically, he chose to major in administrative justice, a course usually selected by students going into police work. He used information gleaned from course study to evade police. He was so successful that authorities suspected the perpetrator could possibly be a cop.

Krajcir selected unsuspecting, defenseless women he had stalked and peered at through their windows to learn their habits. He attacked under the cover of darkness to lessen the possibility of witnesses.

Many victims were assaulted in their beds as they slept or were over-powered when they returned home, finding Krajcir inside. Others he abducted, raped, killed, then dumped their bodies many miles from their home. He killed in several police jurisdictions and four states (Illinois, Kentucky, Missouri, and Pennsylvania) knowing that it was rare for local agencies to share information.

He constantly changed his MO. Some of his victims were shot, others strangled with bare hands or items found in the home such as phone or curtain cords. Still others were knifed to death or bludgeoned. He chose black and white victims, ranging in age from 21 to 65.

He was a loner and talked to no one about his crimes.

In 8/2007, DNA evidence linked Krajcir to a 1982 murder. He was already incarcerated on lesser charges. Eventually he confessed to nine murders and numerous assaults in a plea deal that took the death penalty off the table.

BACKGROUND: Krajcir was born Timothy Wayne McBride to a 16-year-old mother. His father abandoned the family when he was only a year old. His mother remarried when he was five, and her husband legally adopted the boy two years later. Reportedly, his mother kept her son at a distance, most likely resenting the responsibility of a child at such a young age.

As a boy, Krajcir was obsessively attracted to his mother both emotionally and sexually. He secretly watched her in stages of undress and was caught peeping at female neighbors through their windows. Local authorities charged him with petty thefts during his childhood and early teens.

At 17, he enlisted in the Navy but was dishonorably discharged within a year after being convicted of rape.

At 18, he married his 17-year-old pregnant girlfriend. Three months after the wedding, he raped two women, seriously stabbing one victim with scissors. One month after his daughter was born in 5/1953, he was sentenced to 25 to 50 years for two rapes and one attempted murder. His wife divorced him while he was incarcerated. He only served 13 years of his sentence and was paroled in 1976. Within a year, he was again breaking into homes to steal and rape or abducting his rape victims after brandishing a weapon.

On 8/12/1977, Krajcir committed his first known murders. He broke into an empty house he had stalked and waited for the woman to come home. Unfortunately, when she arrived home her grown daughter was with her. Krajcir immediately overpowered them using a gun, bound them side by side on a bed, raped the daughter, then shot both women in the head. Afterwards, he robbed them.

Between 1977 and 1979, Krajcir assaulted and killed four more women but was never caught. He was sent to jail in 1979 for child molestation but authorities recommended an early release after psychological evaluations. Three months after that 6/1981 early release, he assaulted and stabbed a woman in her home but she survived the attack. (This was his second attack on the same woman, but when questioned in custody, he claimed the attacks were coincidental.)

In 1982, he killed three more women and assaulted, raped, and robbed an unknown number of victims. Again, he evaded authorities.

In the spring of 1983, he was arrested sitting in his car in a shopping center parking lot with a gun in his possession. Evidence tied him to assaults in Pennsylvania. He was sentenced to two and a half to five years. This time he served his entire sentence. A botched jail escape unfortunately failed to add any time to his sentence but a parole violation did. In 1989, while serving that additional time, he stopped all participation in his court-ordered programs for sexual predators, a requirement for parole. Krajcir claimed he needed to stay in prison so as not to hurt anyone else. *"I've made the decision to spend the rest of my life incarcerated.... I've accepted the fact that I am pretty twisted." "I should've never been put back on the street. You know, I was a walking time bomb."* Officials had still not connected Krajcir to any murders and it would remain that way until 8/2007, 30 years after his first two kills and after Krajcir had been incarcerated almost 20 years on lesser charges.

OUT OF THE MOUTH OF THE SERIAL KILLER:

"From '77 to '78 I think I just went a little crazy."

"I said to myself, 'the first good-looking gal that comes up by herself, I'm gonna assault.'"

"Don't leave no witnesses. For some reason this just stuck in my brain."

"I don't know why some of them I killed and some of them I didn't. I don't know what, what the trigger was."

"A lot of the women I killed resembled my mother, you know, age wise, body build."

"Sad part about it was, I was smart enough to, like we were talking about yesterday, to fool the counselors and psychologists."

When asked about the nipple he cut off a S7-year-old victim postmortem: *"I was gonna take a souvenir."*

"I didn't have reason, hardly, to kill any of these women."

At his sentencing when he was spared the death penalty in a plea agreement: *"I don't know if I could have been so generous if I were in the same situation. Thank you for sparing my life."*

Additional Facts:

- Krajcir has one daughter who has never met her father.

- His prison psychological evaluation stated he had an average or slightly lower than average I.Q. Later his I.Q. was tested 125.

- He graduated in 12/1981 from Southern Illinois University, Carbondale with a major in Administrative Justice. While he was in college studying criminal justice, he killed and raped six women, one a student at that school.

- It is unknown how many victims he attacked and robbed but did not murder.

- Krajcir was hired as an ambulance driver and EMT when he was released from prison in 1976. He had completed the EMT course in prison, earning an associate degree from Shawnee Community College in 1974. Immediately, he used his position to stalk women and cover up his attacks on victims, including three murders. His co-workers considered him a friend and a compassionate EMT.

- The Illinois Innocence Project at the University of Illinois in Springfield reported that Grover Thompson, a man who died in prison in 1996 while serving a 40-year sentence for the attempted 1981 murder of a woman, received the first posthumous exoneration in state history in 2019. In 2007, Timothy Krajcir confessed to her murder and the murder of eight more women when DNA technology caught up with him. At the time, Krajcir was serving a 20-year prison term on lesser charges.

REX KREBS 2 Kills

DOB: 1/28/1966 ID

SENTENCE: Received the Death Penalty 7/2001

Facility: San Quentin, CA INMATE D69844

THE CRIME: When sexual sadist Rex Allan Krebs was arrested in 1999 on suspicion of murder, he had spent more than 11 of the last 15 years of his life incarcerated for other crimes including burglary, car theft, a violent rape, and an attempted rape. He was a registered sex offender.

On 11/12/1998, Krebs over-powered a female California college student, beat her into unconsciousness, abducted her, threw her into his pick-up truck, and carried her to an abandoned house. There he raped her, hog-tied her, and left. He claimed she strangled herself to death trying to escape and he discovered her dead the next morning when he returned.

Four months later, 3/11/1999, he broke into the apartment of another California college coed he had stalked, knocked her unconscious, abducted, raped, and strangled her to death at his residence.

His parole agent read about the two missing women in the newspaper. He alerted authorities to the possibility that Krebs might be a likely suspect since aspects of these cases mirrored Krebs' 1987 crimes.

At Krebs' home, a distinctive eight-ball key chain, missing from the second victim's apartment, was located and traces of blood from the first victim were found on his truck's jump seat.

On 4/22/1999, Krebs led police to the remains of both women. His second victim was buried in a shallow grave on his property. His first victim was buried close to the abandoned house down the road.

BACKGROUND: Rex Krebs was physically abused by his father from birth. His mother divorced him when Kreps was five-years-old but quickly remarried a man who was also physically and emotionally abusive to the child, his siblings, and his mother. While Krebs' alcoholic mother was not violent, she was neglectful. It was the habit of the parents to keep the children waiting for hours in the parked car outside a bar while they were inside drinking and eating.

The stepfather continually called young Krebs a "little bastard" and seldom referred to him by his given name.

Krebs defecated in his pants as a young child. His stepfather would beat him and then force the boy to wear diapers to school. When Krebs was 10, the mother turned her back on her son and sent Rex to live with his abusive biological father. The father continued his practice of violently beating the boy, his only son. Krebs' sister testified in court that her father often beat her brother bloody.

Time spent at school was no better. Krebs was bullied by classmates and frequently got into fights. He was not a popular student among teachers. School records show one teacher had noted that he constantly craved attention. He ran away from his father's home several times because of the beatings.

Krebs began to peep through windows. When he was 13, he broke into a neighbor's house who reported to authorities that Krebs was discovered in their daughter's closet masturbating. The court mandated psychological counseling for the child, but his father failed to follow through with the treatment program. The father later justified this by saying, *"They wouldn't do it unless I was there and I figured, oh, they're counseling me, not him. And I thought, shit, I'm not the one that's window-peeping."*

When Krebs was 15, he was taken to the hospital by his father for a severe head injury. The hospital staff suspected abuse but both father and son claimed an accident was the cause of the injury.

Krebs began to break into homes to steal. In 1981, he derailed a train for fun and a conductor was badly hurt. His father relinquished his son to state authorities who placed him in a juvenile home for troubled boys. Ironically, Krebs was happier at the boys' home than he had been in any of his childhood homes. His attitude improved and he was even given a good behavior award. Still his records there indicated that Krebs had poor impulse control, easily lied, and was already abusing alcohol.

At 17, he was returned to his father's home and the abuse continued. At 18, he spent three months in jail for beating a 12-year-old girl and attempting to rape her after he plied her with alcohol. Later that same year, he was sentenced to three years in prison for stealing a car. He was released after 18 months.

In 1987, 21-year-old Krebs moved to California to live with his mother and her fourth husband. Krebs was not welcomed with open arms and was forced to live in her garage. That same year, he was tried and sentenced to 20 years for rape, attempted rape, and burglary. He served 10 of those 20 years and was paroled in 1997. In 1998, Krebs killed his first known victim.

OUT OF THE MOUTH OF THE SERIAL KILLER:

"If I am not a monster, then what am I?"

"Have a nice day." (Said to his 1987 rape victim as he fled.)

Additional Facts:

- Krebs was known to abuse both drugs and alcohol.

- At the time he was raping and killing, Krebs' long-time girlfriend was pregnant with their child. She later gave birth to a son.

- Two innocent California college students, Rachael Newton, 20, and Aundria Crawford, 20, were violently attacked, raped, and killed. Krebs was described by mental health professionals as outwardly appearing socially acceptable and upbeat. At his work, he was considered a model employee.

- At the time of Rex Krebs' arrest, his father, Alex Krebs, was out on bail for drug trafficking. Previously, his father's sister and brother had been violently murdered in separate incidents. Another brother once shot and killed a man during a road rage incident. At one time, Alex Krebs had been a suspect in the murder of a prostitute but was never charged. He was, however, once convicted of rape and served time in prison on that charge as well as several other drug related charges.

- One sister testified in court that she witnessed her father often beat her brother bloody.

- At trial, even the lead prosecutor said of Krebs' father *"...one of the meanest guys on the planet, and he took it out on his son."*

CHARLES NG and LEONARD LAKE 13-25 Kills

LEONARD LAKE

DOB: 10/29/1945 CA

DOD: 6/6/1985, age 40 by SUICIDE

CHARLES NG

DOB: 12/24/1960 HONG KONG

SENTENCE: DEATH

FACILITY: SAN QUENTIN, CA INMATE P-46001

THE CRIME: Cain and Able had nothing on Leonard Thomas Lake. Lake killed his brother, Don, and best friend, Charles Gunnar, who had been the best man in Lake's second marriage. He killed both in order to rob them and steal the identity of the friend. In Lake's defense, family values were not high on this clan's list. He had grown up with a maternal grandmother who urged him to take pornographic photos of his sisters and turned a blind eye when he paid those sisters for sex.

Lake, working in partnership with Charles Chi-Tat Ng, killed between 13 and 25 men, women, children, and infants simply to satisfy base sexual sadistic needs. Their killing ground was Calaveras County near Wilseyville, CA, an area approximately 150 miles east of San Francisco. Their murder spree spanned from 1983 through 6/1985.

Lake built a cinder block outbuilding next to his cabin that included a small hidden room that was described as a hostage cell. This is where he and Ng bound, tortured, and eventually killed their prey. Women were raped and videotaped during their ordeal. Among the more disturbing of their victim choices were two young families with infant children. Beside the building was an incinerator where authorities unearthed almost 50 pounds of pulverized and charred human bones, five complete bodies and a part of a sixth. The search also revealed vehicles and articles belonging to victims, plus an extensive hand-written journal Lake kept with lurid details of his crimes, including names and dates. According to his writings, all women should be merely used as *"sex slaves."* That journal implicated Ng in many of the slayings, torture, and rapes.

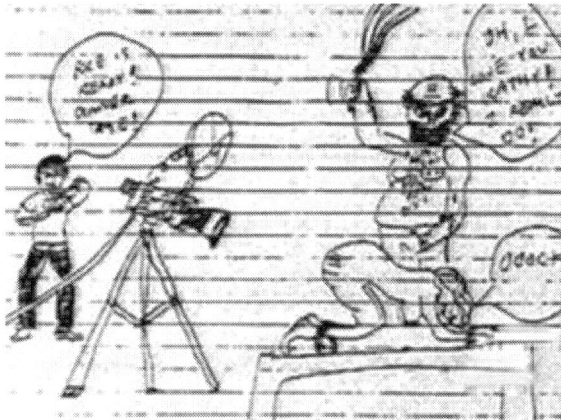

One of several disturbing cartoons authorities uncovered drawn by Charles Ng. (Photo source: Pinterest)

Authorities believe that in the case of the two families, the men were quickly shot and the infants were killed shortly thereafter. Women were held captive for days while they were being tortured and raped, then killed. Men were chosen as victims because Lake and Ng could profit from them: IDs, vehicles, money, video equipment, jewelry, etc.

THE CAPTURE: Charles Ng had been a thief most of his life. This flaw led to the capture of the aberrant duo. Ng was caught shoplifting a $75 bench vice from a lumberyard and ran when spotted. Lake, who was with Ng in the store and fearing the police would be summoned, offered to pay for the item, but the store owner called the authorities. One astute officer was immediately suspicious of Lake. A quick check of his bogus license and vehicle registration led to his immediate arrest. In custody, Lake realized he had been caught. He quickly gave up his real name and the name of Charles Ng to authorities before he killed himself by swallowing a cyanide capsule he had hidden in his clothing.

Ng fled to Canada and fought extradition for six years before being returned to California in 1991 to face justice. A slow learner, Ng had been apprehended and jailed in Canada for shoplifting in 1985. A U.S. jury sentenced him to death 5/3/1999. The videotapes of him and Lake torturing women were shown in court and sealed his fate. Since Lake killed himself in custody, the full scope of his and Ng's crimes will forever remain a secret that he took to the grave. Ng has refused to cooperate.

BACKGROUND: Leonard Thomas Lake was born in San Francisco to married parents who argued and fought continuously. His mother was said to be a promiscuous woman. They divorced when he was six-years-old. Neither parent wanted their four offspring so they were shipped off to a maternal grandmother. She was not mentally stable and her rearing had a negative effect on the children. A favorite childhood activity of Lake's was to capture mice and submerge them into various chemicals to watch them die.

He graduated from high school in 1964 and joined the Marines. He did two tours of duty in Vietnam but saw no combat. Most likely service officials knew better than to put a loaded gun in his hands. He was hospitalized during his first tour of duty when it was noticed he was exhibiting the beginnings of psychotic reactions to ordinary situations. In 1971, Lake was discharged on medical grounds after spending two years in the Oakland Veteran's Administration

Hospital on a mental ward. He was diagnosed with a schizoid personality disorder.

Returning home, he melted into the 70s hippie, drug, commune scene in San Francisco. He found unconventional work as a porn star in amateur productions and preferred roles in bondage and torture films. By 1981, Lake became entranced in the survivalist movement and began to prepare for a nuclear holocaust. He also became passionate about guns and arms. He advertised in a survivalist magazine and Charles Ng reportedly responded. Other accounts say Ng and Lake met through mutual acquaintances. Whatever the circumstances of their meeting, a deadly partnership was formed.

It did not take long for a fanatical Lake to come under the scrutiny of the police. He was arrested for burglary, grand theft, and possession of explosives and automatic weapons. In 1982, Lake jumped bail in Mendocino County. At the time of his death, he had been hiding out from authorities using stolen IDs on a two and a half acre secluded property with a cabin. There he had built a cinder block bunker in preparation for the forthcoming apocalyptic doom. It was stocked with supplies, stolen video equipment, and an arsenal of weapons. It was also equipped with a torture chamber.

BACKGROUND: Charles Chi-Tat Ng was born in the lap of luxury. His father was an affluent Hong Kong businessman who, by his own account, was a strict disciplinarian. Unfortunately, his son was a born thief and a disciplinary problem that most likely deserved an even stronger hand. Despite being the beneficiary of a privileged upbringing, Ng was constantly in trouble and that trouble usually revolved around his stealing.

He was expelled from numerous schools in Hong Kong before his wealthy parents sent him to an expensive English boarding school where an uncle was an instructor. Ng stole from other students at school and from local Yorkshire shops. Even his uncle could not stop his expulsion.

His exasperated father eventually procured Ng a student visa to enable him to travel to California where he was enrolled at Notre Dame College in Belmont. Unrepentant, Ng was soon arrested for trying to flee the scene of an accident.

He joined the Marines in 1979 to avoid a trial. Over-looked was the fact that he was not a legal immigrant. In 1981, Ng and two accomplices broke into a Hawaiian Marine Armory where he was stationed and stole over $10,000 worth of machine guns, grenade launchers, and other deadly weapons. Ng was caught but escaped a few days later and fled to California, a wanted man.

Grim fate at play, Ng and Lake met and became friends. He moved in with Lake and his second wife, all living in a motel that Lake managed. In 1982, he and Lake were arrested on a burglary and weapons charge. Lake jumped bail but Ng was court-marshalled and incarcerated at Leavenworth. Upon release in June 1984, he should have been deported. Instead, Ng returned to San Francisco, an area that was familiar to him, and reconnected with Lake. He began to frequent Lake's remote cabin property and a deadly partnership was formed.

OUT OF THE MOUTH OF THE SERIAL KILLERS:

(Ng to victim, Brenda O'Connor, on tape) *"You can cry and stuff, like the rest of them, but it won't do any good. We are pretty (laughs) cold-hearted, so to speak."* (On tape, when Brenda begs for information about her baby, Lake says) *"Your baby is sound asleep, like a rock."*

"The world would be better off without Don." (Lake speaking about the brother he most likely killed.)

(Written in Lake's journal) *"God meant women for cooking, cleaning house, and sex. And when they are not in use, they should be locked up."*

(Written in Lake's journal) *"If you love something, let it go. If it doesn't come back, hunt it down and kill it."*

"Mercenaries do it for money." (Logo on tee shirts both Lake and Ng liked to wear.)

"By cooperating with us, it means you will stay here as a prisoner. You will work for us, you will wash for us, you will fuck for us. Or you can say no in which case we'll tie you to the bed, we'll rape you, and then we will take you outside and shoot you. Your choice." (Lake speaking on tape. When authorities listened to this tape, they were especially shaken by the sound of crying children in the background.)

(Lake in custody speaking of the article Ng had stolen) *"I didn't think a lousy bench vise would bring me to this."*

"What I want is an off-the-shelf sex partner. I want to be able to use a woman whenever and however I want. And when I'm tired or satiated or bored or not interested, I simply want to put her away. Lock her up in a little room. Get her out of my sight. Out of my life." (Lake speaking on videotape.)

"The main purpose of that cell and the main purpose hence of the building, will be the imprisonment of a young lady who probably at this moment is unknown to me. I know I'm dangerous. If society knew what I was up to, they would be afraid." (Lake speaking on videotape.)

Leonard Lake's Suicide Note he placed in his shirt pocket before taking poison: At the time of Lake's arrest, he and his second wife, Lyn, were divorced. She was living in San Bruno but she and Lake remained close.

Dear Lyn,

I love you, I forgive you. Freedom
is better than all else. Tell (Fern?) *I'm sorry.*
Mom, Patty and all. I'm sorry for all
the trouble.

Love, Leonard

Posted in bunker were six typed rules, all in caps:

1. I MUST ALWAYS BE READY TO SERVICE MY MASTER. I MUST BE CLEAN, BRUSHED, AND MADE-UP WITH MY CELL NEAT.

2. I MUST NEVER SPEAK UNLESS SPOKEN TO. UNLESS IN BED, I MUST NEVER LOOK AT MY MASTER IN THE EYE, BUT MUST KEEP MY EYES DOWNCAST.

3. I MUST NEVER SHOW MY DISRESPECT, EITHER VERBALLY OR SILENTLY. I MUST NEVER CROSS MY ARMS OR LEGS IN FRONT OF MY BODY OR CLENCH MY FISTS AND, UNLESS EATING, I MUST ALWAYS KEEP MY LIPS PARTED.

4. I MUST BE OBEDIENT COMPLETELY AND IN ALL THINGS. I MUST OBEY IMMEDIATELY AND WITHOUT QUESTION OR COMMENT.

5. I MUST ALWAYS BE QUIET WHEN LOCKED IN MY CELL.

6. I MUST REMEMBER AND OBEY ANY ADDITIONAL RULES TOLD TO ME. I MUST UNDERSTAND THAT ANY DISOBEDIENCE, ANY PAIN, TROUBLE, OR ANNOYANCE CAUSED BY ME TO MY MASTER WILL BE GROUNDS FOR PUNISHMENT.

Additional Facts:

- Leonard Lake used the aliases, Leonard Hill, Charlie Gunner, and Scott Stapley. He is known to have killed Gunner and Stapley.

- Lake had one blue eye and one brown eye.

- Lake was briefly married in 1975 but his wife divorced him after discovering he was acting in amateur porn films. He married his second wife, Claralyn Balasz, in 1981. He nicknamed her, *"Cricket."* She acted in porn films with him and in bondage films he produced. They were also into wife-swapping. She testified at Ng's trial under a grant of full immunity.

- One of the most bizarre entries in Lake's journal was his intended plot to use sex slaves to repopulate the world after a nuclear catastrophe.

- The bunker was built on Lake's second wife's family land. It was demolished by authorities in the search for bodies.

- The hidden cell in the bunker was approximately 7 feet by 3 feet and contained a ply board plank that was most likely used as a bed. It also had a bucket and toilet paper, plus a small window that proved to be a one-way mirror looking into the cell.

- Books were found in the bunker. Of special interest was the novel, "The Collector" by author, John Fowles. It is the fictional story of a man who keeps a woman captive, much like the butterflies he collects. Reportedly, Lake discovered the book when he was a teenager and referred to it in his journal. He called his own plan to enslave women as his "Miranda Manifesto" after the female captive in the novel.

• Lake fell into a coma almost immediately after ingesting the poison. Lake lingered, brain dead for four days until his mother, Gloria Eberling, permitted her son to be removed from life support.

• Lake had previously asked for a paper and pencil to scribble a note to his wife. He placed that note into his shirt pocket shortly before committing suicide. (See note.)

• Ng's mother and father testified at trial in his defense, both were brought to tears on the stand. His father claimed to have regrettably been too strong a disciplinarian when Ng was a child.

• The extensive trial of Ng was estimated to have cost between $14,000,000 and $20,000,00 which makes it one of the most expensive State of California tribunals in history. On reporter sarcastically penned, *"After Ng, California's legal system should be placed on trial."*

DERRICK LEE *"The Baton Rouge Serial Killer"* 7-19 Kills

DOB: 11/5/1968 LA

DOD: 1/21/2016 LA age 47 Natural Death From Heart Disease

SENTENCE: DEATH

THE CRIME: Dianne Alexander is the only known survivor of Derrick Todd Lee. On 7/9/2001, Lee forced his way into her home, beat, strangled, and raped her. She was saved from certain death by the chance arrival of her son. He chased Lee out the back door and noted the make and model of the get-away car. His mother remembered her attacker's face and described him to a police sketch artist. She also testified against Lee during at his murder trial after he was finally apprehended and brought to justice.

His known killings started on 8/23/1992 and would not end until 3/3/2003 when he viciously killed a 21-year-old woman. She was to graduate in a few days from LSU, the youngest student in the history of the school to receive her MBA. She was attacked in her residence during the middle of the day. She lived in a high traffic area near the LSU campus yet there were no witnesses and there was no sign of a forced entry. The coroner noted the victim had been bludgeoned with an iron, stabbed over 80 times with a screwdriver, stomped, plus her throat was slit from ear to ear. She was also raped and robbed. Authorities responding to the crime scene reported that *"there was blood from one end of her apartment to the other"*.

Lee's killing fields were the Baton Rouge, Zachary, and Lafayette areas of Louisiana and around Louisiana State University. His victims were what authorities considered low risk victims, victims who led normal, everyday lives, with no record of criminal offences nor drug abuse. The exact number of his murders is unknown but It is estimated that he killed between seven and 19 women before he was caught and sentenced to death.

BACKGROUND: Derrick Todd Lee's early life was a blueprint for the making of a monster.

He was born to an impoverished single mother. His biological father abandoned the family early. At the age of, 3, his mother married a man who was physically abusive to the boy. Reportedly, he beat Lee severely while his mother stood by, refusing to intervene or come to his defense. She was cold and domineering and Lee never felt loved nor wanted at home.

Lee was born with a slight mental deficiency and put into special education classes at school. Peers teased and ostracized him, giving Lee the cruel nickname, "Retard." It did not help that the undersized, dull child also sucked his thumb and called one teacher, *"Momma."*

By elementary school, he was regularly peeping into windows and torturing animals. He once sadistically killed a mother dog and her small puppies. He also wet his bed into his teens.

In 1981, the 13-year-old was arrested for burglary and vandalism and released with a slap on the hand. In 1985, he was arrested for second degree murder but not prosecuted. That was the same year he set fire to his own car, then successfully collected insurance money. In 1988, he was again arrested for burglary but the charges were dropped to a misdemeanor.

At age 20, Lee married. He had problems maintaining steady employment and the arguments at home escalated. His wife called the police on several occasions claiming Lee beat her. He was arrested once, but not charged and quickly released. He had learned early how to talk or charm his way out of trouble and was a person who never accepted responsibility for his actions nor saw himself in the wrong.

On 8/23/1992, Lee killed his first known victim. He bludgeoned a white female to death with a hammer. Her body was not found until 9/2. She had been dumped in a vacant lot in Baton Rouge. Police were not able to locate a viable suspect.

OUT OF THE MOUTH OF THE SERIAL KILLER:

"I've been watching you." (Whispered into the ear of Dianne Alexander while Lee beat, strangled, and raped her. She survived and testified against him at trial.)

Additional Facts:

• Lee was black and the task force wrongly believed that most serial killers were white. (Since 1990, most serial killers in the US have been black.) There were also erroneous eyewitness accounts that pointed to a white perpetrator.

• Lee was incarcerated at Louisiana State Penitentiary at Angola until he died of natural causes awaiting execution. He always claimed he was innocent. DNA eventually linked Lee to the murders of seven women and the rape and attempted murder of one, but authorities suspected he was responsible for as many as a dozen more of the cold case kills during those years. His victims were women, both Black and Caucasian.

- Lee's IQ tested 65 at trial but 91 as a child in public schools. He dropped out of school in the 10th grade but obtained a GED. Lee's defense council argued that Lee was not mentally competent to be tried. That plea was denied.

- His biological father was committed to a psychiatric institute in later life.

BOBBY JOE LONG *"The Classified Ad Rapist"* 10 Kills

DOB: 10/14/1953 WV

DOD: 5/23/2019, Lethal Injection, age,65

SENTENCE: Death, plus additional charges including life sentences.

Facility: Death Row: Union Correctional Institute, Raiford, FL

THE CRIME: Robert Joseph Long was able to get away with brutal rapes in both California and Florida from 1981-1983.

He would answer classified ads for bedroom and other furniture for sale. If he found a woman or teenage girl alone, he would brutally rape and rob her. It is estimated that he assaulted over 50 females before he was apprehended, two of his victims were as young as 12 and 13.

Long moved to the area near Tampa, FL in 1983. In early 1984, he escalated from rape and robbery to murder. During an eight-month period, he abducted, raped, tortured, and killed 10 women. Authorities knew it was the work on one killer because of ligature marks still visible around the victims' necks, plus the dumped bodies were posed, flaunting the kills.

Long preferred to prey on prostitutes, exotic dancers, and drug addicts since he knew these women would not be quickly reported missing. Most of the bodies were not found before decomposition had occurred.

He coaxed or forced each woman into his car, quickly brandished a weapon, took them to various private areas. He bound the women for total control, then raped and brutally murdered them. Most were strangled, but one victim was shot and one had her throat slit.

On November 16, 1984, Long was arrested and charged with kidnapping and sexual battery. He had held and raped a teenage victim in his residence for 25 hours, then allowed her to go free. She helped lead police to Long but, unfortunately, not before he killed his final victim.

During interrogation, Long confessed to 10 murders but was not given an attorney when requested. His incriminating statements were thrown out of court but the survivor's identification, combined with forensic evidence, tied Long to the crimes. The most important forensic evidence was the red fiber from Long's car carpet that was found on multiple victims.

Two death sentences were overturned but he received a third death sentence on 7/21/1989 for his last murder, known victim #10. His guilt was never in question, but Long continued his lengthy appeals and trial proceedings in an unsuccessful effort to eliminate the death penalty. He was executed by lethal injection on 5/23/2019 at age 65.

BACKGROUND: The early years of Bobby Joe Long's life were a textbook formula for the making of a dysfunctional adult.

His married mother was a mentally unstable, sexually permissive bar maid. After she left her husband and moved to Florida with her young son, she paraded a long line of male companions past her son in their one-bedroom apartment. She allowed Bobby Joe to sleep in her bed until he was a teenager.

Long sustained several serious accidents in childhood resulting in head injuries that left him unconscious. At age seven, he was hospitalized for days after being hit by a car. At age 20, he suffered a serious head injury in a motorcycle accident.

At puberty, it was discovered that he was born with an extra X-chromosome resulting in breast development and wide hips. The shy, over-weight, and socially inept teenager suffered even more damage to his already fragile self-image from the constant teasing he received from peers due to his body changes.

Long always claimed his mother neglected his basic needs by never providing him the proper necessities. At age 13, he shot his pet dog because he perceived the dog was fed better food than himself, thus loved more by his mother. He shot the female dog in the vagina.

His hatred of his mother grew throughout his life and, as an adult, that hatred turned outward to encompass all women. He was an X-ray technologist in a hospital setting but was known to abuse his position with some female patients by requiring them to unnecessarily undress before the procedure.

He was verbally abusive to female co-workers and seemed to genuinely enjoy their embarrassment when he would say something sexually shocking, either to them or within earshot. He was briefly married from 1974 until 1980 and fathered two children, a son and a daughter. The marriage ended in divorce when his wife left him and took the children, citing verbal and physical abuse that included choking her to the point she lost consciousness.

OUT OF THE MOUTH OF THE SERIAL KILLER: In response to a letter from the author to Long that simply asked "Why?" 5/2016: IN HIS UNEDITED WORDS:

No I do not want to participate in your project, or, to be included in it. There's already more than enough lies out there written by blood-sucking parasites, and wanna-be authors, trying to profit off other peoples (sic) pain. So you know, my lawyer and I are preparing to take legal action against several of those mentioned above-including the Flowers cow, who seems to have made a career out of spreading lies, and un-substantiated bull-shit about me, and my life. Things that have never been testified about, or put on any record, anywhere...because they are all lies, and bull-shit, all, only too available from cops & prosecutors trying to act like they have all the answers.

I'd advise you to be careful what you write about me. And unless it is part of the court records, not to write anything at all, unless you too want to be part of that "Legal Action" I mentioned.

LEAVE ME ALONE!

DO NOT WRITE ANYTHING ABOUT ME!

"Give a bitch a choice between getting dicked and getting hurt, you know what she's gonna pick."

"Mostly I did it for the thrill of it."

"...(the) intimidation factor...(of my) sharp, nasty blade."

(When asked why he killed:) *"That's my secret. I'm going to my grave with it."*

Additional Facts:

• Bobby Joe Long had an effeminate appearance. It has been suggested that by binding victims, especially with his signature choke hold collar with its leash-like attachment, he was finally able to feel both powerful and in complete control.

• Long was on probation during his murder spree for sending an inappropriate sexual letter and photo to a 12-year-old girl.

- Celebrity defense attorney, Ellis Ruben, was one of many of Long's lawyers.

- Law enforcement from three Florida localities and the FBI worked together to solve this case.

- Long's attorneys had tried to halt his execution claiming that Florida's lethal injection drugs might cause Long to have a seizure during execution. Long suffered from epilepsy. That argument was denied.

- He was executed by the State of Florida for the 1984 murder of Michelle Denise Simms, 22. She had been bound and her throat had been cut.

- Bobby Joe Long died without a final statement. He closed his eyes and would not look at the witnesses.

- *"The peace that came over me is a remarkable feeling."* Lisa McVey Noland in 2019 speaking of the peace she felt as she watched the execution of Bobby Joe Long. She was riding her bicycle home after work at a doughnut shop when he abducted her. Lisa is Long's only known survivor. She eventually was responsible for his capture but sadly not before he killed his 10th victim. Today she is a sheriff's deputy and school resource officer in Florida.

HENRY LEE LUCAS *"The Confession Killer"* 11-50+ Kills

DOB: 8/23/1936 VA

DOD: 3/12/2001 TX (HEART FAILURE. HE DIED IN HIS SLEEP WHILE INCARCERATED, age 64.)

SENTENCE: DEATH BUT COMMUTED TO LIFE IN 1998.

Facility: Texas State Penitentiary, Huntsville, TX

THE CRIME: Henry Lee Lucas has always claimed that he killed his first victim when he was 15, a 17-year-old girl he forcibly abducted at a bus stop, beat, raped, then strangled to death. This claim has never been substantiated. Proven, however, Lucas stabbed his mother to death in 1960 during a drunken brawl. He then had sex with the dying woman.

During another drunken fit of rage in August 1982, he stabbed to death his common law wife, a mentally challenged young girl 30 years his junior he married in 1975. She was the niece of his homosexual crime partner and lover, Ottis Toole, and she had been molested by Lucas since the age of 12. After killing his wife, he dismembered her and scattered her body parts but later returned and buried them. In September 1982, he stabbed to death an octogenarian landlady and had sex with her body before burning the corpse.

He was arrested in 1983 on a weapons charge and inexplicitly confessed to both murders. ***"I done some bad things."*** It is suspected that Lucas and Toole started roaming the country in 1979, killing and raping numerous victims. Lucas would eventually confess to hundreds of crimes, just short of the sinking of the Titanic. While most of those confessions would later be debunked, it is thought that the sexually deviant duo is probably responsible for a minimum of 50 kills from 1979-1983.

Lucas and Toole were partners in crime and lovers. It is suspected that the pair started roaming the country in 1979, killing and raping numerous victims, the exact count unknown.

(Photo source: www.Murderpedia.org)

BACKGROUND: One would be hard-pressed to find anyone in America with a bleaker or more savage childhood.

Henry Lee Lucas was born into abject poverty to an alcoholic prostitute who had no love nor compassion for any of her nine children. Seven were taken by the state and placed in foster homes. Henry, the youngest, and his oldest brother were the unlucky two who remained at home.

By seven, Henry was fitted with a glass eye after two accidents. Around the age of eight, his mother struck him over the head with such force that the bone in his scalp was exposed. He lay on the home's dirt floor for three days, unattended and unconscious, until a boyfriend of his mother, "Uncle Bernie", took him to the hospital.

His mother often forced him to dress as a girl and made no secret of entertaining men for money in front of Henry and her cowering common-law husband, "No Legs" Lucas, who was reportedly Henry's biological father. "No Legs" had lost both legs in a train accident in 1947. In 1950, the man froze to death after passing out drunk in the snow, but not before he had turned 10-year-old Henry into an alcoholic by plying him with moonshine from his still. The alcohol kept the boy from complaining constantly about hunger.

Uncle Bernie introduced Henry to sex with dead animals. By age 13, Henry was actively engaged in sex with animals he slaughtered as well as copulating regularly with a half-brother. In 1952 and 1953, he spent time at Beaumont Reformatory for Boys, the harshest juvenile detention center in Virginia that was reserved for the most hardened offenders. He and two half-brothers had been arrested and charged with numerous burglaries. Henry always claimed he enjoyed his time at Beaumont since this was the first time in his life that he had electricity, running water, and enough food. He willingly participated in sexual acts with other juvenile offenders.

At 18, he was arrested for burglary and served four years in the Richmond, Virginia Penitentiary, again willingly enjoying homosexual acts with fellow inmates.

In 1960, 24-year-old Lucas stabbed his mother to death after a drunken argument and had sex with her while she died. He was sentenced to a prison term of 20 to 40 years. After trying to kill himself in prison the first year, he was transferred to the Michigan Iona State Hospital for the Criminally Insane where he spent the next four years. He returned to Jackson State Prison, a Michigan maximum security institution, until his early release in 1970. He had only served 10 years of his 20 to 40-year murder sentence. Within a few months Lucas was arrested for the attempted armed abduction of two teenage girls. He was sent back to Jackson to serve a four to five-year-sentence but only served a little more than three years.

In 1975, the diagnosed schizophrenic sexual deviant murderer with a low IQ and an elementary school education was released back into the world on an unsuspecting public.

Additional Facts:

• Henry Lee Lucas died of heart failure in prison after confessing to as many as 3,000 unsubstantiated murders. While Lucas is credited with 11 confirmed kills, law enforcement suspect that he could be responsible for many cold cases since he proffered details that only the killer would know. In concert with his crime partner, Ottis Toole, the most accepted number is approximately 50 kills in a four-year killing spree.

• A diligent reporter exposed Lucas' confessions as a scam and the media circus died down. Lucas gave a later interview saying he felt like a rock star and *"was more important than Elvis."* He received financial gain from his many interviews but more importantly to the penniless drifter who had never achieved any merit, he felt important.

• Lucas' death sentence was commuted to life in 1998 by then-Gov. George W. Bush based on the lack of well substantiated evidence presented in his capital murder trial often referred to as the "orange socks" case. Lucas claimed he killed a female hitchhiker in Texas wearing orange socks on 10/31/1979. He was convicted of the crime but later it was discovered that he was not in Texas on that date. The victim has still not been identified nor the murderer apprehended.

• Ottis Toole was officially declared the murderer of Adam Walsh in in 2008 and the case was closed even though no physical evidence linked Toole to the crime. Reportedly, Toole confessed on his death bed to his niece, plus he had long been the prime suspect. Six-year-old Adam Walsh was abducted, tortured, killed, and decapitated in 7/1981. His severed head was found in a canal a few days later. His body was never recovered. Adam was the son of John Walsh who went on to host "America's Most Wanted" and become an ardent crusader in fighting crime. Lucas was in jail at the time of the crime so he could not have been a co-conspirator.

DICK MARQUETTE 3 Kills

Dick Marquette was the first person to be added as No. 11, "A Special Addition", to the FBI's 10 Most Wanted List.

DOB: 12/12/1934 OR

SENTENCE: LIFE, with no possibility of parole 6/11/1975

Facility: Oregon State Penitentiary Salem, OR INMATE 1908466

THE CRIME: Richard Lawrence "Dick" Marquette committed his first murder in 1961 at the age of 27. He was sentenced to life. The jury recommended leniency even though the then-governor of Oregon called the killing *"the most heinous in Oregon history."* He was released in 1973 after serving less than 12 years, a model prisoner.

He committed another murder in 1974 but authorities were not made aware of the crime until Marquette confessed to that murder while under arrest in 1975 for his third murder.

He was sentenced to life in prison with no possibility of parole. (Oregon abolished the death penalty in 1964. The Supreme Court reaffirmed the constitutionality of capital punishment for aggravated murder on 7/2/1976.)

Marquette trolled bars for women for sex. He coaxed them to his residence and always claimed that the sex was consensual. However, mental health professionals theorized that rejection set off a deadly and violent chain reaction.

It was Marquette's custom to strangle the woman to death, drain the body completely of blood, mutilate and dismember the body, then bury or scatter the body parts. Some parts of each victim were never found.

Background: Not much is known of Marquette's background.

In 1934, there were few school records or other records maintained in Oregon. We do know that his parents divorced early in the marriage, a rarity for the times, and his mother was known to have sexual relationships with many men during his early years. Some of the men lived with the mother and Marquette always claimed he has no fond memories of those men.

His mother stated he was a polite, shy, withdrawn child and was extremely jealous of her attention. *"He never could get enough love."* She also claimed that at school and at home, he became violent if punished.

OUT OF THE MOUTH OF THE SERIAL KILLER: An UNEDITED letter dated May 25, 2015 to the Author when asked *Why did you kill?*:

"From my point of view- I've been down over 44 years- Never getting out- A book about me would only cause hate-discontent towards me. Writers like you are like woodpeckers-in the tree-you care very little about the effects on trees-me-what your words do to make other inmate (sic) *cause me problems-"*

"I knew the FBI would get me sooner or later."

"'I wish I could live it all over again."

Additional Facts:

- Before being arrested for murder, Marquette had been arrested in 1955 for attempted rape and disorderly conduct. He served minimal time in jail on both charges. In 1957, he was arrested for robbery and spent a year in jail. He was released early for good behavior.

• Marquette's second victim would never be identified. He had strangled her, mutilated and dismembered her body, then buried her remains in two locations. Her head was not recovered and Marquette couldn't remember her name nor give an adequate description.

• Some speculate that Marquette bought his first parole in 1973 from a corrupt system. It has been said that he received a disability check monthly but was broke when paroled. These accusations were never proven.

• Marquette told police he dismembered his first victim to make disposal easier. At the time, he did not own a vehicle to carry an in-tact body away. However, he owned a vehicle when he killed and dismembered his next two victims. Police speculated he enjoyed the experience and noted the dismemberments were done with a practiced surgical skill.

BLANCHE MOORE *"Black Widow"* 4 Kills

DOB: 2/17/1933 NC

SENTENCE: DEATH

Facility: North Carolina Correctional Facility for Women, Raleigh, NC INMATE 0288088

THE CRIME: If you are born to a father who is a fire-and-brimstone ordained North Carolina Baptist minister but who is also a violent alcoholic, womanizer, and a really inept gambler who prostitutes you out to pay bad gambling debts, then you're probably not going to turn out well. Blanche Kiser Taylor Moore did not.

On 9/18/1966, her father died of a presumed fatal heart attack at age 62. Blanche, the loving daughter, had spent time bedside caring for her father before his death. When Blanche came under suspicion for trying to kill her second husband with arsenic in 1989, the body of her father was exhumed and showed high levels of arsenic poisoning. Apparently, Blanche killed her father and men who fatally reminded her of her father, or at least she tried her hardest to kill them.

Her second husband, Rev. Dwight Moore, survived what doctors called the highest level of arsenic poisoning ever found in a human that lived. Her first husband, his mother, and a boyfriend were not so lucky. When seeking a solid motive other than the veiled psychological one, it did not escape authorities' notice that one victim left her a lot of money and another one would have if he had only cooperated and succumbed to the arsenic.

Four bodies of persons known to Blanche were exhumed and tested, all showing signs of arsenic poisoning. She was only convicted of one count of first-degree murder in the death of boyfriend, Raymond Reid. A jury recommend death. She was not prosecuted for any other alleged crimes. North Carolina saw no need to occur the enormous expense of additional trials since she had already received the harshest sentence possible. To date, Blanche Moore is the longest sitting female on North Carolina's death row. She still claims she is innocent of all charges and is reportedly fighting cancer for the second time.

BACKGROUND: Blanche Kiser was the fifth of seven children born to a back-woods preacher and his wife, Flonnie Blanche Honeycutt Kiser. The Rev. Parker Davis Kiser chased women, drank heavily, beat his wife and kids, and gambled away most of the household money meant for food, shelter, and clothing. Eventually he abandoned his family for a younger woman, leaving them destitute, but not before he had paid bad gambling debts at the price of his daughter's moral soul. When Blanche was 19-years-old, she married James Taylor seeing him as a ticket out of a bad home situation. Unfortunately, for 21 years she repeated much of her own bleak childhood with two daughters of her own to raise and never enough money. When James Taylor died unexpectedly of a heart attack in 1971 at age 45, few tears were shed by Blanche. She had emotionally moved on years before.

Blanche was forced to join the work force in 1954 due to the financial strain at home. She went to work in a Burlington, NC Kroger Grocery Store as a check-out girl. By 1959, she had worked her way up the line to head cashier, the highest position Kroger offered a woman at that time. She started a secret adulterous affair with Raymond Reid in 1962, the store manager, but this churchgoing, sanctimonious woman had experienced several brief trysts with men before she seduced Reid. He was married at the time the affair started and the father of two small children. Very soon after her husband's funeral in 1971, Reid left his wife and he and Blanche made their relationship public.

By 1984, a year before Reid's death, their relationship had cooled, most likely because Blanche was also involved in an overlapping relationship with a Kroger regional manager, Kevin Denton. When that liaison ended, Blanche sued the Kroger Grocery Store chain in 1985, claiming sexual harassment by management and won a reported $275,000 settlement in 1987. Blanche claimed in her suit that she was now unable to form an amorous relationship or even a social contact with any male as a result of her horrifying ordeal. At the time, she was in fact romantically involved with Rev. Dwight Moore and the two kept their affair quiet because of the pending litigation. Authorities would later discover that Rev. Moore had purchased an arsenic-based ant poison for Blanche, at Blanche's request.

In 1987, after the lawsuit was favorably settled, Blanche and Rev. Moore began openly courting. In 1989, they were married. Rev. Dwight Moore fell ill on their honeymoon and was eventually diagnosed with acute arsenic poisoning.

OUT OF THE MOUTH OF THE SERIAL KILLER:

"I know arsenic was found in these people but it's not because I put it there, because I didn't do it." "I have never physically harmed an individual." "I am a very giving person." "I've tried to be here for others and help whenever I can."

Additional Facts:

- Acquaintances claimed Blanche could quote scriptures or talk sex with equal enthusiasm and expertise.

- Blanche testified at trial in her own defense. On the stand, she alternated between crying and bristling when questioned by the state. The jury trial lasted four weeks.

- She was considered an excellent employee by management, but fellow workers called her *"vindictive"* and *"two-faced."*

- In 1984, Blanche set fire to her house in Burlington, NC and blamed it on ***"a pervert"*** she reported having seen around her home. She collected from a small insurance policy and purchased a mobile home. That dwelling was also destroyed by a mysterious fire, Blanche again blaming the pervert and again collecting an insurance payment.

- She was only convicted of one count of first-degree murder in the death of paramour, Raymond Reid. Blanche collected approximately $65,000 from Reid's death.

- While incarcerated, Blanche conducts bible studies and is a model prisoner.

- *Her hobby is writing poetry.*

- As of 2020, Blanche Moore is the longest sitting person on North Carolina's death row. She still claims she is innocent of all charges and is reportedly fighting cancer for the second time.

Herb Mullin 13 Kills

DOB: 4/18/1947 CA

SENTENCE: LIFE, eligible for parole in 2025. Sentenced to 2 counts of first-degree murder and 8 counts of second-degree murder. He was never tried for three murders. (California did not have the death penalty when Mullin killed his 13 innocent victims.) The plea NGRI (not guilty for reason of insanity) was denied.

Facility: Mule Creek State Prison, Ione, CA INMATE B-51410

THE CRIME: From 10/13/1972 to 2/13/1973, when apprehended, Herbert William Mullin killed 13 people in and around Santa Cruz. His motive: To keep California safe from another deadly earthquake. In Mullin's thinking, only a blood sacrifice would forestall an earthquake striking California. He also claimed on the stand in his own defense, that all his victims consented telepathically to their murder. ***"Every Homosapien communicates telepathically. It's just not accepted socially."*** All but two of his victims were complete strangers.

On 10/13/1972, 25-year-old Mullin clubbed a homeless old man to death who was hitchhiking. A few weeks later, he stabbed a young female coed hitchhiker to death and calmly drove away from her disemboweled body after he had thrown the organs along a secluded roadside.

On 11/2/1972, he stabbed a Roman Catholic priest to death in a church confessional and in January 1973, he shot to death three members of a family, the youngest victim was only four-years-old. That child was also stabbed in the back. He continued his brutal killing spree by shooting and stabbing to death a friend and that friend's wife in an over-kill rage. He justified killing his friend claiming that friend had tried to destroy his mind by introducing him to marijuana. (The sequence of the January 1973 murders was disputed in the NGRI plea. The Prosecutor successfully argued that Mullin left, shot and stabbed his friend and the friend's wife, killing them, then returned to kill the mother and children to silence witnesses. This action would prove that Mullin knew right from wrong. The Defense argued the mother and children were killed first. Mullin's NGRI plea was denied.)

In February 1973, he shot to death four teenage boy campers who had invited Mullin to join their campsite. They were trapped inside their tent when he opened fire.

His last victim was an old man he spotted gardening in his front lawn. Mullin stopped his car and shot the man, claiming he again heard voices telling him to kill. An eyewitness to that shooting helped lead the police to Mullin who was arrested without incident. Until his murder spree, Mullin had only minor run-ins with police.

BACKGROUND: Herbert Mullin grew up in a two-parent, middle class, devoutly religious Catholic household. His father was strict but fair and loving. Neither parent was abusive. Their only son was cheerful, intelligent, and highly social. He attended church every Sunday and was an altar boy.

In high school, the handsome Mullin was popular among peers and teachers, played sports, was an honor student, and was voted "Most Likely to Succeed" his senior year.

Shortly after graduation, however, Mullin's mental health began to decline. A best friend was killed in a car accident and Mullin was devastated. He began to delve into the immerging 1960's drug scene and experimented with various drugs. Both incidents are thought to have triggered his budding Paranoid Schizophrenia Disorder, a mental illness that causes the person to become delusional and to hear auditory hallucinations. That person may also experience a feeling of being persecuted or have delusions of grandeur, or both. Paranoid Schizophrenia is a long term or even a lifetime mental illness and often triggers suicidal thoughts or actions.

In 1969, 21-year-old Mullin was first committed to a mental institution. Over the next few years, he was in and out of several facilities and demonstrated bizarre and often self-abusive behaviors such as burning his penis with a lighted cigarette. His drug use escalated.

OUT OF THE MOUTH OF THE SERIAL KILLER: A UNEDITED letter to the author dated 6/19/2016 was accompanied by a 20-page thesis, *"Apologies and Insights"*. The letter, several pages of his thesis, and the summary page of his thesis are included. It was of interest to note that in the entire thesis that is dated 2008-2014, Mullin was never able to write "I killed". Instead, he always referred to the 13 murders of innocent people, two of which were young children, as *"his crimes"*.

Dear M. R. Brett I received your 5/16/2016 letter-Enclosed you fill find a 20 page thesis which describes & explains my point of view concerning my crime spree. These explanations are written at different times and each description dated…they are in sequential order.

When you have the time, maybe you could write me back and indicate that you have received this information.

Also, maybe you could get me a private psychiatrist &/ or psychologist to read this thesis and make comments -perhaps he or she would pose some questions to me?

Thank you for taking an interest in me and my legal struggles-Yours truly, Herb Mullin

(Last pages of Mullin's "Apologies and Insights" thesis dated 11/1/2014:) *The* (Lifer Support Group "prep" questions) *assignment poses some questions-What brought me to forgive myself?*

1. *I saw that I was basically a good person who desires to give & receive beneficial blessings. Life, here in the U.S.A., California, is truly a blessing-. I want to share.*

2. *Have I forgiven my background, upbringing, my rage-who particularly? Yes, by all means! But the idea and concepts that brought me to even suspect their involvement, have not gone away. My parents, aunts & uncles, sister & cousins, friends & neighbors, schools, churches, brother-in-law, etc., etc., all in all have disappeared from my life-. Whenever I meet with a parole board, or psychological review board or case worker, we always discus the relavance* (sic) *&/or pertinence of those people and institutions. But my forgiveness is real and sincere.*

3. *Have I forgiven the prison system? Yes! In fact it is the prison system that has assisted me in overcoming the paranoid undifferentiated schizophrenia that caused the crime spree-* (Something marked out and illegible.)

4. *Have I forgiven the victims and the victim's families? Yes, by all means! I hope that the God of American can somehow reimburse them and console them for their loss. God Bless America and God Bless the victims, their families, and their friends! I am very very sorry for having committed the series of crimes & I honestly show true remorse*

in my daily prayer life-. (Something marked out and illegible.)

Additional Facts:

• When Mullin's best friend was killed in a car accident, Mullin built a macabre shrine to him in his room with his friend's pictures being the focal point. He became obsessed with seeing his friend again and immersed himself into reincarnation and world religions. He also became abnormally afraid of impending death from natural disasters.

• He believed the utter devastation he felt at the loss of his best friend indicated he had homosexual or bisexual tendencies even though he was then in a long-term relationship with a girl.

• In 1972, the Coast Guard refused his application based on his psychological evaluation results. He later was accepted into the Marines but never joined based on his refusal to follow through with documentation.

• Mullin registered with the draft board as a conscientious objector. His father, at his son's urging, wrote a letter supporting his declaration even though the father was a proud WWII Vet.

• The Defense allowed Mullin to take the stand in his own defense. He lectured the courtroom and claimed he was *"the designated leader of his generation."* Mullin believed that since Albert Einstein had died on his birthday, he was reincarnated as Einstein to lead the world.

• In 3/2005, Mullin was denied parole on three objections:

1. Because of the cruel and callous manner in which he carried out his crimes. (Most kills were considered rage kills/ over-kills.)

2. The fact that Mullin has yet to accept responsibility for those crimes.

3. The continuing danger he still poses to society.

Speaking at the hearing, a Commissioner said, *"You are not the victim here. The victims and their families are the victims. You are the individual that made them victims."* Apparently, the Commissioner was not impressed by Mullin's continuing habit of blaming others and other things for his crimes. Parole was denied. At the parole hearing, Mullin had blamed his crimes on a mental condition, his parents whom he felt should be criminally punished, and drugs. He did not, however, mention his calling to protect society from an earthquake.

He is now eligible for parole in 2025.

WILLIAM LEE CODY NEAL 3 Kills

DOB: 10/7/1955 VA

SENTENCE: Three DEATH SENTENCES 9/29/1999; Confessed to all; Death Sentences overturned and commuted to life without parole in 2003 after a Colorado's law was declared unconstitutional.

Facility: Colorado State Penitentiary, Canon City, CO INMATE 103804

THE CRIME: Being a girlfriend of William Lee Cody Neal might be short-lived. Literally.

On 6/30/1998, a six-day rampage in Colorado left three past girlfriends dead and another girlfriend raped and brutalized.

Neal bludgeoned three women to death with an ax or mallet after telling each unsuspecting victim he had a surprise for them. He bound his fourth victim and made her watch as he killed the last woman, then forced her to commit oral sex before he raped her at gun point. She was held hostage for three days in the home with the bodies of the dead women.

All crimes took place in his residence that was owned by one of his victims.

At trial, the prosecution claimed Neal killed the women to cover up the fact that he had stolen money from them.

7/9/1998, he surrendered peacefully after successfully negotiating a deal with police. He demanded a public defender guarantee him he could make a telephone call, that he would be placed in solitary confinement, and he would be provided cigarettes.

Neal acted as his own lawyer after firing his court-appointed attorney and told the judge, *"I am guilty without a doubt."*

BACKGROUND: Cody was born in Virginia, the youngest of five children. Reportedly, he was his mother's favorite child she called her *"golden boy"*. His father, an Air Force officer, was strict, administered corporal punishment, but was not abusive. Cody claimed his father enjoyed teasing him in front of friends and he greatly resented this.

He was caught stealing from a store when he was, 10, but there were no consequences imposed so he continued to steal his entire life. His first sexual encounter was with an older, married woman when he was 13-years-old.

He abused and killed animals even into adulthood.

After high school, he joined the army and served with the Airborne Rangers. He married and divorced four times and is the father of one daughter with whom he has had little contact and only minimal involvement in her life.

Cody tended to live well beyond his means and was never able or willing to maintain long-time employment. He made a habit out of living off the women in his life until they left him or he killed them.

OUT OF THE MOUTH OF THE SERIAL KILLER: In an UNEDITED letter to the author dated July 11, 2016 when asked Why did you kill?:

Dear Mary,

Hello! Thank you! For your letter dated July 7, 2016. Please call me "Cody".

I must say your letter got my attention on a few points you made. I've been in the process of making a decision on various offers from best selling authors, TV producers, journalists, & big screen producers on movie, etc- I have been turning down offers since 1998. As I do not want to glorify evil or promote violence.

I am a very deliberate man. I say this to you respectfully Mary,

Are you interested in the "whole" story? Can you handle it? As I'm going to do it once if I decide to do so.

I need you to answer questions I have too Mary. & I have some requests too. & concerns.

> *1. Request: Please send me your letter dated 7/1/2016 on o Jpay letter to me @ www.ipay.com with your full name & address & exactly as you wrote it to me. I assure you on my word I mean you or yours no harm Mary. I just have to be careful who I write when it comes to such sensitive subject.*
>
> *2. Request send me a jpay $10.00 in funds so I can afford to write you. www.jpay.com*
>
> *3. Request send me info & ISBN #s on the (3) books you said you wrote.*
>
> *4. Request send me info about your education etc & also a photo I need to know your age too. But not your birthdate.*
>
> *5. Request t need to know about your religious beliefs*
>
> *6. Request tell me about yourself? are you single or married.*
>
> *7. Request have you ever been convicted of a crime? or been a crime victim?*
>
> *8. Request Do you believe there is a Devil? Demons etc?*
>
> *9. Please as a Request provide me with your Email address.*

10. Are you a "cop"? FBI? etc?

11. Please know Mary I have no problem with you sharing anything I tell you with the authorities. But please always be sure you are always up front with me. Believe it or not I am a gentleman. & there is a "Line in the Sand". The body count who crossed it is like the mark of the beast as in digits. & I say this respectfully. I have to fight every moment of everyday "always on guard" to keep myself from killing again. As I sincerely never want to harm anyone else ever again.

12. We need to get to know each other.

13. Write soon

Peace, Cody

"…There wasn't anybody here in Denver that I trusted. I was involved in illegal activities -theft, extortion, fraud, embezzlement, forgery. I could keep listing them. I knew they'd be potential snitches. I was right - none of them were trustable."

"They pushed me to my limit. I don't want to say I "snapped". All three had fair warning."

"It was deliberate, it was calculated. I needed time to carry out what I needed to do-"

"I always believed in the death penalty, myself. And I still believe in the death penalty. I do have a heart and I do have a conscience."

Additional Facts:

- Neal is now claiming to be a Born Again Christian, finding God in prison.

- Neal has one daughter from his third marriage who was born in 1993. He had little contact with her.

- At the time of his killing rampage, he was heavily in debt and unemployed.

- It was estimated that during the two years he lived with his first victim in her townhouse, he stole over $60,000 from her. She was in the process of kicking him out when she was murdered by Neal.

- He urinated on the body of his second victim.

- It was important for Neal to stress his victims were not tortured. *"I didn't torture the deceased. I did it as instantly as I could and they never saw it coming, because I did care about them."*

- Neal is a participant in www.Prisonerpal.com, an internet site for pen pals writing prisoners.

- The U.S. Supreme Court ruled in 2003 that only jurors can decide whether a convicted murderer will be executed. This ruling affected previous death sentence convictions in Colorado, Arizona, Idaho, Montana, and Nebraska that had allowed judges to hand down death penalties. In Colorado, a three-judge panel could previously impose a death sentence. Because of this ruling, Neal's 1999 death sentence was over-turned.

WILLIE PICKTON *"The Pig Farmer Killer"* 60+ Kills

Authorities believe that Willie Pickton killed 60 or more victims. Not one dead body located on the Pickton pig farm was found intact. It is probable that Pickton ground up victims and sold it to the public mixed in with pork.

(Photo source www.123people.com)

DOB: 10/24/1949 BRITISH COLUMBIA, CANADA

SENTENCE: 12/9/2007 LIFE in prison with no chance for parole for 25 years, the harshest sentence for murder under Canadian law.

Facility: Kent Institution, Agazziz, B.C. Canada

THE CRIME: ln 2007, Robert William Pickton, the multi-millionaire Canadian pig farmer who lived in filth, was convicted of 6 counts of second-degree murder. He was given the strongest sentence allowed under British Columbia law: 25 years in prison before parole.

Willie Pickton has admitted to killing 49 Eastside Downtown Vancouver sex workers from 1995 until he was apprehended on 2/22/2002 and was *"...gonna do one more and make it 50"* but claimed he got *"sloppy"*. Authorities believe his kill number is closer to 60 or more.

A warrant for Pickton's arrest on an illegal arms charge initially brought the authorities to his Port Coquitlam, B.C. pig farm. Ultimately, authorities would discover the partial remains and DNA of 33 women. Personal effects of several missing women were also found.

His victims, prostitutes and drug addicts, would be lured to the farm with the promise of drugs, money, and a good time. Once there, they would be bound by handcuffs or wire, raped, sodomized, then shot or strangled to death. He also enjoyed injecting women with windshield wiper fluid, telling the victims it was drugs.

He butchered the women in the same manner and with the same tools he used to butcher his pigs. He then ground up the remains and fed them to the livestock. Authorities strongly believe that Pickton's younger brother, David, was involved in or at least aware of the killings, but he has never been officially named nor prosecuted. David lived on the same property until around 1995 when he moved a short distance down the road. They remained close and often socialized together at David's owned party site, "The Piggy Palace Good Times Society."

On 3/10/2004, the British Columbia health authority issued a public warning after missing women's DNA was found to be present in some of the processed meat in freezers on Pickton's farm. It was alleged that Pickton may have ground up human flesh and mixed it with pork that was being sold to the public.

At present, after over a decade behind bars, Pickton is claiming that he is innocent and was merely *"a fall guy"*.

He has suggested in his penned autobiography, *"Pickton In His Own Words"*, the DNA found was simply from various auctioned, impounded, or wrecked vehicles on his property he salvaged. He also blames the Hell's Angels for some of the killings. The book's manuscript was smuggled out of Pickton's maximum security prison, under the noses of the prison guards and administration.

Authorities suspected that Pickton's brother, David, was involved in the killings or, at the very least, knew of his older brother's crimes, but to date he has not been charged.

BACKGROUND: Willie Pickton was born to pig farmers living in primitive, squalid conditions. He was the middle child and had a younger brother, David, and an older sister, Linda. Both parents were uneducated and anti-social. The family stayed mostly to themselves and did not often leave the farm.

The father was distant and had little interaction with any of his children. He and Pickton were never close. His mother was the dominant force in the home, often described as cold, demanding, and strong willed. Her devout religious beliefs were rooted in the Catholic Church. Pickton claimed he and his mother were close, ***"two peas in a pod."***

The boys were required to do many chores around the farm but were either not taught or not allowed to regularly bathe. In school, Pickton was shunned and friendless. He was a slow child requiring special education classes, plus he and his brother often reeked from the pig farm's foul odors. Children taunted them with the unkind chant *"stinky Pinkies."* Pickton dropped out of school at 14 and spent the next four years learning the butcher trade. ***"But like I says, I mean some people can make it right through school, some people can't."***

Pickton was psychologically scarred by two childhood events: at age 12, he came home from school to discover a beloved pet calf he had raised by hand had been slaughtered by his father. *"Anyways, there's my calf upside down, cleaned out, butchered it. I couldn't talk to anybody for days...And I finally realized that we're not here forever. We're here for the time we're here for."* and, as an 18-year-old teenager, he witnessed his mother rolling a gravely injured boy into a deep water-filled ditch where the child drowned. His younger brother, an inexperienced driver, had accidently hit the youth and his mother aided in the cover-up. The child's demise was ruled an accident and his brother was never connected to the death. Later in life, Willie Pickton would tell certain acquaintances, with pride, that his mother always knew just what to do.

In 1970, Pickton took over the full-time running of the farm. His father was aging and his brother was away at an university. It was around this time that Pickton began visiting the seedier streets of Eastside Downtown Vancouver, picking up prostitutes and drug addicts. He had money so he was able to buy sex from prostitutes and companionship from the men and women who frequented the forlorn bars. For the first time in his entire life, he felt superior to his "friends", the desolate street people with their bleak lives. *"I have 100s of friends. I like to help...to help even if they steal from me."*

Pickton's only known serious female romantic relationship was with an American pen pal he started corresponding with when he was 20-years-old. They talked of marriage but the relationship ended when neither Pickton nor the young woman would agree to relocate. Pickton visited her once, but they ended their long-distance correspondence around 1974 and lost touch. *"I didn't even have sex with Connie neither."*

Pickton's father died in January 1978, and his mother passed on 4/1/1979. David Pickton moved into the family home and Willie moved into a trailer on the property. His first known violent attack was in 1980. Pickton picked up a 14-year-old drug addict and violently raped her at knife point before throwing her out of his truck. There were no other known or documented attacks by Pickton for well over a decade.

In 1994 and 1995, Plckton and his two siblings sold three parcels of their farm for over $5M. Pickton, now wealthy, became addicted to drugs, mostly crack cocaine. He neglected the farm. In 1996, Dave Pickton requested and received a government subsidy by claiming to use his recently purchased property a short distance away for non-profit humanitarian events. Dave and Willie dubbed the so-called non-profit society "The Piggy Palace Good Times Society". They would host raves and wild parties there for large crowds that occasionally included members of the Hells Angels motorcycle club. Drugs and sex were openly enjoyed. After parties, Willie would return to his trailer with a prostitute. Soon the scene turned from kinky sex to death and violence.

In 3/1997, the tables turned one evening on Pickton.

After sex, he tried to handcuff a prostitute but she broke free and fled his bedroom- Enraged, he chased her and the woman fought for her life. She grabbed a kitchen knife and stabbed Pickton in the neck and arm. ***"Got knifed back in '97".*** He stabbed her several times but she escaped. Nearly naked and gravely wounded, she fled the trailer and was picked up on the road by his neighbors who called for help. The woman was taken to a hospital in an ambulance. She arrived with no pulse but the medical staff was able to resuscitate her. She was treated for two stab wounds to her abdomen, slashes to her hands and arms, and a knife wound to her right side that had punctured her lung. She still had a handcuff attached to one wrist.

Pickton drove himself to a hospital. The police initially charged Pickton with attempted murder but the charge was stayed in 1/1998. Crown prosecutors believed they could not win a case where the word of a drug-addicted prostitute with a criminal record would be pitted against testimony from a millionaire local farmer represented by an expensive attorney.

In 8/1997, another prostitute would not be so lucky. Pickton killed and dismembered a 24-year-old heroin addict after sex in his trailer. Soon women started disappearing from Eastside Vancouver: 49-year-old Willie Pickton had discovered a lust for murder. Ironically, authorities did not pay much attention to the few disappearances that were actually reported, chalking it up to the transient lifestyle of street people. Plus, no dead bodies had surfaced that required an official investigation.

By early 2001, over 60 women had gone missing. The authorities could no longer ignore the obvious. A task force for missing women was formed and a large reward was offered for information leading to an arrest. Tips flooded in and Pickton's name was mentioned several times but, sadly, with no follow-up until a credible witness told police of illegal guns he had glimpsed on Pickton's farm.

A search warrant was granted for a weapons search and Pickton was arrested on 2/22/2002. A thorough search of his property resulted in much more than expected. The stunned authorities quickly discovered the shocking evidence that linked Pickton to multiple gruesome and macabre slayings.

OUT OF THE MOUTH OF THE SERIAL KILLER:

In his hand-written autobiographical manuscript referring to the judge: ***"The blind leading the blind."***

Referring to the prosecutor handing the jurors: *"...down a crooked and dark pathway."* His manuscript is peppered with biblical references.

Additional Facts:

• Pickton was a regular at the police salvage yard auction where he purchased impounded vehicles, towed them back to his farm, and salvaged parts.

• He was also initially charged in the deaths of an additional 20 women, but these charges were stayed by the Crown in 2010. These charges would have constituted a second trial for Pickton.

• Prostitutes that worked the streets of Eastside Downtown Vancouver called Pickton, a regular on the scene, *"Uncle Willie."*

• ln 1997, David Pickton was sued by Port Coquitlam officials for zoning violations to halt the "Piggy Palace Good Times Society" parties on his land that, at times, included crowds of as many as 2000 people. He ignored the pressure from the officials and held a 1998 New Year's Eve party. Authorities then banned him from hosting any future parties and ordered the arrest of any and all persons attending. David Pickton's non-profit tax status was rescinded.

• According to a bartender that knew Pickton, he was a want-to-be Hells Angel.

• Pickton was able to smuggle out a hand-written book he penned in prison entitled, "Pickton ln His Own Words". He passed the manuscript to a former cell mate, Grant White, who then mailed it to a friend on the outside living in California named, Michael Childress. Childress typed the pages and sold the project, mistakes and all, to Outskirts Press, a Colorado publisher. The book sold for $20 per copy and Childress was credited as the author. Pickton signed over the rights and all profits attached to the book to White. Pickton, who originally admitted to killing 49 victims, now claims he simply wanted his tale of innocence told. British Columbia has no law in place that prohibits a criminal from profiting from his crimes. White, a convicted sexual sadist in his own right, planned to use the proceeds to hire a lawyer to prove his own innocence. The publishing company has since stopped the sale of the book after realizing that Pickton, a convicted serial killer, was the actual author.

• Pickton had an IQ of 85. His lawyer used this fact when presenting his defense.

• His sister, Linda, was sent to town to live with relatives as a child. Their mother believed that a pig farm was no place to raise a daughter. There was some resentment on the boys' part. Linda was able to enjoy herself in town and they were left at the farm and worked hard by the mother. *"That's about it. Never me and Linda was close."*

DOROTHEA PUENTE *"Death House Landlady"* 9+ Kills

DOB: 1/9/1929 CA

DOD: 3/27/2011 CA, age 82 Died of Natural causes: colon and liver cancer.

SENTENCE: TWO LIFE SENTENCES without parole for murder in the first degree and a concurrent 15-year sentence for second degree murder

Facility: Central California Women's Facility (CCWF), Chowchilla, CA

THE CRIME: Prosecutors claim that from 1982 until apprehended in 1988, Dorothea Puente murdered at least nine victims for their social security benefits or to silence witnesses to her crimes. The Defense claims their client admitted to illegally cashing benefit checks of deceased boarders but maintained they all died from natural causes.

In the 1980s, Puente ran an unlicensed boarding house at 1426 F Street in Sacramento, CA. She took in the elderly, the mentally impaired, the ailing, and people living on the fringe of society. She selected boarders who had few or no friends or relatives who would inquire should they go missing. Unfortunately for Puente, a street social worker took an interest in one of her missing clients and pressured the police to investigate his disappearance.

On 11/11/1988, his body was found buried in Puente's yard, along with six other previous boarders. One female body was found with her head, hands, and legs missing. Puente calmly walked away from the active crime scene that was swarming with police, media, and spectators and went on the lam. She was captured in Los Angles when a man she met in a bar recognized her and turned her in. Puente reportedly befriended him after learning he was collecting disability checks.

Further investigation led to two more bodies, one a former boyfriend that was found in a wooden box in the Sacramento River.

At the time of her arrest, Puente was on parole for using drugs to disable elderly victims so she could rob them. She did not take the stand to defend herself in court but went to her death claiming innocence.

BACKGROUND: Dorothea Helen Gray Puente was born in Redlands, California to tenant farm workers. Both parents died within a year of each other, leaving nine-year-old Dorothea an orphan. She spent time in an orphanage until relatives took her in.

By age 15, she was married. By the age of 19, she had given birth to two children, given both up for adoption, had a miscarriage or abortion, and been deserted by her husband. Shortly after her spouse left, she was charged with check forgery and spent 6 months in jail.

Paroled, she had a brief relationship with a man, got pregnant, and surrendered that child for adoption immediately after birth.

In 1952, she married her second husband. The volatile and abusive marriage lasted 14 years.

In 1960, she served two 90-day sentences in jail for running a brothel and on a vagrancy charge.

She went to work as a private duty nurses aid caring for the elderly and infirm. Soon she found a position managing a boarding house for room, board, and pay. In 1966, 37-year-old Dorothea married 19-year-old Roberto Puente. The marriage ended after two years. She began to spend time in bars, trolling for older men who received assistance checks. She was caught forging checks, charged with 34 counts of treasury fraud, and sent to prison.

Out on parole, she continued her same pattern of crime. In 1982, she rented the upstairs rooms of her home at 1426 F Street to boarders and stole their benefits checks. This time she upped the crime and killed at least nine infirm or elderly victims by drug overdoses. Puente's first victim was her friend and business partner. Dorothea killed her with an overdose of drugs so she could rob her for fast cash. She reported to the authorities that the woman committed suicide.

On 8/18/1982, Puente was sentenced to five years behind bars on three charges of theft involving an elderly man. She spent the time in jail developing a love relationship with a 77-year-old Oregon pen pal named Everson Gillmouth. Even with her extensive criminal record, Puente only spent 3 years behind bars. Everson Gillmouth, smitten, picked her up from jail in his truck February 1985. By November 1985, his bank account was drained, his truck bartered for work, and his body dumped into the Sacramento River in a wooden coffin-type box. On New Year's Day, 1986, fishermen informed police of a suspicious box washed up close to the riverbank. Gillmouth's badly decomposed body would remain unidentified for 3 years. During that time, Puente cashed his benefits checks and corresponded regularly with his family in Oregon, writing cheery letters about the couple's happy life together.

She managed her charade for three more years. Neighbors complained about foul smells, but Puente always blamed the odor on fertilizer she regularly spread in her garden. She had been ordered to have no dealings with elderly boarders or to handle government issued checks. Parole officers visited her home regularly but never cited her for the 40 or more boarders who came and went. After her arrest in 1988 due to the diligence of a social worker, it took five years to bring her to trial. The jury deadlocked on the death penalty, voting seven to five for life. The presiding judge declared a mistrial and sentenced Puente to life in prison with no possibility of parole. She died of natural causes after almost two decades behind bars. She was 82.

OUT OF THE MOUTH OF THE SERIAL KILLER:

"I am innocent."

"... (they all died) of natural causes."

"I don't even know what I'm going to do when, if and when I get out, because there's uh no place I can go without uh without being known."

Additional Facts:

• The same drugs were found in many of the bodies, including evidence of an overdose of the drug used in her first kill, a 61-year-old female friend and business partner who moved into Puente's home in 4/1982.

• Attorneys for Puente claimed she was afraid to report the discovery of a tenant's body because she violated her parole by running a boarding house for the ill or the elderly.

• It was five years before the start of Puente's trial due to various delays. Arguments for a change of venue accounted for two years of delay.

• Her murder trial was moved to Monterey County due to the deluge of local media coverage that followed the discovery of bodies buried in Puente's downtown Sacramento yard.

• The jurors deliberated for over five months, the longest trial deliberation in the history of the

California court system. They deadlocked on six of the nine murder charges. The jurors voted 11-one for convictions on all murder charges with one lone dissenting juror who finally agreed to vote for a conviction on only three murder charges.

• Investigators dubbed one room of the home as the "killing room". There was an odor permeating the room and evidence that Puente had stored bodies there awaiting burial.

• It is estimated that Puente stole over $87,000 from illegally obtained monthly stipend checks. She spent a portion of the money on a face lift.

• She told police that she was 70 when she was only 59-years-old. Part of her ploy was to appear like an innocent, helpful, and kindly little old lady, the grandmotherly type.

• The 1895 Victorian boarding house that was the scene of the crime is now a refurbished home and part of the City of Sacramento's Old City House Tour. New owners purchased the house at auction in 2011 for $215,000. A tongue-in-cheek sign was originally displayed at the home stating *"Trespassers will be drugged and buried in the yard."*

DENNIS RADER *"The BTK Killer"* 10+ Kills

DOB: 3/9/1945 KS

SENTENCE: 10 CONSECUTIVE LIFE SENTENCES WITH NO PAROLE (175 YEARS)

Facility: El Dorado Correctional, KS INMATE 0083707

THE CRIME: On 1/15/1974, four members of the Otero family were found murdered in their Wichita, Kansas home. The telephone lines had been cut and there were signs of forced entry. Dead were Joseph Otero, 35, his wife, Julie, 34, and their two children, Josephine, 11, ***"I remember problems with Josephine because her hair was in the way"*** and Joseph, Jr., 9. Both parents and the young son had bound hands and feet. The mother was gagged and the boy and his father had plastic bags placed over their head. The daughter was found, partially naked, hanging from a basement pipe. She was also gagged and bound. Her panties had been pulled down and Dennis Rader, The BTK Killer, had masturbated, apparently sexually excited by the sight of the child's small dead body. A splash of his semen was present on her leg. All four had been strangled to death with lengths of cord cut from venetian blinds, brought to the scene by the killer. The Otero's 15-year-old son discovered the bodies of his murdered family when he returned home.

In 1973, Rader had worked with Julie Otero at the Wichita Coleman Outlet Factory. Nine months after the killings, media attention surrounding the unsolved murders was waning. It was then the local Wichita newspaper received an anonymous phone call directing them to a specific book in a named library. Inside the book was a typed note detailing the crime and claiming responsibility for the Otero murders. Rader had become enthralled by the attention his crimes excited in the media and he soon made a habit of taunting police and media sources with letters and poems, sinisterly signed BTK, an acronym for *"bind, torture, and kill."* This narcissistic, egotistical trait would be his undoing.

BTK resurfaced in 2004 after a long hiatus, again provoking authorities and the media in his bizarre bid to capture publicity. Included in a letter confessing to the 1986 murder of a 28-year-old woman was a copy of her driver's license and three photos of her dead body. Authorities opened a communication line with BTK and he naively believed authorities when they stated they were not able to trace the source of computer discs. Rader mailed a confessional disc he had prepared on his church's computer that detailed past crimes. It took the Wichita police's computer expert only a few moments to name Dennis Rader as the BTK Killer.

Rader was incredulous that authorities had lied to him. At his initial interrogation, he challenged the detectives: *"You lied to me."* In his wake, this sexual sadist left behind 10 dead (many believe the tally higher), all innocents killed by stabbing, hanging, suffocation, or strangulation, all savagely murdered merely to satisfy his sick and perverted sexual lust.

BACKGROUND: One Dennis Lynn Rader persona: the average college graduate, married man with two children who owned his own home in a quiet suburb. He was a former boy scout, now a boy scout leader, plus President of the Church Council at his local Christ Lutheran Church. Rader was considered trustworthy enough to be hired to install ADT security systems in private homes from 1974 to 1988, and in 1990, he passed the FBI background checks necessary to allow him to participate in the national census. He was made a field supervisor.

The other Dennis Rader persona was a narcissistic sexual sadist who spent most of his waking hours fantasizing about lurid, debased sexual acts involving the bonding and torturing of women. He often photographed himself posed in self-deprecating positions and practiced erotic asphyxiation on himself as he masturbated. This Dennis Rader was able to kill men, women, and children without the slightest trace of remorse.

Rader was the oldest of four sons. He was an above average student but was slow to make friends among peers. He admitted that he had fantasies about bondage and the torture of girls from an early age. Annette Funicello, a Mickey Mouse Club TV Mouseketeer, was a favorite object of those fantasies. After graduation from high school, he worked briefly at a grocery store before joining the Air Force in 1966. He voluntarily signed on to avoid the draft and being sent to Vietnam. He rose to the rank of Sergeant before being discharged in 1970 and was awarded the Good Conduct Medal. Rader returned to his hometown to serve his required two years in the national reserves and was employed by the Coleman Company factory that produced camping and outdoor needs.

He married in 5/1971. In 1974, he accepted a position installing ADT security systems in private homes. Ironically, the BTK Killer was kept busy installing security systems for frantic customers who were rushing to secure their home against the BTK Killer.

In 1973, Rader attended Butler County Community College in El Dorado, Kansas, earning an associate's degree in electronics. In 1979, he graduated from Wichita State University with a bachelor's degree in Administrative Justice. In 1975, his son was born and in 1978, a daughter was born. During these normal and often joyful times, Rader viciously killed five in 1974 and two in 1977. During that timeline, he also attempted to kill two others and stalked many women, seeking his next *"project."*

In 1990, Rader was hired as a Park City compliance supervisor. Reportedly, he was the "strictly by the book" arrogant type who enjoyed throwing his weight around. He was also over-zealous in his rush to euthanize captured or stray animals. He later admitted in interviews that he had tortured and killed small animals as a child. He had enjoyed hanging stray cats and dogs.

He was still employed at this job when he was arrested in 2005.

OUT OF THE MOUTH OF THE SERIAL KILLER: When authorities asked Rader if he knew why he was being arrested, he said, *"Oh, I have suspicions why."*

"It's hard to control myself. You probably call me 'psychotic with sexual perversion hang-up." Reportedly, Rader claimed he never raped a victim because it was wrong *"to cheat on my wife."*

"When this monster entered my brain, I will never know, but it's here to stay."

"I did Mrs. Otero. I had never strangled anyone before, so I really didn't know how much pressure you had to put on a person or how long it would take, but…(drifts off subject).*"*

"I had many what I call them projects. They were different people in town that I followed, watched. Kathryn Bright was one of the next targets." (Kathryn Bright, age 20, was Rader's 5th victim, stabbed to death on April 4, 1974.)

"You go through the trolling stage and then a stalking stage."

"The final victim is my wife. That and my family."

Additional Facts:

- Rader prolonged the death of most victims, allowing them to come-to after strangling only to strangle them again. He never raped his victims but his sperm was found near or on his victims or on the victim's undergarment. *"The Sexual Thrill is My Bill."*

- He was stalking his 11th victim when he was arrested on 2/25/2005, 31-years after his first murders. *"She was to be my opus."*

- Rader's victims: 1974 (5 kills); 1977 (2 kills); 1985 (1 kill); 1986 (1 kill); 1991 (1 kill). There has never been a clarification nor explanation from Rader for the spacing of his murders. A few authorities suspect that there may be other kills he is responsible for, but to date, he has not been forthcoming with any additional confessions.

- After his fifth kill, Rader started taking his killing tools with him in a satchel. He called this his *"hit kit."*

- He liked to take underwear from his victims and would wear them.

- His family knew nothing of his secret life. His wife divorced him after his arrest.

RICHARD RAMIREZ *"The Night Stalker"* 14 Kills

DOB: 2/29/1960 TX

DOD: 6/7/2013 CA

Facility: San Quentin, CA, age 53

SENTENCE: 19 DEATH SENTENCES but he died from medical issues (complications secondary to B-cell lymphoma) before he could be executed.

THE CRIME: Always remember to lock your doors at night.

Richard Ramirez's usual MO was to break into an unsecured residence or pry a window open while the innocent victims slept, then rob and kill them. If he found a couple inside, he would quickly kill the male with an execution-style shot to the head, then rape and sodomize the female. On one occasion, he had sex with a dead body before fleeing the crime scene.

His murders and attempted murders were all savagely executed on both male and female victims, the young and the old alike. He would beat his victims with hammers, tire irons or available object, shoot them, stab them with knives, or slash them with a machete. He frequently employed more than one means to murder his victim. He was also known to torture his prey and mutilate the bodies of the dead. He removed the eyes of one female victim postmortem and kept them as a souvenir.

Most of his murders were classified as rage-fueled over-kills. His crime spree lasted from June 28, 1984 until he was apprehended on 8/31/1985.

During his trial and incarceration, Ramirez received fan mail, love letters, and visits from admirers. Some women found him extremely attractive despite his heinous crimes, rotten teeth, and reportedly poor personal hygiene. Prison officials reported fights in the prison parking lot between jealous women.

Ramirez liked to wear large black sunglasses. Many female admirers found him exotic and erotic. One actually married him in prison.

(Photo source: www.Murderpedia.org)

BACKGROUND: Ricardo Leyva Munoz Ramirez was the youngest of five children and known as "Ricky". Two of his siblings were born with birth defects. He grew up in a strict Mexican American Catholic home with a kind and docile mother but under the reins of a violent, raging father who strongly believed in corporal punishment.

His biggest and most damaging influence growing up was his older cousin, a psychotic, who had been a Green Beret serving in Viet Nam. He showed young Ramirez gory photos of Vietnamese women he had tortured, raped, killed, then mutilated and entertained the boy continually with gruesome war stories that Ramirez found both exciting and fascinating.

One Polaroid photo showed the cousin holding up the head of a woman he had raped and decapitated with a machete. The cousin often provided Ramirez with marijuana and LSD. He liked to demonstrate to Ramirez the use of various weapons and how to sneak up on a target without detection. He also introduced Ramirez to the practice of Satanism. That cousin would later shoot his wife in the head, killing her in the presence of 11-year-old Ramirez. He was found not guilty by reason of insanity and only served 4 years in the Texas State Mental Hospital. His release in 1977 coincided with Ramirez's first juvenile conviction the same year for a series of petty criminal offences.

In 1982, Ramirez received probation for a marijuana conviction. Later that year, he moved to Los Angeles where he became addicted to cocaine and supported his habit through home burglaries and stealing cars. He also continued his habitual "peeping tom" nighttime exploits that he first experienced as a young teenager. In 1983, Ramirez was apprehended and received a jail sentence for car theft. He served 6 months. On 6/28/1984, Ramirez committed his first known murder. He savagely beat, raped, and murdered a 79-year-old woman in her own home. This was the beginning of a killing spree that escalated quickly. His male and female murder victims would range in age from nine to 83-years-old and most were brutalized in their homes while they slept.

OUT OF THE MOUTH OF THE SERIAL KILLER:

"We are evil in some form, way, or another, are we not?"
"I believe in the evil in human nature."

"I didn't particularly care for people."

"There were desires where if I didn't give in to them I would be crushed by them."

"Even psychopaths have emotions if you dig deep enough. Then again, maybe they don't." 11/2009

"Yes, I am evil. Not 100% but I am evil." 11/2009

"I have felt powers that were evil." *"I love all that blood"*

"There is no protection against a mad killer, a mass murder."

"Serial killers do on a small scale what governments do on a large one. They are a product of the times and these are blood thirsty times" 11/2009 (Possibly a veiled referral to the Viet Nam War and/or his older cousin's actions during that war.)

Ramirez raised a hand with a pentagram drawn on it and yelled, *"Hail Satan!"*

"Killing is killing weither (sic) *done for duty, profit, or fun."*

"I love to kill people. I love watching them die. I would shoot them in the head and they would wiggle and squirm all over the place, and then just stop. Or I would cut them with a knife and watch their faces turn real white. I love all that blood. I told one lady to give me all her money. She said no. So I cut her and pulled her eyes out." (Speaking of innocent victim, Maxine Zazzara, 44.)

Ramirez received 19 death sentences on November 7, 1989. He showed no remorse when hearing the verdict. *"No big deal. Death always comes with the territory. I'll see you in Disneyland."*

Additional Facts:

- Ramirez was diagnosed with epilepsy at age 10 and experienced seizures. At age two, and later at age five, he suffered accidental head injuries that rendered him unconscious.

• To escape problems at home, he would run off and, at times, spend the night in a cemetery.

• He was a confessed Satanist. Many of his victims were made to swear to Satan during and/or after attacks. At times, he left an inverted pentagram on the victim or at the scene as a mark of the devil.

• Several female admirers attend the court proceedings dressed in all black to show macabre support for their cult hero.

• Ramirez was captured by a crowd of angered citizens who recognized him from a circulated wanted poster. The arrival of police on the scene probably saved his life.

• His trial took approximately four years. It took over one year to amass 12 jurors and 12 alternates who were able to honestly swear they were impartial.

• In 1996, he married Doreen Lioy in a ceremony at San Quentin. She had been writing to Ramirez since 1985. Lioy had vowed to commit suicide should her husband be executed but they had separated before his death.

ROBERT RELDAN *"The Charmer"* 2 Kills

DOB: 6/2/1940 NY

SENTENCE: LIFE IN PRISON PLUS 30 YEARS

Facility: New Jersey State Prison, Trenton INMATE 557463

THE CRIME: On 10/27/1975, the body of 26-year-old Susan Heynes, a Briton newlywed, was found in the woods in Bergen County, NJ. The next day, the body of Susan Reeves was located two miles from Heynes' body. Both had been murdered in the same manner: pantyhose tied with a stick, making a crude garrote. Both were nude.

On 10/14/1975, Susan Reeve, 22, had disappeared. She worked that day and had taken a bus home. She vanished on the short walk from the bus stop to her parent's house, but her body was not located until 10/28. Susan had also been raped. She was a recent college graduate and was engaged to marry. A toll attendant reported a man who was acting suspiciously and playing his radio very loudly. She heard what she believed were a woman's screams for help coming from the vehicle's trunk. The attendant picked Reldan out of a group of mug shots of sex offenders recently paroled. Reldan was asked to come in for questioning. The police requested a lie detector test but Reldan refused until he could speak with his lawyer. He was expected to return to police headquarters but failed to show.

10/31/1975, Reldan was arrested for attempting to burglarize a home. A search warrant was executed for his residence and automobile. In Reldan's car, evidence was found linking him to the crimes. He was also identified as the man who first pawned then bought back the unusual engagement ring belonging to Susan Heynes.

Reldan was tried for both murders, convicted, and received a life sentence plus 30 years on 5/15/1989. However, it took three trials and over a decade to get a conviction to stick. The first trial ended in a mistrial and the second trial, a conviction, was overturned on technicalities. Ironically, Reldan defended himself at his third trial, thus sealing his fate and proving yet again that a suspect acting in his own defense has a fool for a client.

In 1982, Redan was convicted of hiring an outside hit man in 1979 to kill his loyal and loving wealthy Aunt Lillian Garis Booth and her companion, with instructions to make the crime look like a robbery gone amiss. He received an additional 5-year sentence. His aunt never believed the authorities and in a letter she wrote, *"I did not believe my nephew would hurt me, nor do I today."* The plan was foiled when an undercover cop, acting like the hired killer, taped Reldan twice in prison giving instructions for the murder. He wanted his aunt's throat slit.

Reldan was allowed by the courts to keep $200,000 from the $10M Trust from his aunt upon her death in 2007. Susan Reeve's parents successfully sued him for $10M in a wrongful death suit in 2010. He currently receives $2,080 annually deposited directly into his prison account from interest on that $200K.

BACKGROUND: Robert R. Reldan was born Robert Nadler, but later reversed the spelling of his sur name. When he was 11-years-old, his parents and younger sister, Susan, moved to Bergen County in New Jersey. This was an affluent suburban community, just across the George Washington Bridge from New York City. His parents were a loving, hard-working, upper middle-class couple who owned the "Sweet Sue Coffee Shop" near 5th Avenue with its up-scale stores and restaurants. His mother doted on her only son, but much of her time was spent working in the family business or tending to his younger sister who had contracted polio. A strong influence on Reldan's life was his mother's sister, Lillian. Aunt Lillian had married an elderly multi-millionaire who was a son of a founding partner of IBM. He left her a very wealthy 40-year-old widow after a decade of blissful marriage. She invested well and turned her $50 million inheritance into a $200 million estate. She had no children but liked to spoil her nieces and nephews. Her favorite was Reldan whom she lovingly called, "Bobby." Unfortunately, Bobby was over-indulged during his formative years to the point that there were no consequences at home for his bad behavior. He felt entitled and learned early that rules did not apply to him.

His parents never acknowledged their son's bad behavior or, in later years, his criminal activities and always defended him. His aunt used her prestige and bank account to hire the best defense council and believed her favorite nephew could do no wrong, as well.

When Reldan was 17-years-old, he received indefinite probation for assaulting a woman and stealing her purse in an elevator. The judge classified Reldan as a juvenile delinquent. Neither the stern admonishment by the court nor probation stopped Reldan from continuing to break into homes to steal. The court, either showing mercy or recognizing extreme problematic behaviors in the young offender, ordered Reldan to undergo psychiatric observation in lieu of incarceration. Medical professionals categorized him as having a narcissistic personality and a *"strong repressed hostility towards women"*.

One month after graduating from high school, Reldan was arrested for car theft. Mercy was once again shown by the courts. It is probable that his wealthy aunt had inserted her influence in the matter. Instead of jail, Reldan was ordered to undergo further observation at a state mental hospital. The 18-year-old tall, handsome, engaging teen was then diagnosed as a sociopath with anti-social reactions. On Christmas Eve, 1958, he returned to his parents' home after spending only four months under observation. Two months later, Reldan was again arrested for car theft. Since he had violated his probationary guidelines, he was given a three-year sentence at a New York reformatory. He was released in 1/1962.

In 2/1962, he committed his first known sexual attack. He assaulted a 14-year-old girl during a home invasion but was not convicted. An excellent and expensive attorney was hired to defend Reldan. A hung jury set him free. This would be the first of three hung juries that would eventually let Reldan off without any punishment guidelines.

His crime spree continued on an almost daily basis. One month after being set free by the hung jury, he was arrested for a half dozen robberies that occurred in both New York and New Jersey. Reldan received a five-year sentence. He served two years and was released early. Within six months, he was arrested for rape. The nature of the crime was sexual so, at the discretion of the judge, he was given an open-ended sentence at a treatment center, a sentence not to exceed 30 years. Reldan was diagnosed as demonstrating *"a compulsive pattern of sexual behavior"* and knowingly perfecting *"ingratiating and manipulative"* behaviors. Despite this diagnosis by medical professionals, despite his criminal background and previous psychiatric evaluations, Reldan was released, with parole, after only serving three years.

Within five months of release, he was arrested for raping a woman at knifepoint. He was sent to prison on a five to seven-year term. By 1975, 34-year-old Reldan was out on the street. He married on 6/17/1975. On 10/6/1975, he killed his first victim, a 26-year-old newlywed, and on 10/14, he killed a 22-year-old woman who had recently graduated from college and was engaged to marry.

OUT OF THE MOUTH OF THE SERIAL KILLER:
An UNEDITED letter to the author dated 7/15/2016:

Dear Ms. Brett, Thank you for your letter of inquiry of 1 July. The delay in response is due to the inaccuracies in my address, which caused a delay in delivery. Thank you for the SASE, too, but as you see, they don't let us have 'outside' stamps so it was ripped off.

At any rate, I will not be contributing to your book, for a number of reasons: despite the fact that the case is almost 42 years old there is still litigation and parole factors ongoing. The enclosed article might give you a clue as to how my case was handled back then, but at this stage, 'it's water under the bridge.' Plus, I have absolutely no interest, nor do I care how "history remembers me." Those who knew and loved me then, and those who know and love me now, know who I am.

As far as the 'humor' in my name change goes, the enclosed letter might shed some light on my motives. First, the warden's name was Howard L. Beyer, and my petition was for Howard B. (Beyer) Junior. Since, under the law, middle names or initials have no legal bearing, my name would have been Howard Junior.

Knowing they were too obtuse to notice that and knowing they would ascribe some sinister motive to my request, I hoped the press might notice, so I went forward. As you can see, they completely denied that they were torturing a 98 year old (the states oldest inmate at the time), Russian immigrant, who barely spoke English, and who was partially paralyzed by a stroke. He was confined in a bare cell, where the water faucets are controlled by buttons he could not push, and when I went into his cell his sheets were so stiff from encrusted urine and feces that they actually cracked when I tried to fold them. (Howard L. Beyer, Administrator of New Jersey State Prisons, denied these accusations in a letter dated November 16, 1990.)

Of course, despite my protestations and accusations, they were in complete denial, and it was only after my name request that I managed to get the Public Advocate and some attorneys interested. Two days after this letter of denial was received he was taken to an outside hospital, and the hospital, not wanting to be responsible for him, sent him to a private hospice where he died two days later. The official cause of death was listed as "renal failure due to extreme dehydration."

This was not as altruistic an act as it might seem, but only a realization that if they could do that to him and get away with it, they could do the same to me as I entered into my old age. They have since continued to do it to others, though not to such an extreme.

Otherwise, if you want to get to know me further you might be interested in two works I've had published; one, is a book of poetry called "Loss", under my name at buybooksontheweb.com, and a novel, "Birds of Karma", under the pen name R. Dan Roberts, available on Amazon or lulu.com, in print or ebook. This would make an amazing screen play and movie, so if you may be interested in its promotion I'd be interested in hearing back from you.

Well, I guess I've covered everything for now. Wishing you good luck with your future works, I remain

Sincerely yours, Bob Reldan

Additional Facts:

- Reldan did well in school, was popular, and ran with the wealthy crowd. He was funded by gifts from his Aunt Lillian. She regularly gave Bobby $1,000 at Christmas and even purchased a new Volkswagen convertible as a gift upon one early release from incarceration. He was given trips to Europe and expensive skiing excursions. She indulged his every whim. Aunt Lillian paid for such things as scuba diving, horseback, and flying lessons. The more she gave her nephew, the more he resented not receiving even larger monetary gifts and more expensive items and trips.

• In 1993, Robert Reldan tried to legally change his name to Howard B. Beyer, Jr while incarcerated in the New Jersey State Prison in Trenton. The warden's name was Howard L. Beyer. His request was denied.

• He was eligible for parole 9/27/2017 and denied. In the unlikely event he should ever be released, he will receive $50K a year from his aunt's trust

• WHILE INCARCERATED: In 5/1975, Reldan appeared on the David Frost TV Show, "The Unspeakable Crime." He spoke of the need for more psychological help and compassion for inmates charged with sexual crimes. He was selected as the spokesperson because of his handsome, clean-cut, polished, and intelligent demeanor, the exact opposite of characteristics most people imagine in a sex offender. He claimed he was innocent of the two murders for which he was charged and convicted.

• WHILE INCARCERATED: Awaiting his second trial on 10/15/1979 for the murders of his two innocent victims, Reldan attempted an escape. He sprayed two deputies with mace, jumped from a second-story window, broke both ankles, still ran, stole a car, but was shortly apprehended when he ran the car into a ditch. He had smuggled in a handcuff key he used to free himself.

• WHILE INCARCERATED: The week before his attempted escape, Reldan had tried to bribe five jurors in his murder trial with cash amounts ranging from $100 to $900.

• WHILE INCARCERATED: Needing money for his legal defense, he put out a failed 1979 hit on his Aunt Lillian in hopes of collecting an early inheritance. He requested that her throat be slit.

• WHILE INCARCERATED: In 4/1981, Reldan faked an injury that required outside hospitalization. Waiting with a gun and ammunition in a shopping bag in the hospital lobby was Sherry-Anne Stevens, 29, wearing a bad disguise. She had been a frequent visitor and believed herself in love with Reldan. She was arrested and jailed.

GARY RIDGWAY *"The Green River Killer"* 71-90+

DOB: 2/18/1949 UT

SENTENCE: LIFE WITH NO PAROLE, plea bargain

Facility: Walla Walla, WA INMATE 866218

THE CRIME: On 11/30/2001, the most prolific serial killer in our country's history was arrested and charged with the murder of four women. DNA profiling led police to Gary Leon Ridgway, thus ending a 19-year killing spree.

He was spared a trial and the death penalty in lieu of life imprisonment with no chance of parole. Authorities made the hard decision to accept a plea bargain in an effort to solve several cold case files and close many missing person cases in an effort to bring closure to victims' families. Ridgway agreed to work with police in locating and identifying undiscovered bodies. Authorities soon realized the monster they were dealing with. He was eventually charged and convicted of 49 murders, he confessed to an additional 22 more, and police strongly suspect that he is guilty of at least 90 or more total killings. It is probable that even Ridgway has no idea how many women he slaughtered.

In 1982, Ridgway started hunting female street prostitutes, transients, drug addicts, and young runaways. He raped and strangled the victims, then dumped many of their bodies along the overgrown banks of the Washington state Green River in or in forested and heavily weeded areas. He would return to the scene of the crime, often having sex with the decomposing bodies. Some bodies were staged; many bodies were found in groups. All were naked.

He had been put under surveillance shortly before his arrest. That apprehension was speeded up when Ridgway was observed one night trolling the streets in search of another victim.

Frustrated authorities locate another body found during Ridgway's 19-year-killing spree. The exact number of his kills will never be known but the estimate is 90+.

(Photo source: Pinterest)

BACKGROUND: Gary Leon Ridgway was the second born of three boys. Relatives described his mother as domineering and aggressive in manner when dealing with her husband and sons. Ridgway did poorly in school academically and was tested with a low IQ of 82. He wet his bed into his early teens and was belittled by his mother for this.

Reportedly, his mother dressed provocatively and wore a lot of make-up, presenting herself publicly and privately in a trashy manner. Ridgway admitted during interrogation to being sexually aroused yet also embarrassed by his mother's appearance. He had fantasies about killing the mother. All through childhood and even after he married, he aspired to please his mother.

During the psychological examination he underwent while incarcerated, it was uncovered that he had once purposefully smothered a cat and set fires as a teenager.

At 16, he lured a young boy into the woods and stabbed him with a pocketknife. He admitted to laughing as he committed the crime and said later *"I always wondered what it would be like to kill someone."* The boy survived and, for whatever reason, the police never followed through on the attack. Ridgway did not graduate high school until age 20, due to failing two grades.

He joined the Navy after school, spent time in the Philippines, and here the newly married Ridgway experienced his first contact with prostitutes. He contracted gonorrhea and this enraged him. His new bride was having an affair at home and the marriage ended in divorce in less than two years. *"My first wife turned into a whore."*

He quickly remarried but his is second marriage also ended in divorce due to adultery, both partners at fault. It was during his second marriage that Ridgway became fanatical about religion, even going door-to-door to spread God's word. Reading or hearing the scriptures read would often bring him to tears.

His confirmed killings started shortly after his 1981 second divorce and continued during the three-year courtship and 1988 marriage to his third wife, although it is believed the murders slowed down considerably during those years. He claimed he genuinely loved his third wife. His wives and girlfriends describe Ridgway as having an insatiable sex drive. Reportedly, he also enjoyed sex in inappropriate public places as well as secluded areas, ironically, some of the same secluded locations where his murder victims were later found.

Early in 1982, Ridgway was questioned by police when he was found parked with a known prostitute, Keli McGinness. No action was taken. McGinness would later become a Green River victim. In 4/1982, he was arrested in a prostitution sting on the seedy SeaTac Strip where many female victims had last been seen. He was arrested again one month later, also in a prostitution sting.

His first serious run-in with the law was also in 4/1982 when a prostitute accused Ridgway of choking her. The charges were dismissed. Ridgway first came under suspicion in 1983 when he was questioned in the Marie Malvar murder case investigation. The boyfriend of the prostitute had last seen her getting into Ridgway's truck. No action was taken.

In 1/1984, the Green River Task Force was formed. That same year, Ridgway was given a lie detector test but passed. He would pass a second lie detector test in 1986. In 4/1987, the Green River Task Force detectives searched Ridgway's home, vehicle, and locker at work but found nothing incriminating. However, hair and saliva samples were taken.

The Task Force, with no results and a drop in the number of new killings, was reduced in numbers. Five members remained by 1990 and by 1992, that number was down to only two. In 2001, hard work, millions of dollars, and years of dedication finally paid off when newly developed DNA testing linked Ridgway to four Green River victims.

On 11/16/2001, Ridgway was again arrested on prostitution charges. He was placed under round-the-clock surveillance while detectives made their case and on 11/30, he was arrested for the murder of the four women based on those DNA results. Paint samples found at the crime scenes also led directly to Gary Leon Ridgway.

He was married to his third wife when he was arrested for murder. She was convinced her husband was innocent and described him to authorities as a gentle and loving husband, her best friend.

OUT OF THE MOUTH OF THE SERIAL KILLER: In speaking to Sheriff Dave Reichert regarding body locations: *"And where I killed them, you had to, you were the one who recovered* (the bodies)." *"Finding any new bodies, I just can't draw any pictures of where they're at."*

"I always wondered what it would be like to kill someone."

"And for 1992-95, I didn't do many killings because I was in Amway and going to church and being really busy. I didn't have time to kill."

"I drug her down the hill feet first."

"I can count to 60 and they're dead." (Choking was) *"more personal and more rewarding."*

In court records: *"I killed so many women I have a hard time keeping them straight."*

"I picked prostitutes as my victims because I thought I could kill as many of them as I wanted without getting caught."

At sentencing: *"I am sorry for causing so much pain to so many families."*

Ridgway often revisited bodies to have sex. Rather than seeing this as a deviant behavior, he explained to authorities it was *"a matter of economics and convenience."* He did not have to pay for sex and he did not have to *"hunt"* for another prostitute.

He claimed he believed he was doing society a favor by eliminating what he saw as degenerate females. *"The plan was, I wanted to kill as many women I thought were prostitutes as I possibly could."*

Additional Facts:

- After his second divorce, he met most of his girlfriends and third wife at "Parents Without Partners." He preferred this setting to bars.

- He reportedly once told police after his arrest that if he had only strangled to death his second wife he would not have killed again.

- Ridgway was employed as a painter for more than 32 years at the same company and was working for them at the time of his arrest. He repainted his own truck several times to throw off suspicion. Co-workers described him as *"meticulous"* and *"hard-working"* but most said he was somewhat strange. *"He was just a different type of a person."*

- After his arrest as "The Green River Killer", his brothers, their wives, a son, and his third wife all stood by him, convinced the wrong man had been arrested. They often visited him in jail until he confessed after accepting a plea bargain.

JOEL RIFKIN 17 Kills

DOB: 1/20/1959 NY

SENTENCE: 203 YEARS, EIGHT MONTHS

Facility: Clinton Correctional Facility, Dannemora, NY INMATE 95A6514

The Crime: If you are going to transport a dead body around in your vehicle, you might want to first make sure that vehicle is sporting a license plate. This is a lesson that Joel David Rifkin learned the hard way.

On 6/27/1993, state troopers tried to pull him over during a minor traffic stop. Spooked, Rifkin tried to outrun the officers and ended up wrecking his truck. The troopers approached with guns drawn and could not help but notice that there was a dead woman under a tarp in the bed of the truck. The victim was a 22-year-old prostitute Rifkin had killed three days earlier. After strangling her, he had wrapped her remains in a tarp tied with rope and hid her corpse in the trunk of his mother's car. His mother unexpectedly drove the car the next day and Rifkin was left to sweat it out until she returned, hoping she would not open the trunk. Not willing to chance that again, he quickly retrieved the body and stowed it in the back of his truck. Most likely he was on a mission to dispose of the body when he had the unexpected run in with the law. Arrested, then interrogated, 34-year-old Rifkin admitted to 17 murders, all prostitutes he had manually strangled to death.

Rifkin's killing ground was in and around Manhattan, NY and his first known kill occurred in March 1989. His mother was out of town. He brought a 25-year-old prostitute home, had sex, then bludgeoned her before strangling her to death. He mutilated the body, cutting off her head, slicing off her fingertips, and pulling out each tooth with pliers. He placed her head in a paint can and the remainder of her dissected body into several garbage bags before dumping the bags in woods and the East River.

He repeated his prior performance in early 1990 but was less enthusiastic about the exhaustive dismemberment. It seems he calmed down committing later kills or just got lazy. His usual MO was to pick up a prostitute, strangle her manually, then discard the body in a secluded area or in a body of water. When police searched his room at his mother's home, they found over 200 items that had belonged to his victims, collected as souvenirs.

BACKGROUND: Joel David Rifkin was the product of an unwanted pregnancy. His birth parents were college students and both agreed to surrender the infant at birth. He was adopted when he was a few weeks old by a childless Jewish couple. Three years later, the couple would also adopt a daughter. By all accounts, he grew up in a loving middle-class family that lived in a comfortable suburban home in East Meadow, Long Island.

As a child, Rifkin was shy, clumsy, gangly, and a poor student who suffered from dyslexia. He stuttered slightly. He slouched and walked so slowly that peers gave him the unkind nickname, "Turtle." Rifkin's mother was a stay-at-home mom when her children were young and his father was an engineer. Rifkin and his father were not close and Rifkin felt he never measured up to this man who had excelled both academically and athletically during his own school days.

Rifkin claimed he was first a lonely child and then an angry child, but says he worked hard at controlling his rage.

Sometime in his adult life he lost control of that inner rage, costing him jobs and friendships. He became addicted to sex and found paying for it made women readily available for his *"primal urge."* During interrogation, he told detectives that he first started paying prostitutes for sex when he got his driver's license in 1975. True or bravado, he was picking up women for sex as early as August 1987. We know this because he propositioned an undercover policewoman and was arrested.

In 3/1989, that "primal urge" eventually included murder. He justified killing prostitutes by thinking of them as only *"drug addicted hookers with no self-respect."* He also considered them easy targets that shielded him from detection. *"No family. They can be gone six or eight months and no one is looking."*

At the time of his arrest, Rifkin was living with his widowed mother and was unemployed. In 1988, he had been fired from his job at Planting Fields Arboretum in Oyster Bay, NY even though he had been awarded an internship after completing two semesters of a two-year horticulture program at the State College of Technology in Farmingdale, NY making straight A's. Cited was his inability to get along with fellow co-workers, disinterest exhibited on the job, and his failure to regularly show for work. He sporadically worked through a temp agency after his termination.

OUT OF THE MOUTH OF THE SERIAL KILLER:

"...a 25-cent mistake." (He was referring to his missing license plate that resulted in his capture. He had failed to properly secure the plate with a nut and bolt.)

"I was surprised I didn't get caught sooner."

"I dumped them hundreds of miles apart."

"America breeds serial killers. You don't see any in Europe." (This is not true. Serial Killers are present in every country in the world.)

"Girls advertise for $1,000 a night. Most guys who aren't serial killers can't afford that."

"I became addicted to sex and companionship"

"You carve 'em like a turkey."

"I killed 17."

"That's their job, to get into a stranger's car."

Additional Facts:

- Rifkin has an IQ of 128 but was a poor student most likely due, in part, to his dyslexia.

- He claimed he never had a girlfriend and picked up prostitutes at times for companionship.

- Rifkin's first victim's head was found on a golf course. All he remembered about her was that her name was Susie. It would be 24 years before she would be identified. Police working a cold case were able to piece together file information, a forensic reconstruction model, and parental DNA to identify her as a 25-year-old prostitute who went by the street name, "Susie."

- In 1994, Rifkin got into a yelling match with mass murderer, Colin Ferguson, resulting in Ferguson punching him in the mouth.

- In 1996, Rifkin was put into solitary confinement for four years at Attica for being disruptive. Later he was transferred to Clinton Correctional Facility and exhibited the same behavior resulting in isolation.

- Rifkin had pled not guilty by reason of insanity (NGRI) but his motion was denied. He is eligible for parole when he is 238 years old, give or take a few months.

DANNY ROLLING *"Gainesville Ripper* 8 Kills

DOB: 5/26/1954 LA

DOD: 10/25/2006 FL by LETHAL INJECTION AFTER 14 YEARS ON DEATH ROW, age 52

Facility: Florida State Prison, Raiford, FL

THE CRIME: Danny Harold Rolling came to Gainesville, FL on a bus in 8/1990 to make a name for himself. He was fleeing an attempted murder charge in Louisiana. The 36-year-old drifter and loser with an extensive criminal background decided he was going to follow in Ted Bundy's footsteps and become a *"superstar"* in his own right.

Rolling pitched a tent in the woods near the campus of the University of Florida and started his hunt. He followed two freshman roommates to their off-campus apartment and awaited nightfall before entering the unlocked residence of the sleeping women. He violently stabbed one co-ed to death, then bound, raped, and violently stabbed the other roommate in the back several times with a hunting knife before mutilating her body: the breasts were partially amputated postmortem. She had been washed with dish detergent to remove evidence of intercourse.

On 8/26, police discovered a Santa Fe Community College coed murdered in her apartment. She had been bound with tape, raped, and stabbed in the back with such force that her heart had ruptured. Her breasts had been mutilated, she was partially gutted, and the 18-year-old had also been decapitated. Rolling staged the bloody scene for shock value: her head was placed on a shelf as though staring at her own body that was displayed in a sitting position at the foot of her bed. She had not been home when Rolling broke into her residence, so he calmly waited for her to return.

More carnage was discovered the following day. A male and female student from the University of Florida had been stabbed to death in their apartment that was near the other crime scenes. The male student had been ambushed while he slept and savagely stabbed multiple times before the killer's rage had been unleashed upon the female. She was bound, raped, and stabbed three times in the back. Rolling crudely staged her body after he washed it. Neither body was mutilated, leading authorities to suspect he was interrupted before finishing.

A wall near The University of Florida campus on SW 34th Street in Gainesville is painted with the names of Rolling's innocent victims, hearts, and "Remember"

(Photo source: Wikipedia)

THE CAPTURE: In 1/1991, authorities caught a break. Rolling had been jailed south of Gainesville in Ocala, FL and was awaiting trial on a robbery charge. His arrest so near Gainesville prompted Shreveport, LA police to suggest that a triple 1989 homicide in Louisiana and the five slayings in Florida had a ring of similarity. Ocala detectives notified Gainesville authorities and Rolling quickly became the main suspect.

The tools he had in his possession at the time of arrest matched the tool marks left behind in the Gainesville apartments of three of the dead students. Authorities were led to Rolling's encampment. There they discovered other damaging evidence, including a tape-recording alluding to the murders. *"I know I have to run the rest of my life, but I'm getting pretty good at it."* In 12/1990, DNA evidence linked Rolling to the three killings, as well.

Rolling was always the main suspect in a 11/4/1989 triple homicide in Shreveport but he was never charged for lack of evidence. The victims were Tom Grissom, 55, his daughter, Julie, 24, and his grandson Sean, eight. He gave a written statement shortly before his execution admitting guilt in all three deaths. His DNA was also linked to that crime.

BACKGROUND: Danny Harold Rolling's mother was only 19-years-old when she married her husband, a police officer. Just two weeks after the wedding, she announced she was pregnant. James Rolling was angered and often claimed that the child was not his. He never wanted children and felt he had been trapped, tricked, or both by his new wife. He regularly beat his wife before and after the birth of their son, Danny. Soon Danny also became the brunt of his father's rage. When he was six-months of age, his father kicked the infant into a wall. A second son was born less than two years later. This child would fare better than Danny, but Danny's abuse escalated after his brother was born. Nothing Danny ever did was good enough for his controlling, cruel, and tyrannical father.

As early as age five, Danny was tied up as punishment. He also witnessed his father abuse, torture, and kill the family dog that Danny loved. By age eight, Danny was being physically abused by his father once or twice a week. The father often forbid holiday and birthday celebrations for his sons, refusing to spend money on such "frivolous" things and claimed that to hug or kiss his children would result in them growing up to be sissies and wimps. Danny was continually berated by his father, called worthless and no-good.

Danny missed a lot of school due to the physical abuse that was covered up as "illness". He failed the third grade twice. He was shy and projected an air of low self-worth. However, if he felt threatened by peers, he became strongly aggressive and lacked impulse control. School officials recommended counseling, but the parents never sought help for their son.

His mother left the father on five occasions but always returned. Danny developed a deep hatred for both parents: his father for beating and berating him and his weak mother for not protecting him.

When he was age 11, he witnessed his mother slitting her wrists during a violent argument with his father. He was traumatized by seeing the blood as she lay on the bathroom floor. He attacked his father and was beaten badly for defending his injured mother. His mother was taken to the hospital and recovered. Danny never did. He began to abuse alcohol he stole or was given by friends. To escape, he self-taught himself to play the guitar and preferred hymns. He also started having sadist fantasies about killing and torture.

When he was 12, his father attempted to murder his mother in front of her sons. Again, Danny was savagely beaten for defending his mother. He turned more and more to alcohol. His father discovered him drunk once and choked him, then threw his son into jail for two weeks to teach him a lesson. When he was finally released, he refused to speak to his mother and begrudged the fact that she had not come to his rescue. He ran away and stayed until hunger brought him back. His continuing fantasies about killing and torturing others became entangled with his nightly dreams of himself being tortured and mutilated by demons.

As a teenager, he spent several hours each week peeking into windows and masturbating. The beatings continued for minor to major infractions.

At 17, he joined the Air Force but his career was cut short. He began to abuse the drug, LSD, and was arrested for possession. He had a hard time following rules and was demoted for failure to obey orders. An Air Force psychiatrist diagnosed him with a personality disorder and Rolling was honorably discharged from the Air Force on medical grounds at age 18.

He returned home to Shreveport and moved in with his grandfather. He became immersed into religion and met and married his wife on 9/6/1974. She was pregnant at the time they wed. The marriage ended in divorce in 1977 after three years of turbulence. Rolling continued to abuse alcohol and drugs, plus he refused to maintain steady employment. He threatened his wife's life on several occasions, once while holding a gun to her head. She frantically called his parents for help. His father responded by threatening Rolling with a knife to his throat.

Shortly after the divorce, Rolling committed his first rape but was never charged. The victim resembled his ex-wife, a pretty and petite brunette with long hair. (That profile became his victims' profile in Gainesville.) He was in and out of jail on robbery and attempted escape charges from

1979 through 1988. In 1989, he killed three people, one a child, but was never charged for lack of evidence. On 5/18/1990, 36-year-old Rolling shot his father in the head and the abdomen during an argument. His father lost an eye and an ear in the altercation. Rolling fled the state with an attempted murder charge pending. In 8/1990, he arrived in Gainesville.

OUT OF THE MOUTH OF THE SERIAL KILLER:
"We're all down here for just a breath anyway."

"The most horrifying kind of death is to come in the night with a knife and you knew you were going to die."

"Thank you...God bless...please pray for me...God knows I need it." (Videotaped robbing a store on 6/12/1990).

(At the penalty phase): *"I regret with all my heart what my hand has done."*

"I do deserve to die, but do I want to die? No. I want to live. Life is difficult to give up."

(His written confession to the 1989 murders in Shreveport): *"I know that sorrow, that heartfelt bane, that dross th' mortal flame. Stone 'pon stone th' final throw ... etched hither tow — th' captive soul." Danny Rolling* (He saw himself as a country singer and song composer.)

"In order to fulfill all things that no stone be unturned. Here by I make a formal written statement concerning the murders of Julie, Tom & SEAN GRISSOM in my hometown of Shreveport, Louisiana ... HAL CARTER, Julie Grissom's former fiancee is 100% INNOCENT — TOTALLY PURE of that crime. I, and I alone am guilty. It was my hand that took those precious lights out of this ole dark world. With all my heart & soul would I could bring them back. Being a native son of Shreveport, I can only offer this confession of deep felt remorse over the loss of such fine — outstanding souls. Have wept an

ocean of tears ... By which mournful doth float 'pon a sea of regret." Danny Rolling

Rolling showed no remorse for his Gainesville crimes, however, nor made any final statement to victims' families or witnesses at his execution. He stared straight ahead and sang: *"Thou art the alpha and omega. The beginning and the end. The sound of thy voice stills a mighty wind. None greater than thee oh Lord. None greater than thee."*

Additional Facts:

- Rolling's IQ was 89.

- He tried to claim he suffered from a multiple personality disorder. However, at trial, all three experts dispelled that claim.

- Rolling confessed to a psychologist he had wanted to kill eight people, one for each year he had served in prison on previous convictions. (He served time for robbery in Georgia, Alabama, and Mississippi.) However, authorities believed that Rolling would have continued to kill until caught.

- In prison, Rolling was diagnosed by psychiatrists. He was found to have a severe borderline personality disorder characterized by deep anger, substance abuse, anxiety, extreme mood swings, plus impulsive and immature reactions to most situations. He was also said to suffer from Paraphilia (a sexual disorder) and anti-social behaviorisms.

- Fear had strongly gripped the picturesque college town of Gainesville. Students fled to their parents' homes, 700 never to return. Parents flocked to the school to retrieve their children or to stay with them. The school closed its campus for a week and sorority and fraternity houses hired uniformed guards. City security heightened, including adding an aerial surveillance team. A task force was quickly formed and the F.B.I. was asked to provide a profile of the perpetrator. Gun sales soared and large dogs became the most sought-after pet at local shelters.

• An extra row of seats had to be added to accommodate the number of witnesses that elected to watch Rolling's execution. Some of the victims' relatives held photos of their loved ones or wore pins with their pictures. Others carried white roses.

• The families of the victims paid for an advertisement in *The Gainesville Sun* to run on 10/25/2006 defending the death penalty decision and thanking the community for their continued support in prosecuting Rolling. It read: *"We hope you will remember August 1990 and the years that followed without any sense of community shame for what has happened here. You turned a blemish into a rose."*

TOMMY LYNN SELLS *"The Cross Country Killer* 22+ Kills

DOB: 6/28/1964 CA

DOD: 4/3/2014 TX, age 49

SENTENCE: DEATH by Lethal Injection/Texas State Penitentiary, Huntsville, TX

14 years on death row

THE CRIME: Tommy Lynn Sell's crime spree lasted almost two decades, from 1980 (age 15) through 12/31/1999. He was apprehended on 1/2/2000 due to an eye-witness description from a courageous 10-year-old girl he had left for dead after he fatally slashed her 13-year-old friend. Both were asleep when Sells broke into the home and viciously attacked them.

Killing women and children came easy for Sells. In one especially heinous murder spree in 1987, he beat to death a pregnant woman with a baseball bat. When she spontaneously gave birth, he killed the newborn with the same bat. He also bludgeoned her three-year-old son to death and shot her husband. The family's only offense had been to invite Sells to their home for a meal.

Sells often claimed he saw no value in any human being and he never showed remorse for his crimes. He made no final statement before being executed.

Sells was able to evade detection for so long due his transient lifestyle. He has 22 known kills, but authorities suspect him of many more. It is most likely that Sells, himself, never knew exactly how many people he savagely murdered. He once bragged in an interview that he had killed as many as 70 people.

BACKGROUND: Tommy Lynn Sells did not have an ideal childhood.

The identity of Sell's father, or the father of any of his six siblings, is unconfirmed. His mother has been graciously labeled as "uninvolved" with her children when they were young, some say to the point of neglect. Sells had a twin sister, Tammy Jean. Both contracted meningitis when they were 18-months-old. His sister died but Sells recovered.

For whatever reason, shortly after that event Sells was sent to live with a maternal aunt and remained in her home until age five. From age two to age five, his mother never visited nor contacted her son. When she finally retrieved her son, he had no memory of her and begged to stay with his aunt, the only maternal figure he knew.

Sells always claimed that he was molested by a family friend as a child and his mother did nothing to stop the abuse. The man had a known history of abusing boys but Sells was allowed overnight stays. True or not, he blamed this experience for creating his internal lust to kill even innocent infants and children. *"I didn't want them to live through the pain I lived through."*

He had a history of truancy from early grades on and was not forced to attend school. He started drinking alcohol at age seven and smoking ditch weed marijuana at 10. At 14, authorities required Sells to undergo a mental evaluation after he tried to rape his mother. Soon after, he either left home or was forced out of the family unit. By 15, he was a homeless transient who traveled the country continuously by hitchhiking, jumping trains, and stealing cars until his final arrest in 2000.

Sells never owned a home nor a vehicle and he never opened a bank account nor had a credit card in his name. He never filed taxes. Sells occasionally worked an odd job or panhandled to get by, but mostly he committed petty crimes to survive and to support his heavy drug and alcohol addictions.

He served some minor jail terms and, in 1990, he received a 16-month sentence in Wyoming for stealing a truck. During this incarceration, Sells was first diagnosed with several severe mental disorders and addictions. In 1993, he was sentenced to two ten-year-terms for the malicious wounding of a woman he beat almost to death. Again, he was diagnosed with serious mental issues but he was released from jail in 1997 after serving only four years.

In 1997, Julie Rea Harper was convicted of killing her 10-year-old son. Her conviction was overturned when Sells confessed to author, Diane Fanning, that he had killed the boy because his mother was rude to him earlier at a convenience store. Fanning was instrumental in getting the mother acquitted. Her book, *"Through the Window"* is about Sells. ***"Uh, you all haven't asked this, but I will go ahead and tell you this. Do I think I'm the one that killed this kid? Yes."***

OUT OF THE MOUTH OF THE SERIAL KILLER:
"The first time I did a shot of dope, it was the best feeling I ever had in my life. The first time I killed somebody, it was such a rush. It was just like that, a shot of dope every time I did it, it was that rush again, and It started chasing that high."

"I like to watch the eyes fade, the pupil fade. It's just like setting their soul free. I don't have an on-and-off switch. I'm just after that drug, I'm after that feeling."

"I don't like guns. They're dangerous."

When asked how many he had killed: ***"So...I'm not Billy the Kid making notches on my holster...so I know it's been a lot."***

"I am hatred. When you look at me, you look at hate. I don't know what love is. Two words I don't like to use is love and sorry because I'm about hate."

"My life don't make a lot of sense. It don't make sense that I go around the country killing people. Period. It don't make sense doing that."

"I remember seeing columns . . . at the front. Not one-hundred-percent sure, though. I know at some point I killed someone with columns on the front of the door."

PAULA SIMS 2 Kills

DOB: 5/21/1959 MD

SENTENCE: LIFE WITHOUT PAROLE

FACILITY: Dwight Correctional Center, Lincoln, IL INMATE B07074

THE CRIME: On 5/3/1989, six-week-old Heather Lee Sims' body was found stuffed into a black garbage bag and dumped in a Missouri trash can. She had been asphyxiated by a handheld over her nose and mouth. Her mother, Paula Sims, had contacted police on 4/29 to report an unknown person had struck her from behind, knocking her out *"with a karate chop."* She claimed that when she regained consciousness, her infant was gone. Sims' husband, Robert, told police that when he came home from the night shift, his wife was on the floor. The infant daughter was missing but their toddler son was safe in his crib. No physical evidence supported Sims' claims and the medical examiner noted frostbite on Heather's body suggesting the infant had most likely been placed in a freezer for a few days. Sims was arrested, tried, and convicted of murder on 1/30/1990.

In February, Sims broke and confessed to the murder of Heather and the murder of her first-born daughter, Loralei Marie. On 6/17/1986, Sims had told police that a man dressed all in black stole her daughter at gunpoint from the home. On 6/24, the 13-day-old infant's body was found in the woods behind the house. She had been left out in the open, not buried, and animals had disturbed the skeletal remains. An autopsy revealed the child had most likely been dead a few days before her abduction was reported. She had been asphyxiated. The Sims were suspects in the 1986 murder, but there was never enough evidence to pursue a conviction.

Robert and Paula Sims were also the parents of a son born 2/1/1988. Sims later said while incarcerated that she had considered killing him when he was crying but was able to stop herself. The jury spared Sims' life, rejecting the prosecutor's request for the death penalty.

Paula Sims has never shown remorse. Instead she has always offered excuses for the murder of her two infant daughters. She pled not guilty at her trial claiming she had been suffering from post-partum depression. The jury discounted her claim. She appealed asking for a new trial claiming evidence that would prove she was suffering from post-partum depression, plus she cited ineffective legal counsel. Her appeal was denied.

BACKGROUND: Reportedly, Paula Marie Sims was sexually abused by a grandfather starting at age seven. By the age of 13, Paula was already showing signs of a troubled life. She adored one of her two older brothers, Randy, and was his constant companion. Together, they drank alcohol, smoked pot, and regularly stole from local stores. Family noted that Paula was becoming combative when confronted, both at home and at school. She had few friends, preferring her brother's company to other peers, especially girls.

She was an exceptional athlete and played both basketball and softball. By age 15, she was sexually active and taking valium. By age 16, she was experimenting with LSD. She developed an interest in motorcycles and drag racing through Randy and hung out with the mostly male crowd at these events.

On 4/10/1976, she and Randy were in a car wreck. 19-year-old Randy, the driver, died at the scene and Paula received facial injuries that left her permanently scarred. Randy's autopsy showed a high level of both drugs and alcohol in his system. After his death, Paula became completely depressed. She stayed in her room most of the time and avoided social contact. She talked of suicide.

In May of that year, the family moved to Illinois. Paula changed schools and, going against her customary habit, forged a close, long-time friendship with two girls. She was, however, still considered a loner.

After high school, she attended a community college for a year but dropped out before finishing her program. She took a job as a cashier at a grocery store. Later she would be fired from that company for stealing.

In 1979, she met Robert Sims through a friend. In 1981, they married. On 6/5/1986, their first daughter was born.

OUT OF THE MOUTH OF THE SERIAL KILLER:

A script written on the bottom of a letter sent to Paula Sims by the author on 7/1/2016 and returned to the author with the following:

FYI-Paula is not a serial killer! -Paula would like you to know her true story has been told by Audrey Becker in "Dying Dreams." Paula did what she did because she suffered from Post Partum Depression and Psychosis. She was diagnosed by the leading expert in the field while incarcerated. She wishes you well with your book- J.- It is the author's opinion that "J" is Paula Sims and this response was written by Paula.

(Before murdering the infants) *"I actually felt like I was having a conversation with the devil."*

"Due to post-partum psychosis, I had auditory and visual hallucinations. Voices told me to hurt them and said that I was a bad mother. I visualized demons. Dead children

and a masked gunman. At times I was kind of normal but those times were fewer and fewer as the days progressed."

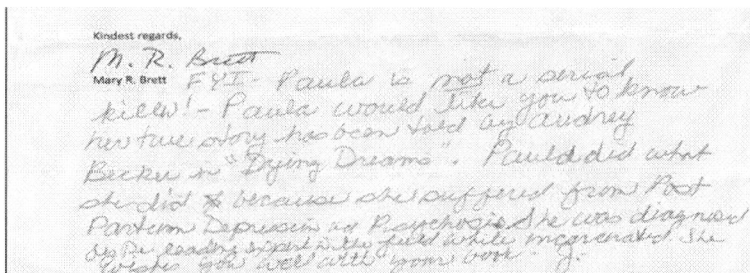

Kindest regards,

M. R. Brett

Mary R. Brett *FYI- Paula is not a serial killer!- Paula would like you to know her true story has been told by Audrey Becker in "Dying Dreams". Paula did did what she did & because she suffered from Post Partum Depression & Psychosis. She was diagnosed after reading about it in the field while incarcerated. She wrote you well with "your book". J.*

Additional Facts:

• Paula named her son after her beloved deceased brother, Randy. The child's middle name was, Troy, named for Robert Sims' father. It has been suggested that by naming the child, Randy, his life may have been spared.

• Sims' oldest brother, David, suffered from seizures as a child. Sims would steal his medications and take them as a teenager.

• Robert Sims was never charged nor arrested but authorities strongly suspected he helped conceal the murders. He testified on his wife's behalf at her murder trial but he filed for divorce eight months after she was sentenced. He was given custody of their son, Randall, then age two.

• Father and son were killed in a car accident in 6/2015, when a drunk driver rear-ended them, forcing their vehicle over an interstate embankment. Robert Sims was 63 and Randall was 27. They were not buried with the two infants. The two baby girls are buried at Woodland Hills Cemetery in East Afton, IL.

JEREMY & JAMIE SLY: *KILLER TWINS:*

JEREMY SLY 7 Kills

DOB: 3/2/1970

SENTENCE: LIFE WITHOUT THE POSSIBILITY OF PAROLE. A plea deal took the death penalty off the table.

Facility: Graceville Correctional Center, Graceville, FL INMATE 719954

THE CRIME: In 2002, Jeremy Bruce Sly was already serving a life sentence in a Florida prison for an unrelated 11/13/1991 murder and armed burglary of an elderly woman when he confessed to the 12/19/1991 in home shooting murders and robbery of a Port Charlotte, Florida retired couple and their dog, plus the shooting murders of four members of a family that included three children. A fifth member of the family, a nine-year-old son, was the only survivor. That child was shot seven times and left for dead. Sly revealed details that only the killer would know.

Both crimes happened the same night and authorities believe the choice of victims was random. The remote location of the homes most likely played a large part in the selection.

A plea bargain took the possibility of the death penalty off the table. Sly would have been eligible for parole in 2017 had he not been charged and convicted of these additional 6 killings.

OUT OF THE MOUTH OF THE SERIAL KILLER:
Unedited statements included in a letter to the author from Jeremy Sly:

"I think you should know that I am not a serial killer; although, I guess you could call me a mass murderer and maybe to a small extent maybe a spree killer. Even so, I thought you should know." "As for your request-I'm not sure that I would fit your topic of discussion, and of course, I don't know if I would feel comfortable airing my dirty laundry to a stranger. If someone was to write about me I would think I would want someone who would write about me from the perspective that I am a human being rather than a deranged psychopath bent on mayhem. I'm not, but that's not to say I didn't have problems- I was pretty bad off psychologically back then. Today, well, I'm not the man I once was-."

At his 2011 sentencing, Jeremy Sly quoted an Anne Rice vampire book and spoke of atoning for his sins. He gave the following statement: *"From the very beginning of my life, my mind has been a fury of chaos and disruption.*

Additional Facts:

- Jeremy Sly has been treated for severe mental illness in his past.

- He is heavily tattooed, with three tattoos of Dale Earnhardt, numerous skulls, a Joker, a cross, a pentagram, a spider web, yin yang, a demon face, Calvin, roses, a dragon, a butterfly, a flame, and a naked lady

- He has an identical twin brother, Jamie Edward Sly, who is also incarcerated for the 11/1991 brutal murder and armed burglary of an elderly woman he committed alongside his brother. Jamie Sly is currently serving a life sentence at Cross City Correctional

Institution in Florida. It remains unclear if Jamie Sly also participated in the six 12/1991 murders. Authorities have always strongly believed more than one gunman was involved in this murder spree but, to date, Jeremy Sly has not implicated anyone else.

JAMIE SLY: 1 Kill

DOB: 3/2/1970

SENTENCE: LIFE

Facility: Cross City Correctional Center, FL INMATE 2L9973

OUT OF THE MOUTH OF THE KILLER: An UNEDITED May 2016 letter from Jamie Sly:

"I'm sorry you must have me mistaken with my Brother Jeremy B. Sly. Sorry I seem to have wasted some of your time and money. Please forgive. I'm also sorry that I can't be of help. Thank you for your time."

BRUCE & STEPHEN SPAHALSKI: *KILLER TWINS*

BRUCE SPAHALSKI 4 Kills

DOB: 12/12/1954 NY

SENTENCE: Four convictions of second-degree murder. Sentenced to 100 years 12/13/2008.

Facility: Great Meadow Correctional Facility, Comstock, NY INMATE 06B3454

THE CRIME: On 11/9/2005, 51-year-old Robert Bruce Spahalski turned himself in for the murder of his friend, neighbor, and fellow drug addict, Vivian Irizarry, age 54. He had beaten her in the head, then strangled her to death while hallucinating on crack cocaine. *"All of a sudden I saw her as a demon. I freaked out."* Eventually, he would confess to 4 murders, the first going back to 1990.

The murder of Moraine Armstrong, 24, on 12/31/1990, had remained unsolved for 15 years. Police discovered Armstrong's naked body with an electrical cord wrapped around her neck. Spahalski was never a suspect even though he lived across the street. He also confessed to the murder of a prostitute and drug addict, Adrian Berger, killed 7/21/1991 in her Rochester, NY apartment. Her body was so decomposed that authorities were never able to classify her death as a homicide. At the time, she was the girlfriend of Spahalski.

He was a suspect in the 10/2/1991 murder of Charles Grande but he was never charged. He confessed to killing Grande with a hammer because the man refused to pay him

$20 owed for performing sex. When his twin brother, at the time incarcerated at Attica, heard of Bruce's confession he reportedly said, *"I thought I was the only murderer in the family. I never knew he killed someone. He never told me, he never mentioned it to me." "Why would he turn himself in? I don't have that kind of brain! I would never turn myself in."*

BACKGROUND: Robert Bruce and Stephen Joseph Spahalski were identical twins born to an unwed mother in Elmira, NY on 12/12/1952. The parents would later marry, then divorce. The twins were inseparable in their early years and displayed the typical strong bond found between twins, especially identical twins.

By the age of 15, Stephen had killed a store owner by stabbing him to death and Bruce was sentenced to jail for stealing a car and setting a flag on fire at his school. Both twins would travel separate paths to prison but each would spend most of their early lives incarcerated.

At one time, they were both incarcerated at Auburn Correctional Facility. Authorities are still not sure which twin once attempted a 1978 escape in a truck leaving the grounds. When exposed, the inmate jumped out of the vehicle and ran back into the prison population. Neither twin would confess so authorities placed both into solitary confinement. Stephan would claim much later during an interview that it was Bruce.

Acquaintances of Bruce say he was a street hustler, ran a male escort service, performed as a male prostitute, was addicted to hard drugs, and has AIDS.

OUT OF THE MOUTH OF THE SERIAL KILLER: In an UNEDITED second letter received from Robert Bruce Spahalski dated 3/12/2018:

Hello again Mary,

hope you are well and prospering in many levels of your life, mentally, physically & spiritually.

You approached me in July 2016 about my homicidal atrocities and including me in a book you were in the process of writing. I have no idea if you've finished that project but I am a person of social integrity and feel I have the social responsibility to further satisfy your curiosity & research of human beings committing murder and the motivational factors behind them. You reached out to me, and I'm here to deliver to you.

After 10 years of mental reflection and self-examination of myself, I'm going to try and explain what happened to me.

As you know, I had a huge crack addiction. In a 15 year period as a crack broker, I helped purchase and smoke at least a ½ million dollars worth of crack cocaine. While I was experiencing that social dysfunction, I was mentally ill with the affliction of homicidal schizophrenia. These 2 definitive mind-sets are responsible for the homicidal carnage, make no mistake about that. You being a researcher, I want you to understand that homicidal schizophrenia manifest itself as evil incarnate. the day I killed those people, this was my mind set. I was not mentally in the reality you and I are now sharing, the reality distortion I experienced at those homicides were voices urging and compelling me to kill people. In this reality you and I are now sharing, I did not premeditatively sanction mentally the killing of those people, I did not. I do not consider myself a serial killer, that mind-set is (unable to read) *and premeditive, and I am socially not that.*

I just finished filming an interview with CNN News, "Inside with Chris Cuomo" they told me my twin brother past away 4 months ago of a congenital heart defect.

We never meant to hurt anybody Mary, but drugs, genetics & mental illness are characteristical nuances in those homicides. Just thought you should know...Robert Bruce Spahalski

One more thing Mary

Here's some mental trivia for you, when I did that interview with CNN Feb 8th, 2018 I recanted the murder confession of Maurice Armstrong an alleged prostitute. I confessed to that homicide to give the mother of that homicide Spiritual & Social closure regarding her daughters death. I let that mother vent her rage & anguish & loss at my sentencing of 25 to life for that homicide just so she could get on with her life thinking that justice had prevailed, it was about closure to me, even though I was in deep shit with the other homicides, maybe I was wrong playing god that day, but my motivations were pure with positive intentions that s how I'm mentally wired.

good-Bye Mary

RBS

Additional Facts:

- According to Stephen, when they were young they were both excellent gymnasts.

- Police first suspected Bruce of the 1971 murder of a man that Stephen later confessed to killing. Stephen claimed the man had made sexual advances towards him. *"He deserved it."*

- In 1980, the City of Rochester hired Bruce as a mechanic's helper after he was released from prison. He was fired within a year for failure to report to work. He was unable to show up because he had been arrested again, this time for stealing an expensive coin collection.

- Bruce killed Moraine Armstrong because the prostitute demanded $100 for sex. He felt he owed her nothing since he had shared a large quantity of drugs with her.

- He killed Charles Grande, a business owner, because he had shortchanged him after sex. He also stole $1000 and a car from Grande.

- Bruce had turned the thermostat all the way up at crime scenes to expedite the decomposition of the body to destroy evidence, proving he was able to differentiate between right and wrong. This meant his attorney was not able to offer the insanity plea he sought.

- At the time of his surrender in 2005, Bruce had been in a 14-year relationship with a girlfriend.

- Bruce's apartment rent was paid by a nonprofit agency that provided help for drug addicts and people with mental health problems.

- Stephen Spahalski was released from Attica. Besides his manslaughter conviction at age 15, he has a rap sheet that included robbery, kidnapping, and parole violations. Reportedly, Stephen had no contact with Bruce from the time of his release until his death in 2017 from congestive heart failure.

TIMOTHY SPENCER *"Southside Strangler"* 5 Kills

Timothy Spencer became the first murderer in the United States to be convicted and executed based on DNA fingerprinting.

DOB: 3/17/1962 VA

DOD: 4/27/1994 VA

SENTENCE: DEATH BY ELECTROCUTION/ six years on Death Row

Facility: Greenville Correctional Centre, Jarratt, VA

THE CRIME: Timothy Wilson Spencer was well-known to Arlington, VA authorities as a prolific home burglar and a suspect in a series of rapes when he came to light as the key suspect in the 1987 break-ins, rapes, sodomy, and torture murders of three Richmond, VA women and one woman in Arlington, VA. All crime scenes had been meticulously free of clues apart from large amounts of semen near the victims' bodies and one hair. Through this, the newly developed DNA profiling was able to link him to the crimes. Timothy Spencer became the first murderer in the United States to be convicted and executed through the technology of DNA analysis. That challenged conviction was upheld by the Virginia Supreme Court.

Spencer was also subsequently convicted of a 1984 woman's murder through DNA, a crime for which another man had been previously charged and convicted.

Spencer's usual MO was to break into a woman's residence and wait for her to return home. He would first bind then rape her while strangling her with any available weapon at hand such as a vacuum cleaner hose, shoelaces, sock, or belt. At least one of his victims had been savagely beaten.

He tortured his victims by strangling them until they passed out, reviving them, and then strangling them again. He continued this sick ritual until they finally died. One victim, a 15-year-old girl, had her mouth taped because family members were asleep in the house but it is easy to imagine that his other victims, alone in their homes, desperately begged for their lives.

Spencer avoided being caught because law enforcement agencies, working with the FBI, were looking for the typical profiled serial killer at that time, a white male.

BACKGROUND: Timothy Spencer was the older of two sons born to a married couple that divorced soon after the second child was born. The children lived with their mother in the Green Valley District of Arlington, VA, an area that was well-known for being crime infested. His mother worked so the boys were often left on their own and unsupervised growing up.

Spencer was a quiet, handsome child but was a poor student and often in trouble at school and with the authorities beginning by age nine. At age 12, he was caught urinating and defecating in a public area of his school as *"a prank."* He was also known in his neighborhood for setting fires and for breaking into homes to steal. However, when his younger brother was caught for stealing candy and brought home by the police, the brother remembers Spencer's stern admonishment: *"Don't be like me. Be better than me."*

He was in and out of jail. In 1987, he was released early to a half-way house in the South Side of Richmond, VA after a three-year jail stint. The rules stated that all occupants had to be inside the house and accounted for at night, but for whatever reason, Spencer was able to come and go as he pleased. On 9/19/1987, he waited for his first area victim to arrive home and brutally murdered her.

OUT OF THE MOUTH OF THE SERIAL KILLER: Spencer always maintained his innocence, never admitting to the crimes, nor showing remorse. At his sentence hearing in 1988, he flipped off the court with his middle finger. He was said to almost swagger into the execution chamber, unassisted by guards, and when asked if he had any final words, he uttered, *"Yeah, I think...."* then said no more. Possibly his bravado had subsided.

Additional Facts:

• On 1/16/1988, another Richmond, VA woman was found dead in apparently the same manner but she had not been raped. It was later discovered that she was killed by her sister's boyfriend when she returned home and caught him stealing money from her. The boyfriend then staged the scene to erroneously point the finger at the Southside Strangler. He subsequently hung himself before authorities could arrest him.

• Spencer served time in jail for a 1984 conviction for burglary, explaining the three-year gap in his killings. He only served three years of his 10-year sentence, freeing him to kill his innocent victims, including a 15-year old student and a married surgeon.

• At the time of the Richmond murders, Spencer was living in a halfway house within walking distance of two of his victims.

• Police were able to prove that Spencer had traveled from Richmond to Arlington to visit his mother for Thanksgiving when the Arlington murder occurred.

• Spencer was the inspiration for mystery writer Patricia D. Cornwell's popular 1990 first novel,

"Postmortem." She wrote it and sold it to a publisher while working at the Office of the Chief Medical Examiner in Richmond, Virginia as a computer tech.

• The oak electric chair at Greensville Correctional Centre was built by prisoners in the 1950s and dubbed, "Old Sparky."

• Prisoner David Vasqyez became the first American to be exonerated based on DNA evidence. Vasquez was granted an unconditional pardon on 1/4/1989 for a 1984 murder that Spencer had committed.

• Spencer's vicious murders rocked the city of Richmond, VA. In 1989, Virginia became the first state to create a DNA database of previously convicted sex offenders.

STEPHEN STANKO 2 Kills

DOB: 1/13/1968

SENTENCE: TWO DEATH SENTENCES

Facility: Lieber Correctional Institution, Ridgeville, SC INMATE 6022

THE CRIME: In 2/1996, Stephen Stanko was arrested after an attack on his long-time girlfriend. He was sentenced to 10 years in prison on charges of kidnapping, plus assault and battery with the intent to kill. He was also charged and convicted on numerous counts of car theft. He served eight and a half years and was released in 2004 with two years of probation required.

Shortly after release, 36-year-old Stanko met a local 43-year old librarian, her teen-age daughter, and a 74-year-old male library patron who became his friend and business associate. He soon moved in with the librarian and her daughter. On 4/8/2005, he savagely beat and choked the librarian to death, then beat, raped, and attempted to kill her 15-year-old daughter by slicing her throat twice. He believed her to be dead. After the attacks, he showered, packed his clothes, then cleaned out his girlfriends' bank account at an ATM and stole her car.

He next drove to his elderly friend's house in Conway, SC, spent the night, then shot him to death in the morning after his friend served him breakfast. Stanko robbed him, traded his dead girlfriend's stolen car for his murdered friend's truck, and drove to Columbia, SC in time for "Happy Hour" at a local bar.

The motive for the murders: he needed money, was broke, unemployed, plus his girlfriend was about to kick him out.

THE CAPTURE: Stanko was arrested after a woman in Atlanta, GA alerted police after seeing him profiled in the media. He had met her in a bar, picked her up, and gone home with her. He was captured without incident. She told authorities that Stanko had already professed his love for her.

BACKGROUND: Stephen Christopher Stanko was born in Guantanamo Bay, Cuba where his father was serving in the U. S. Navy. Later, his family moved to Goose Creek, South Carolina. His father was a Master Chief in the Navy and a strict disciplinarian, but not abusive.

Stephen was the second child born into a family of five children. When he was, 15, a brother died in a house fire that had a suspicious origin. It was eventually ruled arson but no one was ever charged. For whatever reason, Stanko's father grew distant and emotionally turned his back on Stephen after the loss, possibly suspecting his son of the crime.

It was a dream of Stanko to go to the Air Force Academy after graduating from high school. Even though he scored in the 85th percentile in the National SAT's and was an excellent student, a top athlete, and was popular among his teachers and peers, he was denied admission. The rejection and deep disappointment became a turning point in his life.

He briefly attended a local community college but this secondary plan did not work out favorably. Stanko turned to crime. He often proffered a grandiose lie when presenting himself or his employment status to others. Family and friends reported strange, illegal, and even frightening behaviors.

In 1995, Stanko's father barred him permanently from the family home.

From 1993 through 1996, Stanko was habitually stealing from workplaces, mostly car dealerships, and running scams on friends and strangers alike.

OUT OF THE MOUTH OF THE SERIAL KILLER: An UNEDITED undated letter to the author by Stephen Stanko:

Ms. Mary

First of all, Congratulations on the recent publication of your fourth book.

I would, next, like to thank you for considering me for part in your next work. It very much sounds to be quite interesting and a novel approach.

My immediate concern is whether or not you are knowledgeable and aware of my case. You are viewing me as a "serial killer." There were to (sic) *deaths in my incident, but this is not a serial chain of events.*

Further, you ask "why did your father, in essence, blame you for your brother's death?" With all due respect-where did you get that from? I was in the 10th grade in high school, an honor student/athlete and had NEVER done anything but excel at that point, and my brother was MURDERED serval counties away. My father NEVER blamed me for that. Please, where did you get that from? I am not sure where this info. Is coming from, but based on the inaccuracy, I may not be someone you want to consider.

Mary, I am a published author as well. I have had to stay away from projects that discuss my incidents because of the need to protect my appellate procedures.

There has been some real-for lack of a better term-"crap" put out there, however, as a result of mine and my attorney's unwillingness to talk with interviewers and authors. I would like to share an honest story.

With your answer to the above question, would you please add some more in-depth understanding of what you are looking for-word count, chronology., etc.…

Are you aware of my defense? One of the most amazing parts of my case is that there are numerous professional sports figures that are now being almost-exonerated for the same physiologal (sic) *defect that my case provided as evidence for what occurred. Of course, it was called "junk-science" during my trial. It would be wise to see some measure of truth told, but what limits, content, and timelines are you looking for?*

I hope you understand a very restricted level of trust. Thus far, the things written and said were nowhere near the truth. Of course, I did not participate.

Please respond at your earliest opportunity, and thank you, for your considerations. Please excuse the lack of formality. I wanted to give you Quick Response.

Respectfully…I am Stephen

(An excerpt from his book:) *"What I fear most now is that I may carry some of this total institution back into society with me."*

"For 20 years now I've been running this race to try to be something I'm not. Lying to people and everything else."

"I never meant to hurt anybody. It's like there's two of me."

"I know that I'm not a person to hurt anyone. I never would have hurt anyone on purpose. Never."

"She slapped at me and I had a cigarette, and that cigarette lodged in between my glasses and burned me. And that's the last thing I remember."

"I think about Laura every day. I wish I could remember the things that happened, but I don't." (Stanko claimed he blacked out during the attack and came to in the shower.)

Additional Facts:

- Stanko co-authored the book, *"Living in Prison: A History of the Correctional System with an Insider's View"* while serving time in prison for a 1996 assault and kidnapping conviction. The book was self-published after being rejected by a publisher.

- While out on parole in 2004, he started to write a second book, this one about serial killers.

- The night after Stanko killed his elderly friend, he drove to a SC bar and was buying the patrons drinks and claiming to be a wealthy businessman in town for the Augusta golf tournament.

- Two days after killing his live-in girlfriend and attempting to kill her daughter, he was in an Augusta, Georgia bar picking up a woman and going home with her. The next day, a Sunday, he went to church with the woman and was already telling the lady of his intense feelings for her.

WILLIAM SUFF *"Riverside CA Prostitute Killer"* *"Lake Elsinore Killer"* 15-22 Kills

DOB: 8/20/1950 CA

SENTENCE: 12 DEATH SENTENCES plus an additional sentence for attempted murder

Facility: San Quentin, CA INMATE J-83402

THE CRIME: William Lester Suff's first kill was his two-month old baby daughter. He beat and shook the infant to death in 1973 because she would not stop crying. The doctors would discover signs of chronic abuse. He was sentenced to 70 years but served only 10 years behind bars and was released in March 1984.

In 1986, he committed his next kill, a prostitute. He would eventually be tried for the murder of 13 women even though authorities believe that the victim count is closer to 22. All victims were either beaten, strangled, or stabbed to death. Some were mutilated. Others were splayed or grotesquely posed with various objects protruding from their vaginas or stuffed into their mouths. All were working girls from the University Avenue red light district of Riverside City, CA.

On 1/9/1992, Suff was arrested after a traffic stop revealed a knife caked with blood, a rope, and a sleeping bag that would eventually be proven to contain fibers matching those found on several of the victims' bodies. He had unknowingly made an illegal U-turn in front of police to solicit a prostitute on the opposite side of the street. Police were already on the watch for a silver-colored van driven by a white male who wore glasses. A friend of one of the prostitutes that Suff killed had seen her get into the van before her death and alerted the authorities.

It only took the jury 10 minutes to return with a guilty verdict in the murder of 12 women but they dead locked on the 13th victim, 11 to one. Suff was also found guilty in the attempted murder of one prostitute who leapt from his truck after he attacked her. He wept when the verdict was read.

BACKGROUND: His given name at birth was Bill Lee Suff. He grew up in the rural Riverside, CA community. Riverside City is located in the southern part of California, a city not too far from Los Angeles. He was the oldest of five children. His father abandoned the family early and Suff and his siblings were raised by a mother described as cold and non-loving. The dynamics of the home were far from nurturing.

The younger children were always in trouble, ranging from minor problems with neighbors and the school to killing animals and setting fires. In adulthood, one sibling would struggle with drug addiction and another with pedophilia sexual issues.

Suff, the oldest, was forced into the role of head of the household. It became his responsibility to deal with any and all issues that arose regarding his siblings. He graduated from high school in 1968 in the lower half of his class but he was not a disciplinary problem. On the contrary. He never stood out. He was described as the quintessential invisible student. The only academic areas where he showed interest were shop and music. He was a member of his high school band.

Suff was shy and married the first girl who took an interest in him. He met her in high school and they communicated while he was in Air Force basic training, stationed in Texas. When she told him she was pregnant, claiming to have been raped, Suff offered to marry her. They wed on 12/13/1969.

She was 16 and he was 19. Suff arranged for her parents to adopt the baby in California before he and his new bride returned to Texas.

Soon a son was born to the couple and named for his father. Reportedly, Suff never bonded with the child. His wife later claimed that he was physically abusive to the boy and that she often feared for her own safety, as well. Despite this, the couple had another child, a daughter born in 1973. She would live for two months before she was killed by her father. An examination of her small body also showed numerous signs of past injuries.

OUT OF THE MOUTH OF THE SERIAL KILLER:

"Prosecutors, Paula Zellerbach, and the news media have all painted a grotesque picture of me as a cold-blooded, heartless monster. They couldn't have been more wrong about me. I am a caring, loving, and helpful person. Ask anyone who is close to me."

Suff was known to rant about the prostitute problems in his city. He called them *"filthy carriers of disease."*

Additional Facts:

- Suff had unusual habits. He liked to dress his victims in his own clothes or, at times, take their clothes and jewelry to give as gifts.

- Most victims were dumped in citrus groves, in dumpsters, or along the side of the road. One was left in a bowling alley parking lot.

- Suff enjoyed cooking and had a passion for preparing his own recipe for chili. An unfounded story that continually surfaces claims he once served chili made from the breasts of one of his victims in the 1986 Riverside County Employee Chili Cook-Off that he won.

- He went out of his way to be neighborly and helpful. Co-workers thought of Suff as a slightly nerdy employee who was easy going and cheerful.

- At the time of his arrest, Suff was a stock clerk for the County of Riverside. Ironically, he delivered furniture and other supplies to the task force headquarters where authorities were actively engaged in solving his murders. He was friendly and often engaged them in conversations concerning the investigation.

MARYBETH TINNING 8 Kills

DOB: 9/11/1942 NY

SENTENCE: 20 YEARS TO LIFE/ Paroled after 31 years incarcerated. She was 75.

Facility: Bedford Hill Correctional Facility for Women, Bedford Hills, NY INMATE 87GO597

THE CRIME: Housewives with time on their hands often get addicted to a variety of things: soaps, shopping, gardening, Tupperware parties. Marybeth Roe Tinning got addicted to killing her children.

Tinning's third child, Jennifer, was born on 12/26/1971. She died eight days later in the hospital and an autopsy revealed the infant had succumbed to acute meningitis. Friends and relatives noted that Marybeth was relishing being in the sympathy spotlight and acted as though the baby's funeral was a social functioning instead of a tragic memorial to a lost child. Within nine weeks of that funeral, her other two children would be dead.

By 1975, five Tinning children had died in five years. Doctors suggested the problem could possibly be an inherited defect, a "death gene". Family and friends quietly suspected a much darker explanation. Noted was Marybeth's negative reaction unless she was the focus of each funeral or viewing. She very much enjoyed playing the role of the grieving mother.

From 1971 until her arrest in late 1986, more of Tinning's children would die, including Michael, a two and half-year-old bi-racial foster child the Tinnings had adopted. He passed on 3/2/1981. Michael had pneumonia but it was not a severe enough case to cause death. Hospital staff became suspicious since the "death gene" theory would not apply to a non-biological off-spring of a different race.

The Tinning's ninth child, a daughter they named Tami Lynne, was born on 8/22/1985. She was closely monitored by pediatricians and hospital staff. Sadly, four months later, Tami Lynne would die. SIDS was listed as the cause of death. No official investigation pursued.

Once again, Marybeth had gotten away with murder. However, if the authorities were not alarmed, her outraged family, friends, and neighbors were. Hot lines lit up. Even hospital staff members called tips into the police reporting their suspicions.

On 2/4/1986, Schenectady, NY investigators brought Marybeth in for questioning. She broke down and confessed to killing three children, Tami Lynne (ninth victim), Timothy (fourth victim) and Nathan (fifth victim) *"...Just these three, Timothy, Nathan and Tami. I smothered them each with a pillow because I'm not a good mother. I'm not a good mother because of the other children."* Prosecutors successfully argued at trial that it would be ludicrous to believe that a woman would kill her ninth child, a healthy infant, if she had tragically lost many other infants due to medical issues.

BACKGROUND: Marybeth Roe Tinning was born into a two-parent household, the older of two children. She has a younger brother. Her story changes when asked about her childhood. She has varied between saying her father was physically violent with her, cold, disapproving, and locked her in dark closets as punishment to painting him as a caring father who disciplined lightly by switching her with a fly swatter or locked her in her room, but maintained she likely deserved the admonishments.

She was an average student in school, quiet, shy, and blended into the crowd. She was not a stand-out on any level. Marybeth did not date often and maintained a small group of friends. She graduated in 1960 from high school. After working several menial jobs, she took a position at a local hospital as a nursing assistant.

In 1963, a friend set her up on a blind date with Joseph Tinning. They married in 1965. Their first child was born in 1967.

The Tinning Children:

Barbara Ann: 5/31/1967-3/2/1972 (third child to die) Police called by concerned hospital and social workers. Official cause stated as Reyes Syndrome. No charges filed.

Joseph, Jr.: 1/10/1970-1/20/1972 (second child to die) reported as SIDS (no autopsy).

Jennifer: 12/26/1971-1/3/1972 (first child to die) Died of natural causes in the hospital, acute meningitis, and an autopsy was performed. She never left the hospital after birth so most consider this a natural death. Ironically, this loss unleashed a psychological break in Marybeth's mind that would result in 8 more children's unnatural deaths.

Timothy: 11/21/1973-12/10/1973 (fourth child to die) reported as SIDS but **Tinning admits to killing infant.**

1974: Attempted poisoning of her husband.

Nathan: 3/30/1975-9/2/1975 (fifth child to die) reported as heart failure but **Tinning admits to this murder.**

Michael: Bi-racial child adopted 8/1978. Died 3/2/1981 (eighth child to die) reported as pneumonia.

Mary Francis: 10/29/1978-2/20/1979 (sixth child to die) reported as SIDS.

Jonathan: 11/19/1979-3/24/1980 (seventh child to die) reported as heart failure.

Tami Lynne: 8/22/1985-12/20/1985 (ninth child to die) reported as SIDS but **Tinning admits to this kill.**

OUT OF THE MOUTH OF THE SERIAL KILLER:

"...in reflection, they died of other causes. It's in my paperwork, but they did not die by my hands."

"I have to be honest, and the only thing that I can tell you is that I know that my daughter is dead. I live with it every day. I have no recollection and I can't believe that I harmed her." (After her first parole hearing in March 2007, Tinning was still proclaiming innocence. Her parole was denied.)

"I was going through bad times." (Stated at second parole hearing in January 2009. She was denied parole and a board member stated that her remorse *"was superficial at best."*)

(At her January 26, 2011 parole hearing. She was denied release.) *"Two things that I wanted in life was to be married to someone who cared for me and to have children and, other than that, I can't give you a reason." "When I look back, I see a very damaged and just a messed-up person... Sometimes I try not to look in the mirror and when I do, I just, there is no words that I can express now. I feel none. I'm just, just none."*

"My actions and my memories hold me in a prison every day, whether I'm awake or asleep. My heart breaks every day and I grieve every second. No matter where I am, I will live with my actions and continue to pray for forgiveness, and nothing will change that." (Tinning's letter she read pleading for release during her fourth parole hearing in 2013. She was denied.)

"No. After the fact I remembered, but I don't remember why." "It's just — can't remember. I mean, I know I did it, but I can't tell you why. There is no reason." NOTED:

She later recanted her signed confession, but the entire document was presented and read at trial.

Additional Facts:

• Hot line tips received after the ninth infant death prompted police to seek an opinion from a forensic pathologist. He looked closely into the Tinning cases and stated a simple medical fact: Unlike the Tinning infants, SIDS babies do not turn blue but appear normal, as if sleeping. That information spurred authorities to bring Tinning in for questioning.

• Tinning was tried on one count of second degree murder for the death of her ninth child, Tami Lynne, and found guilty. She did not testify in her own defense but maintained she killed no child. At sentencing, she read the statement: *"The Lord above and I know I am innocent. One day the whole world will know that I am innocent and maybe then I can have my life back once again or what is left of it."* Authorities did not pursue charges in the deaths of any other children. Small bodies quickly deteriorate to the point that citing an absolute cause of death from an autopsy would be difficult, if not impossible.

• Marybeth was always alone with the children when they experienced trauma. Her husband, Joe, was never a suspect nor charged in any of the deaths.

• Her husband continued to support his wife and visited her regularly in prison. Admirable, especially since Marybeth poisoned him in 1974 by feeding him a near lethal dose of barbiturates during a tumultuous period of their marriage. No charges were leveled and the couple stayed in the marriage. *"You have to trust your wife."*

- After being paroled in 2018, she returned to live with her husband.

OTTIS TOOLE 6+ Kills

DOB: 3/5/1947 FL

DOD: 9/15/1996 FL, age 49/ Died from cirrhosis of the liver while incarcerated.

SENTENCE: DEATH, later commuted to five life sentences due to low IQ and borderline mental retardation.

Facility: Florida State Prison, Raiford, FL.

THE CRIME: Ottis Elwood Toole is a self-professed serial killer, rapist, Satanist, and practicing cannibal. He claims to have killed hundreds of victims with his lover, Henry Lee Lucas.

Toole was convicted of killing six people, but the exact number of his victims will never be known. Many of his and Lucas' confessions have been proven to be a hoax played on law enforcement and the media for self-serving reasons. Both died in prison of natural causes, taking their secrets to the grave.

In 1979, the two penniless drifters began to travel the country, often together, until Toole was arrested in 1983 in Florida on an arson charge and Lucas was apprehended in Texas on a weapons charge.

Lucas started confessing in his jail cell in Texas and Toole backed up his claims, sitting in a Florida jail. Ironically, both men were able to separately provide detailed recollection of murders, each offering the exact same bits and pieces of information that only the killer or killers would know.

The two had evaded police for years by staying on the run, crossing state lines, changing their MO, and for the most part, victimizing total strangers.

Toole was sentenced to death in 1984 for the 1983 murder of a 19-year-old woman and the 1982 arson-related death of a 64-year old man who had been his lover. Toole locked the man inside a boarding house before setting the building on fire. Both sentences were commuted to life.

Toole is most infamous for the murder of Adam Walsh, the six-year-old son of John Walsh. In jail, Toole confessed to killing the child who was abducted on 7/27/81, beaten, tortured, and decapitated. Although Toole later recanted his confession and no physical evidence linked him to the crime, he was considered by authorities to be the perpetrator. According to a niece of Toole's, he confessed to the murder on his death bed. The case was officially closed in 2008 based on strong circumstantial evidence. Adam's head was located two weeks after the murder in a canal but his body was never recovered. Toole once said he had **"...fed the body to the alligators."** (Lucas was incarcerated in July 1981 so he was never implicated in the Walsh murder.)

BACKGROUND: Ottis Toole was born into abject poverty in Jacksonville, Florida, the youngest of five children. His alcoholic father abandoned the family when Toole was around age five. His mother was an overly devout religious zealot who had a hard time controlling her youngest son. She would continually admonish him for doing the *"devil's work."*

Toole was borderline mentally retarded with a low IQ of 75. He performed poorly in school and was not well liked by his peers nor his teachers. He quit in the sixth grade and was barely able to read or write.

He started running away from home and was in an out of boys' homes. At 13, he had his first serious run-in with authorities when he was apprehended for breaking and entering. As a youth, he set fires and was sexually aroused by the act. True or not, Toole claimed he was sexually abused by relatives and exposed to a Grandmother who practiced Satanism.

At the age of 14, he ran away from home for good and panhandled, stole, or prostituted himself to survive on the streets. He often dressed as a female. He drifted around from one location to the next, embracing the transient lifestyle, and was involved in one homosexual relationship after another.

In 1976, Toole was briefly married to a much older woman but the marriage quickly disintegrated when she discovered Toole was a homosexual.

He was seldom gainfully employed. In late 1976, Toole met Henry Lee Lucas in a soup kitchen in Jacksonville, FL. They became lovers and in 1979, they both moved into the home of Toole's mother that she shared with her daughter, her young granddaughter, and grandson. Immediately, Lucas became sexually involved with the 12-year-old granddaughter, Toole's niece. (Lucas would stab her to death in a drunken rage three years later.)

In 1981, both Toole's mother and sister died within a few months of each other. Toole claimed he would sleep on his mother's grave to be close to her. This touching sentiment, however, did not keep him and Lucas from looting the home and stealing his deceased sister's truck. They hit the road with the two children in tow and continued their crime spree until both Toole and Lucas were separately apprehended in 1983. How many victims either or both killed in tandem remains a mystery to date, but most authorities believe Toole was the leader and Lucas was the more submissive follower.

OUT OF THE MOUTH OF THE SERIAL KILLER:

"I really got into that, got into devil worship all the way."

"Some of 'ems been cut wide open and some of 'ems been with a head, arms, and legs, and all that cut up."

"Some of them would be shot in the head, back of head, and behind the ear, and in the chest. Some of them would be choked to death, and some of them would be beat in the head with a tire tool."

"The Hands of Death killed your father." Referring to a Satanic cult he claimed hired him to kill.

Additional Facts:

- Toole suffered from epilepsy and frequent seizures.

- He once told a reporter he knew he was gay by age 10.

- He claimed to have committed his first murder at age 14. He bragged that he ran over a salesman who had propositioned him for sex with the man's own car. This claim was never substantiated.

- Toole is buried in the Florida State Prison Cemetery. No one claimed his body.

- In 1974, Toole was briefly housed next to Ted Bundy in Florida's Raiford Prison.

- Jeffrey Dahmer has been cited by author, Willis Morgan, as a plausible suspect in the murder of Adam Walsh in his book, "Frustrated Witness." His theory suggests that Dahmer lived and worked within miles of the mall where Adam was abducted, and he claims witnesses reported a man resembling Dahmer at the mall that day talking to young boys.

- John Walsh, supported by his wife, Reve, went on to create "America's Most Wanted" TV show that led to the capture and conviction of many of our country's most vile criminals.

• Adam Walsh's murder drastically changed the way police departments nationwide reacted to missing children and missing persons.

JOE TURE 6+ Kills

DOB: 2/7/1951 MN

SENTENCE: Four Consecutive Life Terms (Huling Family)

Facility: Minnesota Correctional Facility--Stillwater, Bayport, MN INMATE 118968

THE CRIME: It's not polite to stiff a waitress.

Joseph Donald Ture, Jr., a drifter, had a thing for teen-age waitresses, possibly because he could sit and stare at them for long periods of time with just a cup of coffee in front of him. On 9/26/1980, 29-year-old Ture did more than just stare.

Diane Edwards,19, was abducted as she walked home from her restaurant job in West St. Paul, MN. Ture forced her into his vehicle within three few blocks of her house. ***"Tied a rope around her arms in the back of her."*** Several people witnessed the abduction and quickly called police but no arrests were made. Her body was found two weeks later dumped in a secluded location 60 miles away near Elk River. She had been raped and stabbed in the chest.

Weeks later, police in Minneapolis notified local authorities they had Ture in custody on unrelated charges of the rape and abduction of young women. They suggested the two cases could be linked. A search warrant was granted to search Ture's storage locker. Inside was found Diane Edwards' name circled inside a notebook, but that was not enough to prosecute him for her murder.

In 4/1981, Ture was convicted of three counts of rape in Minneapolis and was looking at the next several decades behind bars. Prison life did not suit him. A convicted rapist is not popular among other inmates and Ture most likely had a legitimate concern for his safety. He devised a plan to plead NGRI (not guilty by reason of insanity) in hopes of getting a transfer to a mental hospital. In May 1981, he confessed to the Edwards' slaying and led authorities to where he had disposed of her body.

To make his insanity plea more plausible, on 12/14/1981, he dictated a full four-page written confession to his cell mate implicating himself in two cold cases: the death of 18-year-old Marlys Wohlenhaus in 1979 and the deaths of four members of the Huling family in 1978. (Both Marlys Wohlenhaus and Susan Huling had worked part-time as waitresses.) Ture included specific details of the crimes not previously released to the public and signed the bottom of each of the four pages. When he discovered that his insanity plea was denied, he recanted his confession, claiming he had been tricked by his cell mate. He was not charged.

It would be almost 20 years before the Wohlenhaus and Huling murders would be solved and Ture finally sentenced.

HULING FAMILY CRIME: On the night of 12/15/1978, Joe Ture broke into the secluded Sterns County, MN home of the Huling family, a divorced mother raising four children. He was interested in dating Susan Huling, 16, a part-time waitress and high school student. Earlier that day he had asked her mother for permission. Instead of granting it, Mrs. Huling had demanded he leave her home and called 27-year-old Ture *"a pervert."*

Enraged by the insult, Ture returned with a 12-gage shotgun to exact revenge. He wore a ski mask. He first encountered Alice Huling asleep in her bed downstairs. His original plan was to tie her up, then rape Susan but Mrs. Huling recognized him. He beat and shot her, then went upstairs where her four children slept. He systematically shot

16-year-old Susan and 12-year-old Patti before going to the bedroom of Wayne, 13, and Billy, 11. He shot at them, killing Wayne but missing Billy twice. Billy was able to run two miles through the snow to a neighbor's home for help.

Four days after the murders, Ture was stopped in a stolen car. Inside, authorities found a ski mask, a 27" metal club wrapped in black vinyl, and a toy car. They also discovered a loose-leaf notebook containing almost 200 names of women, mostly waitresses, along with their physical descriptions, phone numbers, the color, make, and model of their vehicles, license plate numbers, places where they worked, how they dressed, and their addresses. Ture was questioned about the notebook while in custody but the ledger, mask, toy, and club alone were not enough to prosecute him. He was released after the stolen car charge was settled. Ironically, the toy car found by police while searching the stolen car belonged to the lone Huling family survivor, Billy. Ture had taken it from the scene as a souvenir.

OUT OF THE MOUTH OF THE SERIAL KILLER:

From his 12/14/1981 dictated and signed confession: *"I got to thinking about Mrs. Huling calling me a pervert. I got real pissed. So I drove back to the Huling house...I grabbed her by the hair and I told her that before she died, she would go through more physical and mental pain than she has ever gone through in her life... I then went upstairs. By this time, I was really going crazy. I shot two girls and a boy in the head."*

From his 12/14/1981 dictated and signed confession: *"I freaked and hit her* (Marlys Wohlenhaus) *3 or 4 times in the head with the hatchet. I heard the dog going crazy upstairs so I left in a hurry."*

From his TV interview for "Cold Case Files": ***"The real killer should be sitting in this chair, not me... Nah, they ain't got no evidence on me. They ain't got nothin'. It's all circumstantial stuff that they manipulate to make me look bad. Like I said, they can indict a ham sandwich in this state."***

From his TV interview for "Cold Case Files": ***"Well, I can't get no justice because I'm a poor man. I ain't got no lawyer, ain't got no family to stick up for me. That's that's*** (sic) ***why I'm locked up. I ain't got nobody."***

(Spoken to a Minnesota BCA cold case detective: ***"It's not my fault all women are nothing but whores and bitches. Everyone has ruined my life and broke my heart."***

"I blew up" (When a victim yelled an insult at Ture after he raped her.) He then stabbed her to death and raped her dead body.

Additional Facts:

• After the TV show "48 Hours" broadcasted an episode on Ture, dozens of women, mostly waitress, came forward and claimed that Ture had attacked them as early as the 1970s. Some callers had lived in other states at the time of the attack. This has led authorities to suspect that Ture could be responsible for additional unsolved murders and rapes.

• While incarcerated, an inmate attacked Ture with a laundry hook and drove it into his skull.

• It is not rare for inmates to confess to crimes they never committed. Authorities discounted Ture's confession after checking, by phone, the work records at the Ford Motors plant where he was employed. Ironically, the time sheet erroneously recited to them was for his father, Joe Ture, Sr., who also worked at the same plant. It would be almost 20 years before the Wohlenhaus and Huling murders would be solved and Ture finally sentenced for their murders. Billy Hurlings's long stolen toy car was the key.

• Ture still claims he is innocent of all murders except for the Diane Edwards slaying.

CHESTER TURNER 15+ Kills and 1 fetus

DOB: 11/5/1966 AR

SENTENCE: DEATH on 5/2007 for 10 murders and a second death penalty in 2014 for an additional four murders. He was also sentenced to time behind bars in 2007 for the murder of the fetus.

Facility: San Quentin, CA INMATE J-69942

THE CRIME: In 2002, Chester DeWayne Turner was convicted of the rape of a homeless woman and a DNA sample was taken. That sample would result in Turner eventually being convicted of the murder of 14 women and one unborn child.

He mostly targeted his neighborhood prostitutes, drug addicts, and homeless women that frequented the South Central, Los Angles mean streets of the 1980's and 1990's during the height of the city's gang and drug wars.

The brawny Turner strangled his victims to death with his hands and abandoned their partially clothed, sexually abused bodies in secluded areas, abandoned buildings, and alleys.

Turner's murder spree lasted from 1987 until 1998. Authorities called him the most prolific killer LA had ever seen. He has never shown remorse.

On 9/8/2003, Cold Case Detectives were notified of a match between the DNA recovered from a murder victim and a known offender, Chester Turner. At that time, Turner was serving an eight-year sentence at a California State Prison for a rape conviction.

Later, they were also informed that there was a second DNA hit matching Turner to a 1996 unsolved murder.

BACKGROUND: Turner's mother left his father when he was five-years-old and moved from Arkansas to Los Angeles.

Reportedly, his mother would lock away food as well as lock Turner out of the home while she worked at a cleaning business she owned. As a child, he was often hungry, cold, lonely, and scared as he waited outside the home for his mother's return.

He occasionally saw his father who had remarried. Turner always felt his father was too strict and favored his half siblings over him. Turner never bonded with his siblings or stepmother and later said he always felt unwanted at both his father's and his mother's home.

He was often in trouble at school and teachers claimed he showed no reserve. He had problems with sexual boundaries and earned the nickname, "Chester the Molester." At 17, he quit school.

Eventually, his mother moved to Utah and left Turner behind with few resources. For most of his adult life, Turner was homeless and lived in shelters, missions, with relatives, or with friends and girlfriends. He had a series of rocky relationships with women, never married, but was the father of four children.

OUT OF THE MOUTH OF THE SERIAL KILLER: In an Unedited letter received 5/1/2016:

"I hope everything is well with you and your family.

I received your letter and out of respected I am responding to your letter.

Thank you, I wouldn't be interesting in being aparted of your book."

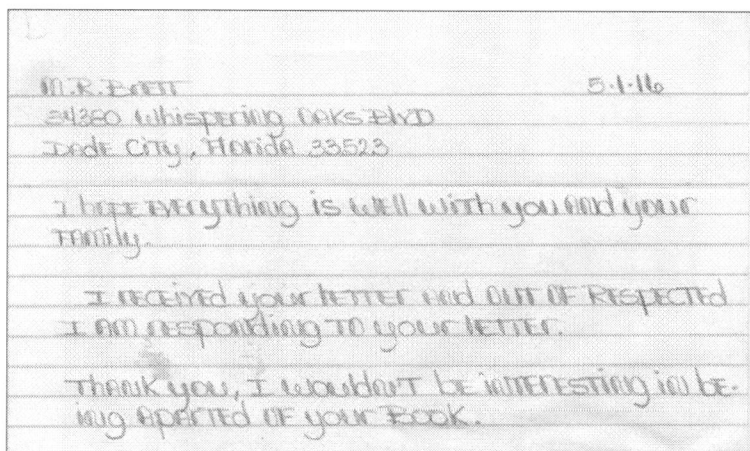

MR. EVETT   5-1-16
24360 Whispering Oaks Blvd
Dade City, Florida 33523

I hope everything is well with you and your
family

I received your letter and out of respected
I am responding to your letter.

Thank you, I wouldn't be interesting in being apparted of your book.

As Chester Turner was led from the courtroom after a death sentence was handed down, he cursed at the Prosecutor and said, *"I'll be back."*

Additional Facts:

- More than 100 women in South Central Los Angeles were killed during the height of the gang and drug wars of the 1980s and 1990s, all thought to be the work of a solo killer the press called the "Southside Slayer." Turner is one of several men now blamed for many of those murders.

- David Allen Jones was erroneously convicted of three murders committed by Turner. Jones, a mentally challenged former janitor, served over a decade in prison before DNA evidence exonerated him and incriminated Turner.

- He worked for Domino's Pizza as a cook and delivery man. He was in a management training program cut short by his arrest for lewd behavior. In 2000, he was required to register as a sex offender.

- Turner's street name was "Cisco" for a wine cooler he drank.

- The mother of victim, Andrea Tripplett and her unborn daughter, claimed in a newspaper interview that Turner, a friend from the neighborhood, attended a gathering of family and mourners at her home after the burial service.

CORAL WATTS *"The Sunday Morning Slasher"* 80+ Kills

DOB: 11/7/1953 TX

DOD: 9/21/2007 MI, age 55 Died from prostate cancer while incarcerated.

Facility: Died in a secure section of Foote Hospital in Jackson, MI

THE CRIME: In 2006, Carl "Coral" Eugene Watts was set to become the first known convicted serial killer ever released from prison.

Watts, not a household name on the serial killer world stage, was one of the most prolific killers this country has ever experienced. He was the quintessential poster child for anyone diagnosed as a misogynist (a strong prejudice against women).

Michigan, Texas, and Ontario were his stalking grounds. Watts was being honest when he factually claimed to have killed over 80 women. These victims were not raped nor were they robbed. They were innocent strangers who were viciously murdered simply because Watts hated women and felt elated after a kill.

Most of his victims were young, thin white females. He would stalk a vulnerable woman walking alone late at night or early in the AM. His usual MO was to approach from behind, place the victim in a choke hold with his left arm, then stab them repeatedly. He also strangled some victims, drowned some in their bathtubs, hung a few in their homes with their own clothing, and drowned one woman in her apartment complex swimming pool. She had fought back with such force that they both fell into the pool. Watts held her under the water until she stopped breathing.

He also broke into many women's apartments and they would awaken to find him touching them. Some he beat into unconsciousness, others he left without causing trauma. He was arrested on 5/23/1982 after a botched murder attempt on two roommates in their apartment.

In 9/1982, he was sentenced to 60 years behind bars. Watts was allowed to plea bargain due to his low IQ. By Texas law, he was declared mentally retarded so the death sentence would not have been considered. Ironically, this mentally challenged monster was able to find a loophole in his defense while incarcerated, challenge his sentencing guidelines, win, and make himself eligible for mandatory parole in 2006. Conversely, Michigan authorities stepped in and successfully prosecuted Watts for the murder of two women in 1974 and 1979. In 12/2004, and in 7/2007, Watts was sentenced to life by two Michigan juries. Two months later, he died in prison from prostate cancer at age 55. He always claimed that if he ever got out of jail, he would kill again.

BACKGROUND: Watts was the older of two children. He had a younger sister, Sharon. His father abandoned the family when Watts was two-years-old. When he was nine, his mother remarried a man with six children and together they had two more daughters.

Watts grew up in Michigan where his mother taught kindergarten art. Watts did not receive a lot of attention from a working mother with ten children and a new husband to care for. Resentment built, especially when his mother gave his step siblings attention and love. According to testimony given by Watts, he started having vivid fantasies about hurting young girls and women by age 12. At the age of eight, Watts was hospitalized suffering from meningitis and a high fever. He missed so much school that the already struggling student was forced to repeat the third grade. This humiliated the sullen and shy boy who was already being teased and shunned at school by his peers.

His first criminal offense occurred in June 1969. While delivering papers one morning, unprovoked, he punched a 26-year-old white woman in the face, then finished his delivery route. She pressed charges and 15-year-old Watts was arrested. *"I just felt like beating someone up."* He never showed remorse. Since this was Watts' first offense, he was sent to a forensic psychiatry center for evaluation in lieu of a reformatory. He was released two months later. The diagnosis showed that the patient was struggling to repress homicidal tendencies towards women. Out-patient treatment was recommended but not received.

Sports became Watts' refuge. He was an all-around great athlete, excelling in football, baseball, track, and boxing. Despite low grades and a below average IQ (Watts could only read on a fourth-grade level), he received a football scholarship to the predominantly black Lane College in Tennessee. A serious knee injury and a stalking charge on campus ended Watts' college career after only three months. He returned home to live with his parents and landed a mechanics job with a local garage.

On 9/6/1972, it is believed that Watts killed for the first time, a 20-year-old woman who was stabbed to death in Taylor, Michigan. The crime was not solved.

In 1974, Watts was accepted at Western Michigan University under the MLK grant program for minorities. He performed poorly at college, attended few classes, and was expelled in October for stealing from the school. The university did not press charges. On 10/26/1974, a woman was choked unconscious in her apartment and another

WMU student was stabbed to death. An apartment manager gave testimony that led authorities to Watts. On 11/16/1974, Watts was arrested and interrogated. In December, Watts broke down and confessed to attacking at least 15 women before demanding legal representation. A search of his residence produced wooden carving tools but little else. Even with the confession that Watts later recanted, police were not able to immediately prosecute him.

In the course of the next six months, he was in and out of two psychiatric hospitals. Watts was not declared insane, but one doctor noted that he enjoyed beating up women, showed no remorse for his actions, and actually experienced a high afterwards. The doctor called him "dangerous." In 12/1975, Watts received an one-year jail term for the assault and battery of two women. He was released after serving less than eight months. In 1980, three women in Windsor, Ontario were attacked, but survived. Watts became the major suspect after the border surveillance cameras recorded the movement of his car after each assault.

On 11/15/1980, 27-year-old Watts was stopped and questioned by police for stalking a woman. A search of his car revealed suspicious articles, but nothing that would warrant an arrest. This did, however, put Watts squarely on police radar. Sensing the police closing in, Watts moved to Texas in March 1981. He obtained employment working 4 PM until midnight, his favorite shift.

Michigan police contacted Texas officials and alerted them. They also sent Texas police their complete dossier on Watts. The Texas police, in turn, began to scrutinize Watts' daily routines. On 5/23/1982, Watts was arrested. He had tried to kill two white female roommates in their apartment but was scared off when one roommate escaped. Both women identified Watts as their attacker.

The judge ordered Watts to be sent to a mental hospital for evaluation. He was declared sane but his IQ in the range of 70 meant he was legally considered mentally retarded under Texas law. Watts was offered a plea bargain: if he would confess to his involvement in any unsolved murders in Texas, he would only be prosecuted on the aggravated burglary and attempted murder of his last two victims. Watts began what would amount to almost 30 hours of confessions and he led police to the location of three of his victims' remains. On 9/3/1982, he was sentenced to 60 years, expectantly a life sentence.

OUT OF THE MOUTH OF THE SERIAL KILLER:

"She had evil eyes." "They have evil in their eyes." "Yeah. She's got evil in her eyes." Watts would often drive around for hours, passing up dozens of women, before he selected a victim.

When asked the question, *"how many women did you kill?",* Watts looked around the interrogation room containing four detectives and said: ***"There's not enough fingers and toes in this room."***

"I'm gonna kill again if they ever release me."

When asked if he had confessed to all his murders in Texas, Watts said he had not. When asked why: ***"I don't want to go down in history as a mass murderer."***

Additional Facts:

- Carl Watts was called *"Coral"* Watts from an early age. Reportedly, younger cousins could not pronounce "Carl", instead drawing out the name so it sounded more like "Coral". Watts liked being called Coral so the nickname stuck.

- He had his first sexual experience with a girl at age 14, but he showed little interest in females for sexual gratification. He was diagnosed by doctors at a psychiatric hospital as having a homosexual predisposition although there is no proof he acted upon this inclination.

• The Ann Arbor, MI media dubbed the then unknown assailant *"The Sunday Morning Slasher"* because three Ann Arbor women had each been viciously and repeatedly stabbed to death early on a Sunday morning in 1980, all within five months of each other.

• He did not rape his victims, so DNA was not an ostensible evidence source.

• Watts had one child, a daughter, born to a girlfriend on 2/3/1979. He never claimed the child as his own.

• He was briefly married from 8/1979 to 5/1980. His wife left him because she claimed he was eerily strange in his actions and mannerisms.

• Watts stabbed his victims with a knife or wood-working instruments.

• He always claimed he killed women that had *"evil eyes."*

• One of his last intended victims claimed that Watts actually clapped, jumped, and laughed as he filled the tub in preparation to drown her and her roommate. She claimed he seemed extremely excited about the prospect of killing.

• On 1/8/1975, Watts attempted to hang himself while being legally restricted to a Michigan mental hospital. A female nurse saved his life.

• Watts did not receive a plea bargain offer from Michigan nor Ontario so he never confessed to any killings in those localities. He is a viable suspect in as many as 80 unsolved murders.

- On 2/20/1983, Watts staged an unsuccessful jail escape in Texas.

- He was considered an exemplary inmate.

AILEEN WUORNOS 7 Kills

DOB: 2/29/1956 MI

DOD: 10/9/2002 FL, age 46

SENTENCE: DEATH BY LETHAL INJECTION. Carried out at Florida State Prison, Bradford County, FL

Facility: Broward Correctional Institution, FL/On death row for 10 years.

THE CRIME: While working as a prostitute, Aileen Wuornos robbed, shot, and killed seven men in a murder spree that lasted a year from November 1989 through November 1990. Wuornos' weapon of choice was a .22 caliber pistol.

She always claimed that she shot all the men in self-defense but later recanted her original testimony except for her first killing, Richard Mallory, age 51, a business owner and convicted rapist who had served 10 years in jail. She never wavered from her original story that Mallory brutally raped her and that she was in fear for her life when she shot him.

Ironically, Wuornos would receive the death sentence for his murder.

BACKGROUND: Aileen Carol Wuornos' (born Aileen Carol Pittman) parents were young when they married, her mother, 14, her father, 17. She never met her father. Her mother took her older infant brother, Keith, and left while pregnant with Wuornos.

In 1960, her mother abandoned her two children, leaving them with her alcoholic parents who later adopted them when it became apparent their mother was not prepared nor willing to reclaim her children.

Her father hung himself in 1969 while serving a prison term for raping a young girl. He had previously been diagnosed with schizophrenia.

Wuornos claimed her violent grandfather beat and sexually abused her and that she and her brother were treated differently than the two other children also living in the home. She and her brother ran away from the home on several occasions and were put in juvenile facilities before being returned to the grandparents.

By 11, she was having sex with her brother and was providing sex to boys at school in exchange for payment. She gave birth to a son when she was 15 and placed him up for adoption. That same year, she quit school, her grandmother died, and her grandfather barred her and her brother from the home.

She moved to woods nearby to live and again sold herself for food, money, cigarettes, drugs, and alcohol. A year later, 16-year-old Wuornos hit the road, a transient hitchhiker.

Her run-ins with the law started when she was 18. She was arrested in Colorado on a DUI charge with additional charges attached. She skipped out on her court date and hitchhiked to Florida.

In 1976, 20-year-old Wuornos married a wealthy 70-year-old man and their wedding announcement made the society pages. The marriage would be annulled in a few weeks and the elderly husband required a restraining order to protect himself from his new bride.

A series of alcohol-fueled run-ins with the law followed resulting in minor jail time. In 1981, she was incarcerated and served a year on a three-year sentence for armed robbery. Other arrests would follow for crimes ranging from check forgery to car theft, but the courts were lenient on her and she spent little time behind bars.

In 1986, she met Tyria Moore in a gay bar. The two quickly became lovers and moved in together. Wuornos supported them through money earned as a highway prostitute.

On 11/30/1989, she murdered her first victim. Wuornos claimed Richard Mallory picked her up in his car for paid sex, but then beat, raped, sodomized, and would have killed her had she had not broken free and shot him in self-defense.

OUT OF THE MOUTH OF THE SERIAL KILLER:

"I killed those men, robbed them as cold as ice. And I'd do it again, too."

"I'm one who seriously hates human life and would kill again."

"I'm as guilty as can be."

"Thanks a lot, society, for railroading my ass."

"...being taken away to meet God and Jesus and the angels and whatever is beyond the beyond."

"I'll be up in heaven while you all ore rotting in hell."

Last Words Before Execution: *"Yes, I would just like to say I'm sailing with the rock, and I'll be bock, like "Independence Day", with Jesus. June 6, like the movie. Big mother ship and all, I'll be back, I'll be back."*

Additional Facts:

• Wuornos attempted suicide several times during her early life, once shooting herself in the stomach.

• In a 2001 petition to the Florida Supreme Court, Wuornos stated her intention to fire her legal counsel and stop all appeals that were pending. *"I am so sick of hearing this 'she's crazy' stuff. I've been evaluated so many times. I'm competent, sane..."*

• Wuornos father was incarcerated at the time of her birth. He was later convicted of sex crimes against children and on 1/30/1969 committed suicide by hanging himself in prison.

• On 7/17/76, her brother Keith died of esophageal cancer and Wuornos received $10,000 from his life insurance. She quickly squandered her inheritance and within a few months was broke.

• Florida then-Governor Jeb Bush lifted a 2002 temporary stay of execution and signed her death warrant after three psychiatrists deemed Wuornos mentally competent.

• She left specific instructions regarding her funeral. She asked that her body be cremated and her ashes returned to Michigan. She requested that the song, "Carnival" by singer, Natalie Merchant be played at her service.

• Tyria Moore, her lover, made a deal with authorities to avoid prosecution. On a taped phone conversation between Moore and Wuornos, Wuornos admitted sole guilt. Moore also testified against Wuornos at trial.

THE DEATH PENALTY

The death penalty is what each of the murderers featured in this book imposed on their victims, their *multiple* victims, so why is it so hard for our society to impose the death penalty upon them? And, if a jury or learned judge does impose that death penalty, convinced all evidence legitimately concludes that this person has committed a crime or crimes so heinous that the death penalty is warranted, why is it so hard to carry out that sentence? According to 2017 statistics provided by Bureau of Justice, the average time spent on death row before execution is 15.8 years. During this time, the convicted can file appeals, frivolous law suits, or force new trials at taxpayers' expense.

We are all born into a world that has established laws designed to protect the innocent from the guilty. Law is the concrete foundation of any civilized nation, but the spirit of the law is vacated when the courts allow the criminals more justice than the abducted, robbed, raped, tortured, murdered, and often mutilated victims.

I will use Florida as an example of a flawed legal system even though Florida is one of our states that leads the nation in capital punishment. In 9/2016, the 1988 death penalty for Florida murderer and rapist, Freddie Lee Hall, was vacated. He is not officially branded a serial killer since he only killed two people in 2/1978, unless you count the unborn fetus of the 21-year-old pregnant woman he forcefully abducted, raped, and murdered. She was snatched outside a grocery store, her only crime purchasing food for her family. Hall and his partner, Mack Ruffin, Jr., also shot and killed a sheriff's deputy.

The pair selected a helpless victim, had an escape route pre-planned down a deserted, less-traveled road, and were savvy enough to know to shoot the deputy in a vulnerable place not protected by his bullet-proof vest. Yet, the Florida Supreme Court was forced by the US Supreme Court to over-turn Hall's death penalty because his total level of intelligence was not fully explored at the time of trial and sentencing.

His IQ tested above 70, an acceptable number in the past to impose the death sentence in Florida, if warranted. However, that law has now been re-written by the state's highest court, in deference to the 2014 US Supreme Court's ruling in favor of Hall's challenge to Florida's established standard for executing offenders considered not intellectually disabled if based solely upon the IQ test. The reason stated: a possible margin of error. Moving forward, IQ results alone will not be enough to establish retardation. Wider range evidence is now required, examples being the evaluations provided by psychologists/psychiatrists, school records, and family members.

Consider this: an IQ number is fact, however, psychologists and psychiatrists provide intangible results, open to interpretation. Most hardened criminals performed poorly in school and dropped out early. Family members are not prone to giving honest testimony if their loved one's life is on the line. Florida had a clear-cut, blind justice, concrete rule to guide us. Now Florida's guideline is ambiguous and open to being manipulated by a smart defense.

Hall is still alive at this writing, one of the longest members of Florida's death row. He is now in his 70s, having been incarcerated four decades. His victims, a young woman, her unborn child, and a devoted deputy sheriff have been dead for over 40 years.

In 2016, Timothy Lee Hurst, a Florida death row inmate, forced a change that will gravely affect past and new capital murder trials in Florida. The new law, imposed by the Florida Supreme Court, now requires a unanimous jury recommendation of death before that penalty can be imposed. Previously, the death penalty was allowed when 10 of 12 jurors agreed upon a death sentence or a Judge recommended death in a separate hearing after the defendant had been found guilty by a jury and that jury's majority had recommended death. The case reached the United States Supreme Court that ruled on 1/12/2016 eight to one that Florida's old law was "unconstitutional".

Timothy Lee Hurst had been tried and convicted of the 1998 brutal murder of his female work supervisor at a fast-food restaurant. The money from the restaurant's safe was missing and her body had been dumped in the freezer. She had been stabbed more than 60 times as she fought for her life.

This new law in Florida will likely open the legal loophole door to allow felons' death sentences to be commuted to life without the possibility of parole and could affect other states, as well. Where is the do-over for the victims?

Texas was faced with over-crowding in their jails due to that state's population explosion in the 1970s. In what could only be called an insane move by their courts, Texas passed a bill requiring mandatory early releases for **ALL** prisoners with good behavior credit convicted from 1977 through 1987. Somehow, they forgot to limit that mandatory early release to *exclude* violent offenders until 1987. The law was amended in 1987, but that amendment only applied to violent criminals convicted *after* 1987. Ready to legally walk out the jailhouse was Coral Watts, a prolific serial killer with 80+ kills to his credit and Genene Jones, a nurse serial killer who murdered 11 to 46 children. Many other killers and rapist packed their bags and awaited their release. The

State of Michigan stepped in and convicted Watts of two murders in that state and Texas sensibly re-indicted Jones for five murders to keep this "Angel of Death" behind bars, but many violent criminals were released back into the community and onto Texas' citizens.

Per 2017 Bureau of Justice stats, 76% of all offenders will return to jail within five years. In most repeats, the crime escalates in gravity each time. How many innocent people have been harmed or murdered by felons released early? How many more will be harmed or killed in the future if we continue to release violent inmates early?

Proponents of abolishing the death penalty argue that it has never been proven that executions diminish murder and odious crimes. I ask them simply, *"What does?"* Surely, just locking away our vilest offenders, those who have unleashed the highest level of inhumanity upon humanity, will never be the correct answer. Imagine they find a legal loophole or escape and show up on your doorstep. Ted Bundy did escape, twice. He killed at least three victims while he was on the run, his last rage-fueled murder was a 12-year-old innocent schoolgirl.

"An eye for an eye" is the oldest cornerstone of law. Civilization is not made more compassionate by deviating from this ancient rule, just weaker. Criminals need to be prosecuted to the fullest extent of our written laws. Compassion and justice should be reserved for victims and their families

Bibliography

48 Hour Mysteries, "Living Nightmare", (Joseph Ture); 1996/1999.

Aamodt, M. G. (2015, November 23). *Serial killer statistics*. Retrieved 5/25/2015 from http://maamodt. asp.radford.edu/serial killer information center/ projectdescription.htm.

American Justice: John Wayne Gacy; YouTube; 12/24/2014.

Anderson, Teresa H.; UPI Archives; "Nurse Genene Jones faces trial in children's hospital deaths"; 1/14/1984.

A&E, The Killer Speaks Gary Ray Bowels "The I-95 Killer", Season 2, Episode 4, 2014.

A&E, Cold Case Files, "Finding BTK", Season 5, Episode 2, 12/22/2005.

A&E, Cold Case Files, "Murder on the Menu"; Season 2, Episode 11, 1/14/2003.

A&E, American Justice, "Lipstick Killer: Was William Heirens Innocent", unknown air time.

Albany Times Union; February 1, 1992.

www.AOL.com.

Bell, Rachael; www.crimelibrary.com; Paul Durousseau: The Killer Cabbie.

Boca Raton News; "Five More Slayings Charged"; 5/21/1981; p. 4A.

Bonn, Scott, *Why We Love Serial Killers: The Curious Appeal of the World's Most Savage Murderers*, Skyhorse Publishing, 2014.

Boster, Mark, photographer, *LA Times*.

Bovson, Mara; www.nydailynews.com; Sicko Juan Corona rots in jail after mass killings on California fruit farms; 2/23/2013.

Celona, Larry; www.nypost.com; Brooklyn Strangler Admits Killing 5; 8/6/2000.

Christian, Jessica;S F Examiner.

Clark County Sheriff's Department, Vancouver, WA.

Cook, Steven; www.dailygazette.com; "Child killer Marybeth Tinning again denied parole"; 1/10/2013.

Culbert, Lori; Vancouver Sun; "Pickton murders: Bloody knife fight left one victim barely alive"; 8/4/2010.

Dailymotion; 11/29/2015; (video) Killer Profile-Serial Killer Timothy "Mamma's Boy" Krajcir.

Denver Post, The; 9/19/1998, online edition of The Denver Post newspaper; Kevin Simpson.

Discovery and Documentary HD Channel; Ed Gein; 5/3/2014.

Docur.co.

Dolan, Maura; "Serial killer's lone survivor torn by conscience"; 11/1/2012.

Elkind, Peter; Texas Monthly; August, 1983; "The Death Shift".

Fanning, Diane; "Through the Window: The Terrifying Story of Cross Country Killer Tommy Lynn Sells"; St. Martin's True Crime; 4/2007.

Florida Department of Corrections.

Forensic Files, Season 3, Ep. 6, "Similar Circumstances".

Fry, George R., *Los Angeles Times.*

Gainesville Sun (Gainesville, FL), 4/20/2004; p.74; "Man Charged in 12 Killings of Women, Girls in Kansas (sic)".

Gnerre, Sam; Patrick Wayne Kearney, the "trash bag murderer"; 11/22/2014; South Bay Daily Breeze.

Herald Tribune; 12/21/2011; "Update: Guilty plea and six life terms for 1991 murders"; Eckhart, Robert.

Herald Tribune; 3/23/2007; "1991 Killing rampage might be solved with indictment of convict"; Kridel, Kristin and Bryce, Erin.

Hicks, Jerry; The Kraft Case: A Special Report: Randy Kraft's Scorecard; 10/2/1988.

Hodges, Jeff; Hollins Magazine, "Justice for Susan"; 6/2/?

Howard, John; AP; Suspected mass killer leaves trail of mystery; 6/16/1985.

ID Investigation Discovery Channel, "Danny Rolling, the Gainesville Ripper", airing date unknown.

KCRA 3 NEWS, 8/13/2013.

Kelly, Bill; "Charles Ng y Leonard Lake The Motherlode Murders"; date unknown.

Kendall, Elizabeth (September,1981). The Phantom Prince: My Life with Ted Bundy (Hardcover, 1st ed.).

Kiger, Patrick J.; www.orangecoast.com; "Why Isn't Randy Kraft Dead?"; 4/22/2013.

Kloepfer, Elizabeth, (writing under a pseudonym) p. 167. Madrona. ISBN 978-0-914842-70-5.

Klein, Julia M.; www.philly.com; "On stand, woman denies poisoning lover or husbands"; 11/9/1990.

Lakowski, Jim; "Charles Albright 'The Eyeball Killer'" (Famous Serial Killers Book 1) Kindle Edition.

Lise, Fisher; "Danny Rolling executed for five student murders". *The Gainesville Sun*; 10/27/2006.

Lundberg, Murray; "Robert Hansen A Serial Killer in Alaska"; 2/11/2000.

Markman, Ronald and Bosco, Dominick; "Alone with the Devil: Famous Cases of a Courtroom Psychiatrist"; New York; Doubleday, 1989.

Michaud, Stephen; Aynesworth, Hugh (August 1999) [1983]. The Only Living Witness: The True Story of Serial Sex Killer Ted Bundy (Paperback; revised ed.). Irving, Texas: Authorlink Press. ISBN 978-1-928704-11-9. p.263; pp. 334-35.

Michaud, Stephen; Aynesworth, Hugh (October 1989). Ted Bundy: Conversations with a Killer (Paperback ed.). New York: Signet. ISBN 978-0-451-16355-4. Transcripts of the authors' Death Row interviews with Bundy. pp. 216-22, p. 250, p.281.

Mills, Steve and Haggerty, Ryan; William; "Heirens, known as the 'Lipstick Killer,' dead"; Chicago Tribune; 3/6/2012.

Missouri Department of Corrections.

Montaldo, Charles; www.crime.about.com; "Marybeth Tinning The Story of the Death of Nine Children and Munchausen by Proxy Syndrome"; publishing date unknown.

Moose Jaw Times Herald, The; Pickton won't face 20 murder charges, but end of legal saga could yield answers; 8/4/2010.

Morel, Laura; Tampa Bay Times; "Man cheers death sentence"; 6/4/2016.

"Most Evil", Discovery Channel; Season 1, Episode 2. 2006.

Mudede, Charles; www.thestranger.com; Death Farm The Geography of Pig Farmer Robert Pickton, the Man Suspected of Having Killed Over 60 Vancouver, BC, Sex Workers; 10/30/2003.

Muti, Richard and Buckley, Charles; "The Charmer: The True Story of Robert Reldan – Rapist, Murderer, and Millionaire – and the Women Who Fell Victim to his Allure"; *Title Town Publishing, 2012.*

New York Department of Corrections.

New School Psychology Bulletin, The"; Volume 5, No. 1, 2007.

Newton, Michael; "Hunting Humans An Encyclopedia of Modern Serial Killers"; 3/90; Breakout Productions.

North Carolina Department of Corrections.

Oregon Department of Corrections.

Palm Beach County Sheriff's Dept.

Pinkham, Paul; *The Times-Union*; "No trials for killer's other cases; 11/9/2007.

Pickton, Robert "Willie" interview by Canadian authorities; 2/23/2003.

Pinterest.

Radford University; Radford, VA Department of Psychology; "Serial killer researched and Summarized" Lorenzo Gilyard, Jr. by Julie Payne, Derek Hommema, Ashley Hash, and Catherine Hosford.

Radford University; Radford, VA Department of Psychology; "Serial killer researched and Summarized" David Alan Gore by Steve Monohan, Kyle Carlson, Renee Arellano, and Danielle Brown.

Radford University; Radford, VA Department of Psychology; "Serial killer researched and Summarized" Tommy Lynn Sells; by Catherine Rowe, Nicole Ruggiero, Christopher Ruotolo, and Jason Smith.

Radford University; Radford, VA Department of Psychology; "Serial killer researched and Summarized" Daniel Blank; by Kristin Foye, Paul Hall, Mathew Helsel and Alia Zaro.

Radford University; Radford, VA Department of Psychology; "Serial killer researched and Summarized" Wayne Adam Ford; by Shanna Woodson, Whitnee Young, & Christina Nolin.

Radford University; Radford, VA Department of Psychology; "Serial killer researched and Summarized" Gary Leon Ridgway; by Brenda Lackey, Carlie Jones, and Julie Johnson.

Radford University; Radford, VA Department of Psychology; "Serial killer researched and Summarized"

Herbert Mullin; by Vernetta Watts, Virginia Douglas, Doreen DeWitt, Erin Walker, Kelly Thompson, Adam anZandbergen, John Stacy, and Benjie Soberano.

Radford University; Radford, VA Department of Psychology; "Serial killer researched and Summarized"

James Daveggio: by Heather Rose and Michael McLaughlin.

Radford University; Radford, VA Department of Psychology; "Serial killer researched and Summarized"

Rex Krebs by Katherine East, Caitlin Dublirer, MaryAnn Ernst, Mike Formichella, and Alexander Dowsett.

Radford University; Radford, VA Department of Psychology; "Serial killer researched and Summarized"

Timothy Krajcir; by Jessica Campbell, Samantha Lynn, and Ryan McCarthy.

Radford University; Radford, VA Department of Psychology; "Serial killer researched and Summarized" Henry Lee Lucas; by Matt Bullins, Chelsea Rakes, Meridith Gombar, Ashley Griffith, Kala Hodge, Alison Plummer, Sarah Pitman, Margaret Kosicki, Lauren Akers, Josette Anderson, Teresa Boyd, Jennifer Dagenhart, Amy C. Hill, Gregory Kerwin, Mary Morrison, Jesse Rosenthal, Jessie Smith, Natilie Flemens, and Jamie Kuback.

Radford University; Radford, VA Department of Psychology; "Serial killer researched and Summarized"

Paula Sims; by Deanna Graham and Denise Graham.

Radford University; Radford, VA Department of Psychology; "Serial killer researched and Summarized"

Stephen Stanko; by Maribel Street, Julia Welt, and Emily Williams.

Radford University; Radford, VA Department of Psychology; "Serial killer researched and Summarized"

Charles Albright; by Victoria Bedford, Maryann Bishop, Jillian Lee Allen, Lauren Blanks, Annemarie Bartholomew, & Ann Spangler.

Radford University; Radford, VA Department of Psychology; "Serial killer researched and Summarized"

David Berkowitz; by Cassandra Carter, Lori Ferguson, Amy Goodman, Susanna Heilbron, Marcus Kilgore, Greg Murphy, Missy Shank, Sherron Shaw, Eric Stokes, Leann Fowler, Teresa Brewer, Charlie Puckett, and Charles Zimmerman.

Radford University; Radford, VA Department of Psychology; "Serial killer researched and Summarized"

Bruce Spahalski; by Sam Miller and Grant Maloney.

Radford University; Radford, VA Department of Psychology; "Serial killer researched and Summarized"

William Cody Neal; by Jillie A. Beck, Meghan Sullivan, and Jessica Horton.

Radford University; Radford, VA Department of Psychology; "Serial killer researched and Summarized"

Charles Cullen; by Jennifer Hash.

Radford University; Radford, VA Department of Psychology; "Serial killer researched and Summarized"

William Suff; by Kitzi Woodard, Jessica Whalen, Cameron Ward, and Lilliam Wilson.

Radford University; Radford, VA Department of Psychology; "Serial killer researched and Summarized"

Robert Redlan; by Robert Weber, Carl Mocarski, Samantha Moran.

Radford University; Radford, VA Department of Psychology; "Serial killer researched and Summarized"

Coral Watts; by Kristy Walter and Christopher White.

Radford University; Radford, VA Department of Psychology; "Serial killer researched and Summarized"

Lawrence Bittaker; by Marcy Chojnack and Ellen Danz.

Radford University; Radford, VA Department of Psychology; "Serial killer researched and Summarized"

Dennis Rader; by Misty Sexton, Melissa Shaw, and Louis Smith.

Radford University; Radford, VA Department of Psychology; "Serial killer researched and Summarized"

Patrick Kearney; by Courtney Cook, Katie Cordova, and Kristin Kipp.

Radford University; Radford, VA Department of Psychology; "Serial killer researched and Summarized"

Dean Corll; by Christopher Williams, Lindsay Woodson, Stacie Wright, and Warren Zaccagnini.

Radford University; Radford, VA Department of Psychology; "Serial killer researched and Summarized"

Joel Rifkin; by Lori Ligon, Ashley Liverman, Nicole Lushbaugh, and Sandra Lyerly.

Radford University; Radford, VA Department of Psychology; "Serial killer researched and Summarized"

Blanche Moore; by Leah Streeper, Michael Kimpflen, and Sara Lupino.

Radford University; Radford, VA Department of Psychology; "Serial killer researched and Summarized"

Kristen Gilbert; by Elizabeth Daly, Kanika Davis, Sarah DeHart, and Michael Palmadesso.

Radford University; Radford, VA Department of Psychology; "Serial killer researched and Summarized"

Ed Kemper; by Michel "Mika" Labergerie, Erin Connors, Diane Duncan, Bonnie Cullipher, John Stone, Paige Borton, Scott Campbell, Donald "Troy" Williams, Sandy Crump, Shae Dunavant, Ashley Carle, A.J. Smith, and Samantha Layne.

Radford University; Radford, VA Department of Psychology; "Serial killer researched and Summarized"

Derrick Todd Lee; by James J. Layman, Brooke Gumm, Kristina Henriques, and Jennifer Hodges.

Radford University; Radford, VA Department of Psychology; "Serial killer researched and Summarized"

Robert "Willie" Pickton; by Kara Gallagher, Stephanie Sodano, and Brandon Speers.

Radford University; Radford, VA Department of Psychology; "Serial killer researched and Summarized"

Robert Hansen; by Emily McLaughlin, Megan Donnally, Carrie Draper, and Jennifer Duncan.

Radford University; Radford, VA Department of Psychology; "Serial killer researched and Summarized"

William Heirens, by Ashley Moyer, Brandy Powell, Christina Powell, Mike Pinn.

Radford University; Radford, VA Department of Psychology; "Serial killer researched and Summarized"

Danny Rolling; by Jessica L. Branich, Michelle J. Gallimore, Kristen E. Hutchison, Holly C. Obispo, Korey L Willis, Lisa Bradford, Crystal Bradner, Bonnie Byer, John R. Casey, Alissa Castellano, Heather Collins, Rual Fuller Jr., Monica N. Jahnigen, Ian Jewell, Kristyn Macready, Antania Morgan, Rose Mullins, Jesse Sherry, Courtney Smith, Melissa Williard.

Radford University; Radford, VA Department of Psychology; "Serial killer researched and Summarized"

Genene Jones; by Kelly Williams, Sarah Waldrop, and Rachel Ward.

Radford University; Radford, VA Department of Psychology; "Serial killer researched and Summarized"

David Carpenter; by George Bartenstein, Lauren Bergsten, Sarah Blake, and Denise Burton.

Radford University; Radford, VA Department of Psychology; "Serial killer researched and Summarized"

Paul Durousseau; by George Ferguson, Emily Downing, Kaylor Eutsler, and David Disque.

Rashbaum, William K.; *New York Times*; "Man Arrested in Killings of Six Women"; 8/5/2000.

Ruda, Geetika; www.abcnews; Nurse Suspected of Killing Up to 46 Kids Set to Leave Prison; August 13, 2013.

Rule, Ann (2000). The Stranger Beside Me (Paperback; updated 20th anniversary ed.). New York: Signet.

ISBN 978-0-451-20326-7. pp. 431-32.

Salinero, Mike, *The Tribune* (Tampa, FL), February 4, 2016, "Hillsborough wants animal abuse registry", p.4.

Sarasota County Sheriff's Office.

Scherschel, Frank/The LIFE Picture Collection/Getty Images.

"The Scotsman"; August 15, 2000.

Supreme Court of California, The People vs. Dean Phillip Carter; S023000; Filed 8/15/05.

"Sunday Times"; July 28, 1991.

The FBI Federal Bureau of Investigation, Reports and Publications, Serial Murder, www.fbi.gov, 2014.

USA Today; posted 3/5/2007; "6 of 13 counts of murder dropped against serial killings suspect".

Van Derbeken, Jaxon; DNA ties Trailside Killer to '79 S.F. slaying; 2/24/2010.

Woodard, Boston; The Prison Press: Conversation with David Carpenter, aka "The Trailside Killer";

8/1/ 2013.

YouTube published 1/25/2014; Serial Killers-Doug Clark & Carol Bundy The Sunset Strip Killers Documentary by Serial Killer World Wide.

You Tube published 3/26/2006; Ed Kemper Interview-1991.

You Tube published 2/22/2010; Ed Kemper Interview-1984. Dailymotion.

YouTube published 11/27/2007; A Conversation with Richard Ramirez-The Night Stalker; Watkins, Mike.

YouTube published 11/27/2005; Jeffry Dahmer Interview with Stone Phillips.

YouTube published 5/31/2014; Serial Killer Richard Ramirez Murder Very Brutal Documentary.

YouTube published 2/28/2013; Serial Killer Tommy Lynn Sells Talks to Martin Bashir (Elizabeth Orr).

YouTube published 5/3/2014; Ed Gein The Red Leatherface Serial Killer.

You Tube published 4/3/2014; Serial Killers - Bobby Joe Long (The Classified Ad Rapist).

You Tube published 1/17/2014; Rex Allen Krebs Documentary.

Weichselbaum, Simon: www.dailynews.com; Joel Rifkin, serial killer of 17 prostitutes, dismissive of sloppy tactics of L. I. maniac; 12/16/2010.

www.123people.com.

www.2Paragraphs.com.

www.25.media.tumbler.com.

www.abcnews.go.com; "Night Stalker" Richard Ramirez Dies in Prison; Clayton Sandell; 6/7/2013.

www.abcnews.go.com; Henry Lee Lucas Dies in Prison; 3/13/2013.

www.abcnews.go.com; "Convicted Serial Killer Tommy Lynn Sells Executed in Texas"; Roxanna Sherwood and Lauren Effron; 4/3/2014.

www.aboutserialkillers.blogspot.com;" The World of Serial Killers"; Robert Hansen; 01/2010.

www.alltruecrime.com; Ed Gein Quotes.

www.americas_most_haunted.com

www.bbc.com/news/magazine; 11/3/2014; Melissa Moore; *"My evil dad: Life as a serial killer's daughter"*.

www.bing.com.

www.biography.com; Jeffery Dahmer Biography.

www.biography.com; Richard Ramirez.

www.biography.com; Bobby Joe Long.

www.biography.com; Dennis Rader.

www.bustle.com; "8 Surprising Facts About Notorious Serial Killer Aileen Wuornos That Will Haunt Your Dreams".

www.cbc.com.

www.cbsnews.com.

www.cbsnews.com/murder-on-his-mind; Forty-Eight Hours; 11/1/2007.

www.cbsnews.com; Leung, Rebecca; "A Deal With The Devil? Coral Eugene Watts could become the first serial killer to be set free"; 10/14/2004.

www.chicagotribune.com; From the archives: Jury convicts Alton mother in baby's death; Michael Tackett; 1/31/1990.

www.chron.com.

www.Cincinnati.com.

www.ctvnews.ca; Serial killer Robert Pickton pens book in prison; 2/21/2016.

www.crime.about.com; Gary Ridgway The Green River Killer; Charles Montaldo; 3/1/2016.

www.crime.about.com; "Dean Corll and the Houston Mass Murders; 5/3/2016.

www.crimefeed.com; "Inside Ted Bundy's Head:10 Twisted Confessions From The Angel of Decay; 6/9/2015; Crime Feed staff.

www.crimezzz.net. (Wayne Adam Ford)

www.criminalminds.wikia.com; Richard Ramirez.

www.cultofweird.com.

www.dailymail.co.uk; 4/12/2012; Beth Stebner; "God Bless all y'all": Serial rapist and Killer dies of lethal injection (after last meal of fried chicken and butter pecan ice cream).

www.dailymail.co.uk; 12/6/2011; "'The Machete Murderer' who hacked 25 farmworkers to death in the 1970s is denied parole"

https://davidmalocco.wordpress.com; PATRICK WAYNE KEARNEY (1939- Serial Killer); 6/12/2015.

www.deathpenalty.procon.org; "Historical Timeline".

www.//dennisraderbtk.blogspot.co.uk/2005/10/childhood-adolescence-adulthood-pre_30.html.

www.derangedlacrime.com.

www.digplanet.com.

www.fbi.gov. Photo of Gary Ray Bowels ca. 1992.

www.fbi.gov. FBI's "10 Most Wanted Fugitives" Program/ Frequently Asked Questions.

www.findagrave.com.

www.forum.goregrish.com

www.fox13news.com.

www.fox19.com; "Police: Anthony Kirkland suspect in several murders" by Sara Gouedy.

www.heraldsun.com.au/news; Howard, Amanda "Backpack killer Ivan Milat & Anatoly Onoprienko among serial killers who did it for thrills"; 8/14/2014; extracted from *Murder on the Mind*.

www.haunted.com.

www.ibtimes.com; "Angel Of Death" Serial Killer Charles Cullen Apologizes On '60 Minutes, Family Members Of Victims Says It's Meaningless; Charles Poladian; 04/29/13

www.imdb.com.

www.inquisitr.com; 10/27/2015; "Douglas "Doug" Clark: Carol Bundy Died In 2003, Sex-Addicted Sunset Slayer Still On Death Row", by Traciy Reyes.

www.irishmirror.ie.

www.krackedkillers.wordpress.com.

www.laweekly.com; "Silent Wraith: Chester Turner" by Christine Pelisek; 5/2/2007.

www.lifedaily.co.

www.media.tumblr.com.

www.medicalnewstoday.com; 5/27/2015; Christian Nordqvist; "Paranoid Schizophrenia: Cause: Symptoms and Treatments".

www.mugshots.com.

www.Murderpedia.org.

www.mylifeofcrime.wordpress.com.

www.nationalenquirer.com.

www.nbc-12.com. 12/21/2011.

www.palmbeachpost.com; Melissa E. Holsman; 4/9/2012; "David Ala Gore: A Killer with no remorse".

www.pibillwarner.wordpress.com.

www.pnj.com.

www.post.task.ca.

www.pysis.com; Paul Durousseau; 6/11/2007.

www.nola.com; 7/9/2009; by Littice Bacon-Blood (blog)

www.northhersey.com; "Family of Demarest woman slain decades ago wins $10 M settlement from Killer"; by Kilbret Markos; 9/16/2010.

www.nypost.com; Jamie Schram; "Why I killed Jeffery Dahmer"; 4/28/2015.

www.nytimes.com; AP; "First Conviction Based on DNA Use IS Upheld"; 9/23/1989.

www.nytimes.com; "Mechanic Held in Series of Killings, Police in Louisiana Say Gambling Habit Motivated Suspect"; 11/17/1997; by Christopher Cooper.

www.nytimes.com; "Murderer Put to Death in Virginia"; 4/28/1994.

www.nytimes.com; "Richard Ramirez the "Night Stalker" Dies at 53"; Martin, Douglas; 6/7/2013.

www.nytimes.com; "For Convicted Murderer, No Escaping His Name"; 12/31/1993.

www.nytimes.com; "Jury Asks for Death Penalty for Convicted Killer of 12 Women"; 8/20/1995.

www.nytimes.com; "Man is Indicted in 14 Killings in CA; 7/30/1992.

www.nytimes.com; "Californian is Guilty in Killing 12 Prostitutes"; 7/20/1995.

www.people.com.

www.quotesdaddy.com; Ed Gein.

www.ranker.com.

www.reddit.com.

www.sanluisobispo.com; "Rex Krebs A Killer in our Midst"; 2/10/2010/; "His own father says Rex Krebs is a "demon seed"";2/10/2010; "Rex Krebs' likes it on death row at San Quinten State Prison"; 2/10/2010.

www.sfgate.com; Rape-Murder Suspect's Jekyll-Hyde Life / Michelle Michaud known as church helper, hooker by Patricia Jacobus, Christopher Heredia, Chronicle Staff Writers; Published 4:00 am, Friday, December 19, 1997.

www.shared.com.

www.smh.com.au; "Saga of a lethal landlady: serial killer Dorothea dead at 82"; 4/2/2001

www.stltiday.com; "Paula Sims trial: Either a maniacal killer on the loose, or Sims was lying, prosecutor says"; by Charles Bosworth, Jr.; 12/31/1990.

www.theadvocate.com.

www.thecreole.com; 4/8/2014; "$30K to possibly execute Daniel Blank? "OK" says Finance Committee."

www.theodysseyonline.com.

www.thisoldhouse.com.

www.transcripts.cnn.com/Transcripts; CNN Larry King Weekend; 10/26/2002.

www.truecrimecases.blospot.com; True Crime XL; 8/8/2012; "The Obscure Streetwalker Strangler."

United States Court of Appeals, 3 cases argued and decided against Timothy Wilson Spencer.

www.vimeo.com; Interview with James Dobson; 1/24/1989.

Washington Post, The; Barker, Peter; "In grim distinction, Va. killer is first to die based on DNA testing"; 4/28/1994.

www.wafb.com; "LA Supreme Court delays execution of serial killer Daniel Blank"; 2/17/16; Stegall, Amber.

www.websluths.com.

www.wickedwe.com.

www.wikiworldbook.com.

www.Wikipedia.org.

*For More Pictures and actual letters from
serial killers, visit the gallery at:*

http://wbp.bz/mouthsserialkillersgallery

*For More News About Mary Brett,
Signup For Our Newsletter:*

http://wbp.bz/newsletter

~

*Word-of-mouth is critical to an author's long-
term success. If you appreciated this book please
leave a review on the Amazon sales page:*

http://wbp.bz/mouthsserialkillersa

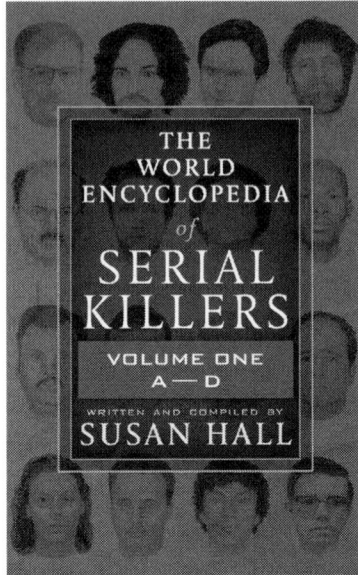

AVAILABLE FROM KEVIN SULLIVAN AND WILDBLUE PRESS!

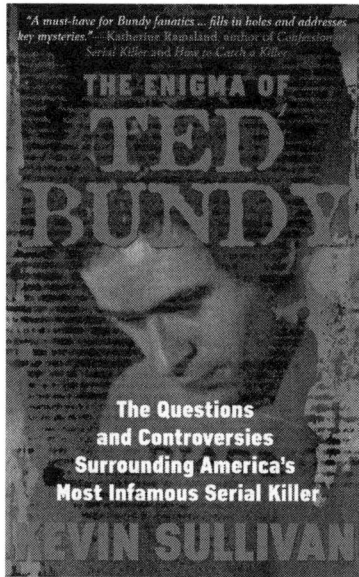

THE ENIGMA OF TED BUNDY by KEVIN SULLIVAN

http://wbp.bz/enigmaa

Printed in Great Britain
by Amazon

56156793R00221